"Don Menzel is a leader at the frontier of public sector ethics research and this new edition of his accessible book explores the challenges of cultivating organizations of integrity. Menzel effectively draws on the best available scholarship, speaks to the concerns of practitioners, offers perceptive legal and historical analysis, and assesses tools for ethics managers. He also focuses on achieving ethical competencies, provides thought-provoking case studies, and develops practical skill-building exercises to examine ethical governance. Ethics in diverse government and nonprofit environments at the local, state, national and international levels are examined. This book is an ideal choice for classroom use."

–Jonathan P. West, University of Miami, USA

"A practical compendium of the who, what, when, and how of ethics management in the public and private sectors. This is the road map for managers who often lose their way through the complexities of ethics management. Truly a resource both students and professionals will cherish."

–Carole L. Jurkiewicz, University of Massachusetts Boston, USA

Ethics Management for Public and Nonprofit Managers

This practical book is dedicated to building ethical organizations. Concise and comprehensive, *Ethics Management for Public and Nonprofit Managers* takes a managerial ethics approach to building and leading ethical public organizations.

The third edition includes:

- a new chapter on achieving ethical competence, exploring a wide range of ethical issues that confront public and nonprofit managers in their efforts to lead and build organizations of integrity
- examples and cases from both the public and the nonprofit sectors, to provide a kind of 'field guide' for ethical behavior
- descriptions and assessments of the tools available to elected and appointed officials at every level
- exercises that build ethical competence skills, asking the reader to judge the ethical competence of key actors in cases drawn from recent headlines.

With a discussion of the U.S. constitutional and administrative environment in which officials carry out their duties, as well as unique coverage of ethics management around the world, this book is written specifically for students preparing for careers in public service as well as for elected and appointed officials, administrators, and career public servants.

Donald C. Menzel is President of Ethics Management International and Emeritus Professor of Public Administration, Northern Illinois University, USA. He served as the 2005–2006 president of the American Society for Public Administration and has published widely in the field of public administration, with a particular interest in local government management and ethics. He is the author of *Ethics Moments in Government* (Routledge,

2010), co-editor (with Harvey L. White) of *The State of Public Administration: Issues, Challenges, and Opportunities* (Routledge, 2011), and co-editor (with Terry L. Cooper) of *Achieving Ethical Competence for Public Service Leadership* (Routledge, 2013).

Ethics Management for Public and Nonprofit Managers

Leading and Building Organizations of Integrity

Third Edition

Donald C. Menzel

Routledge
Taylor & Francis Group
NEW YORK AND LONDON

First published 2017
by Routledge
711 Third Avenue, New York, NY 10017

and by Routledge
2 Park Square, Milton Park, Abingdon, Oxon OX14 4RN

Routledge is an imprint of the Taylor & Francis Group, an informa business

© 2017 Taylor & Francis

Library of Congress Cataloging in Publication Data
Names: Menzel, Donald C.
Title: Ethics management for public and nonprofit managers : leading and
    building organizations of integrity / by Donald C. Menzel.
Description: 3rd ed. | New York : Routledge, 2016. | Includes bibliographical
    references and index.
Identifiers: LCCN 2015050969| ISBN 9781138190153 (hardback : alk. paper) |
    ISBN 9781138190160 (pbk. : alk. paper) |
    ISBN 9781315641256 (ebook)
Subjects: LCSH: Public administration—Moral and ethical aspects. | Civil
    service ethics.
Classification: LCC JF1525.E8 M46 2016 | DDC 172/.2—dc23
LC record available at http://lccn.loc.gov/2015050969

ISBN: (hbk) 978-1-138-19015-3
ISBN: (pbk) 978-1-138-19016-0
ISBN: (ebk) 978-1-315-64125-6

Typeset in Times New Roman
by Swales & Willis Ltd, Exeter, Devon, UK

For Kristi and Ed,
David and Robin
—The best is yet to come

Contents

List of Exhibits

Preface

More than four decades ago I began a journey into an intellectual future that would be filled with the excitement of discovery and new knowledge. Little did I imagine that the journey would take me to the third edition of this text, but it has. The future has arrived for this traveler and, hopefully, with the benefit of his hindsight, insight, and new knowledge, the reader will come to appreciate the power and potential of sound ethics management in public governance.

So what does the third edition have to offer? This edition takes the reader on a road that begins with a thorough understanding of: (1) ethics management in principle and practice; (2) what it means and why it is so important to pursue ethical competence; and (3) why integrity leadership in the public and nonprofit fields is essential to the future of responsive public governance. Chapter 1 introduces the reader to ethics management and governance. Chapter 2, an entirely new chapter, focuses on ethical competence and draws on newly developed exercises to help the reader become competent. Chapter 3 challenges the reader to learn how to lead with integrity. The tools available to managers to lead and build organizations of integrity are carefully examined in Chapter 4. The next three chapters—5–7—place ethics management within the context of local state, national, and international governance environments. Chapter 8 examines the challenges ahead for ethical governance in the twenty-first century.

The third edition builds upon and expands the message in the first edition that ethics management is a very important, although largely neglected, subject in both the classroom and practice. The first edition offered students and practitioners guidance for building organizations of integrity, organizations that are the heart beat of democratic governance in America. Second, while the second edition brought to the fore an emphasis on leadership, the third edition broadens this emphasis by recognizing that ethical leadership demands ethical competence. Thus an entirely new chapter introduces the reader to the challenges of becoming an ethically competent leader.

Further, the third edition recognizes that sound ethics management must take into account the diverse ethics management environments of local state, national, and international governance. Equally important, this edition brings into the ethics management fold the vital role that nonprofit managers and organizations play in fostering effective public governance. The ethical role of managers in the nonprofit sector is integrated throughout the text and given significance in the context of public governance. Thus the major themes of the third edition are: (1) ethical governance is an inclusive reality involving nonprofit and governmental managers and agencies and (2) successful ethical leadership for both public and nonprofit managers demands a thorough grounding in knowledge of the meaning and acquisition of ethical competence.

The failure to recognize the potential and power to lead and build organizations of integrity is in part responsible for the unending stream of scandals and ethical meltdowns in America. It is time to close this chapter and move forward. Thus a major objective of this book is to provide managers with essential knowledge and skills necessary to lead and build organizations of integrity.

Leaders with integrity, men and women who are ethically competent, can only build organizations of integrity. Achieving ethical competence is an endless, yet rewarding, pursuit. It is essential that public and nonprofit managers commit themselves to high ethical standards in the conduct of their work and life. The pursuit of ethical competence is the first step in *learning how* to lead with integrity. There is no place for moral muteness in talk or behavior. Followers know when a leader embraces high ethical standards and promotes integrity in the day-to-day affairs of the organization.

Achieving an ethics-driven workplace is difficult, but not impossible. There are ways and means to strengthen an organization's ethical culture, and it seems rather foolish not to employ those means to lead and build organizations of integrity.

The third edition takes an inclusive perspective toward public governance. Career managers in both the public and nonprofit sectors are encouraged to take a proactive posture toward leading their organizations and serving others. Neither nonprofit nor public-sector leaders can be content to simply "let things happen"; they must seek out best ethics management practices and knowledge to ensure ethical governance is more than a good idea. Putting your organization on an ethical autopilot will not move the enterprise forward.

Do we know enough about leading and cultivating ethical cultures in organizations to guide managers toward sound ethical management practices? Without question. Considerable research has been conducted on this subject, yielding results that can be tapped for best-practice ideas. Among other things, the accumulated scholarship provides ideas and recommendations for resolving ethics and values conflicts, managing ethics-induced stress, fostering strong ethical climates, preventing ethics failures, and even changing organizational cultures to make them more integrity-friendly and responsive to the needs of employees and the community of which they are an integral part.

Accompanying each chapter are two skill-building exercises that allow the reader, either working alone or as a member of a small group, to engage in "hands-on" active learning. The exercises cover a wide range of issues and settings. Some are presented in a city or county setting; some in the nonprofit sector; and others are presented in a state, national, or international context. All are designed to stimulate the reader to think about the day-to-day world of ethics management and to explore the intricacies and complexities of the subject matter.

Acknowledgments

The third edition is the "best" yet, thanks to all who have had a hand in making it so. Of course, this edition would never have materialized without the kind encouragement offered long ago by Professors James S. Bowman at Florida State University and Jonathan P. West at the University of Miami. Thanks to Professor Alicia Schatterman at Northern Illinois University, who responded to my call for material on nonprofit organizations. Equally responsive and helpful was Professor J. Steven Ott at the University of Utah. Linda Hamilton, a seasoned nonprofit manager, provided insightful information. Others who lent a hand were: Calvin Bellamy, President, Shared Ethics Advisory Commission; Professor Taco Brandsen at Radboud University, Nijmegen, the Netherlands; Professor dr. L.W.J.C. Huberts at the VU University, Amsterdam, the Netherlands; Professor Manfred F. Meine, Troy University; Neil Reichenberg, Executive Director, International Public Management Association for Human Resources; and Patty Shreve, Operations Manager with the Utah Nonprofit Association. A special "thanks" to Pam Iorio, President and CEO of Big Brothers Big Sisters of America, for taking time from her busy schedule to share with me the joys of leading a large charitable nonprofit organization.

The author is especially grateful for the constructive comments provided by a half-dozen anonymous reviewers of the book proposal. Those comments were quite valuable.

Finally, my faithful partner and mate of more than 50 years, Kay Fortman Menzel, never wavered in her patience and good will as the hours passed, and became weeks, then months. Our beloved golden doodle, Sammy, and his companion Emmy provided much needed "woof" down time.

1
Ethics Management and Governance

If men were angels, no government would be necessary.

—James Madison, *The Federalist* #51

Men and women are not angels, nor are they devils. Nevertheless, it is human nature to be ambitious and self-serving—and, as Alexis de Tocqueville added in his classic nineteenth-century account *Democracy in America* (1840/2000), Americans "enjoy explaining almost every act of their lives on the principle of self-interest properly understood" (Mayer 1969, 526). The doctrine of enlightened self-interest means "every American has the sense to sacrifice some of his private interests to save the rest" (Mayer 1969, 527).

Men and women of ambition continue to seek power and act out their lives, driven by "self-interest properly understood." Of course, not all do so, and when self-interest consumes the public interest, much trouble is in store. Those who govern and those who are leaders of organizations that serve the public are constrained by a myriad of laws, bylaws, and regulations intended to ensure that the public interest is not sacrificed on the altar of self-interest. Still, it is impossible to construct enough laws and rules to check the behavior of human beings both in and out of government. Thus, self-constraint is thought by many to be the answer to ethical governance. But what are the self-constraints? Where do they come from? How do you know they work? Answers to these questions about human behavior have occupied the attention of philosophers for centuries.

This chapter introduces the important, but largely neglected, subject of ethics management. As the following pages make abundantly clear, there are a number of good reasons why ethics management has not received the attention it warrants. First, it is easy to assume that laws and rules make all but the most egregious behaviors worthy of attention and warranting punishment. Ethics has always been a more elusive, gray matter and therefore receives less attention. Second, while we have no difficult imagining "managing" people, budgets, organizations, and more, it is almost counterintuitive to imagine "managing" ethical behavior, short of a lengthy list of prescriptions and proscriptions regarding what behaviors are (un)acceptable. But this is a narrow view of why men and women behave as they do. This book makes the case for managing people in organizations with a much wider lens perspective.

Third, the focus of professional ethics pedagogy has been, and largely still is, focused on the individual as a morally responsible agent. This focus is certainly meritorious but also limited. It is time to broaden our view and understanding of why individuals do or do not act ethically. Fourth, the public management field of study and practice has only recently begun to escape from the grip of the business sector, a grip that has been to a large extent self-inflicted by academic programs and professional associations enamored with the "magic" of the marketplace. For these reasons and others, ethics management has rarely risen above the status of a poor, unwanted cousin.

But times change and this book reflects those changes. The pages that follow also offer an overview of organizational perspectives that can lead to the development of effective ethics leadership and management strategies. There is no magic potion that can be applied to transform an organization—governmental or nonprofit—into an organization of integrity. Building an organization of integrity—*workplaces where individuals treat each other with respect, take pride in their work, care about one another, promote accountability, and place constituents and public interest over individual and organizational self-interest*—requires substantial time, resources, and commitment. No small challenge, is it? Yet it must be met.

Serving the Public

Neither government nor nonprofits are in the business of producing ethics. Rather, they are in the business of producing public goods and services such as health care, justice, transportation, air and water quality, consumer and occupational safety, national security, and protection from the misfortunes of age, poverty, or illness, to name a few. Thus, managers and elected officeholders are charged with providing those goods and services deemed desirable but often not provided by others, especially private for-profit businesses.

Why, then, do so many people—managers included—believe that ethical governance is so important? The answer is disarmingly straightforward: Without ethical governance, the production of affordable, high-quality public goods and services is not likely to occur; or, as is so commonly illustrated in the experiences of undemocratic and developing countries, the costs and consequences are so great that a vast majority of the population cannot afford whatever goods and services are produced. Moreover, ethical governance is vital to sustaining a robust, healthy democracy. As Dennis F. Thompson reminds us, "Ethics may be only instrumental, it may be only a means to an end, but it is a necessary means to an end" (Thompson 1992, 255). In other words, well-intentioned public and nonprofit managers and elected policy makers must realize that effective public policies and organizations cannot be achieved in an ethical vacuum. Indeed, such a vacuum is likely to swallow up even the most well-conceived policies, plans, and day-to-day operations of governmental and nonprofit organizations.

This apparently undeniable law linking ethics, sound management, and governance has not always taken precedence in the United States. Indeed, as Americans fast-forward into the second decade of the twenty-first century, there is reason to wonder whether such an iron law really exists. Do public managers and elected officeholders understand the vital link between ethics and good governance? Does anyone care if they do, or have we entered an era of "anything goes" governance so long as somebody else will pay for it?

President Barack Obama has taken note of the nation's lapse in responsibility. In his first inaugural address (2009), he exclaimed:

> What is required of us now is a new era of responsibility—a recognition on the part of every American that we have duties to ourselves, our nation and the world; duties that we do not grudgingly accept but rather seize gladly, firm in the knowledge that there is nothing so satisfying to the spirit, so defining of our character than giving our all to a difficult task.

Challenges to Ethical Governance

The vast majority of public servants and nonprofit employees are conscientious, dedicated, competent individuals pursuing public-service careers with integrity and pride. Yet, the ethical challenges facing those who preside and administer over governmental and nonprofit organizations have become increasingly complex. Among other things, the boundary between those things public and those things private has largely disappeared, leaving in its wake much uncertainty about how to do the right thing in the right way. The *age of privatization* is upon us and, with it, the increasing inability of citizens, elected officials, and organizational leaders and managers to distinguish between public and nonprofit and private organizations, public and private managers, and public and private ethics. Oh, you say—but ethics are ethics, no matter the domain or the organization. While it might seem readily apparent to be so, the ethical line may not be as bright as one might think. We shall return to this matter later.

Governance and Government

Governance is a dynamic, inclusive concept that encompasses a wide spectrum of organizations and individuals engaged in making, implementing, and evaluating public policies. This includes government bodies, elected and appointed public officials, administrators and middle managers, rank-and-file members of public organizations, nonprofit organizations, interest groups, political lobbyists, and profit-making corporations and their chief executives. *Government* refers to institutions such as three branches of the U.S. government and the rules and laws that determine how the work of government gets done.

The ethical challenges of privatization are no less daunting than those ushered in first by the *Internet* and later by mobile and web-based *social media* technologies. The future is here: it is now. It is both a virtual "now" and a very real "now." Not only must elected officials and public and nonprofit managers, like their private-sector counterparts, understand and harness information technology (IT) within their organizations, they must be able to understand and manage the human–technical–organizational dynamics that IT brings to the workplace. For example, organizational leaders cannot ignore the depersonalization of relationships in the workplace due to the arrival of e-mail and the sometimes harmful dynamics wrought by the explosive growth of social media. Nor can leaders ignore the desire of employees to carry out their duties in high-performing organizations with strong ethical cultures.

The knowledge explosion wrought by the electronic age of computers and high-speed interactive communication has truly transformed the world, giving meaning to the global village and citizen in ways unimaginable a mere decade ago. The globalization of economies, communication, education, commerce, and even warfare and peace are redefining the nation-state and presenting numerous challenges to public officials in the United States and abroad. Public and nonprofit organizations, like private profit-making firms, must add value to their products and services in order to withstand the ever-increasing pressures of worldwide competition. Responsive, high-performing organizations are a necessity, not a luxury. Neither government agencies nor mission-driven nonprofits are immune to these pressures; political executives and organizational managers know this. They also know that the forces of globalization can tempt all to devalue the ethical overhead that is part and parcel of getting things done. Getting things done and staying competitive can be—but are not necessarily—compatible with high ethical standards.

A person with sound moral character is said to possess *integrity*. When applied to an organization, integrity refers to an environment in which decency, fairness, and honesty abound and respect for others transcends self-serving interests. Building an organization of integrity involves cultivating and balancing a range of competencies and virtues that improve judgment in making decisions.

Ethics Management Is Important

Why is ethics management important? Rarely has this question been asked or satisfactorily answered.[1] Why? Because in the past, reformers and scholars focused heavily, if not exclusively, on the core values of efficiency, economy, and effectiveness.[2] Moreover, it was generally assumed that administrators would be men and women of strong moral character and integrity. Look, for instance, to the words of nineteenth-century civil service reformers such as Woodrow Wilson. In his famous essay of 1887 titled "The Study of Administration," he said that we must clear "the moral atmosphere of official life by establishing the sanctity of public office as a public trust . . . [thereby] opening the way for making it businesslike" (1887/1941, 494). "The ideal for us," he argued, "is a civil service cultured and self-sufficient enough to act with sense and vigor" (501). Thus, there was little reason to be concerned about the need to add a fourth "e"—ethics—to the holy trilogy of efficiency, economy, and effectiveness. But times change. Ethics has become both academic talk and office shoptalk.

The effort to curb wrongdoing in and out of government is driven by several factors. First, incidents of wrongdoing in the United States and abroad have drawn increasing public and media attention. Corrupt acts at the highest levels in local, state, national, and international arenas have not vanished from the earth. Indeed, a persuasive argument can be made that corruption has held steady in developed countries and is rampant in many developing countries. No community or nation is immune to its ruinous effects. Thus, the "why" of ethics management can be tied to stamping out or, at a minimum, reducing the harmful consequences of wrongdoing.

At the same time, there is a second compelling argument for organizations to embrace high ethical standards—an argument tied to the realization among private-, public- and nonprofit-sector managers that productive, high-performing organizations are value-driven. And, most importantly, these organizations place ethics high on their list of values. Insofar as such a link exists between ethics and organizational performance, prudent managers and scholars have focused on understanding the dynamics of the ethical workplace. Additionally, they have examined how professional associations armed with ethics codes can help them cultivate an ethical culture.

Ethics Philosophies

Ethics management has become a reality only in recent decades, although interest in ethics in Western culture can be traced to the age of antiquity (eighth century B.C.E.) and in the Orient to the Chinese sage Confucius (551–479 B.C.E.). The Greek philosopher Aristotle (384–322 B.C.E.) wrote about moral virtues such as courage, honesty, temperance, and responsibility. Virtue ethics, as this approach came to be known, has inspired and motivated human beings in vastly different cultures for centuries. Confucian ethics is considered similar to virtue ethics, although Confucius' teachings emphasized self-cultivation and reasoned judgment.

Other philosophers such as the German Immanuel Kant (1724–1804) offer an alternative to virtue ethics. Kantian ethics focuses on duty, as exemplified in the famous categorical imperative: "Act only according to that maxim by which you can at the same time will that it should become a universal law" (Kant 1785/1989). An act is accorded moral worth if the motive is principled. Ethical humans are duty-bound to do the right thing.

The Englishman John Stuart Mill (1806–1873) offers yet another view, asserting that one can know if an act is right or wrong only by its consequences. Thus, utilitarian ethics as espoused by Mill calls for acts that result in desirable ends. The well-known maxim, "Do the greatest good for the greatest number," continues to undergird the ethics philosophy of many. The view that moral ends justify immoral means is no more acceptable from a public ethos utilitarian perspective than is the view that moral means can be used to justify immoral ends.[3]

Given these philosophies, reasonable questions include: How would we characterize the prevailing ethos of American public and nonprofit managers? Do they subscribe to one of these views? More than one? None? While it is risky to generalize, the answer is that most managers draw on all of these ideas but are closer to what might be called *pragmatic utilitarianism*—that is, they are constantly exploring decision alternatives that generate satisfactory outcomes for their (1) elected and appointed bosses, (2) employees, and (3) clients and citizens. A public-service ethos presupposes that administrators promote the public interest over those of their employees and elected bosses, but doing so is not always so straightforward or clear.

These philosophies—virtue ethics, duty-based ethics, or utilitarianism—rarely serve as pure operating philosophies in day-to-day living. As ethicist Terry L. Cooper explains,

> We identify, or assume, certain principles of duty that are important to us and relate those to the consequences we anticipate by following that duty. The result is that we almost never act purely on the basis of duty to principle, nor purely by calculating the consequences.
>
> (Cooper 2006b)

These great philosophers beget a legacy and presence that remain significant in the twenty-first century. Though different, they share a common bond in identifying and holding the individual responsible for right and wrong behavior. Consequently, moral agency—the capacity to make a choice between right and wrong—is key to understanding ethical choice and behavior. Telling a lie when under physical duress, for example, illustrates a lack of moral agency.

Definitions of *ethics* and *morals* are provided in the following box. While both ethics and morals are concerned with right and wrong, it is important to note that there is a difference. On the one hand, the term *ethics* presupposes that an action has taken place or a certain behavior exists. It is this behavior that matters and, in the end, defines right or wrong. On the other hand, *morals* can exist independently of behavior. Former U.S. President Jimmy Carter's statement in a *Playboy* magazine interview during the 1976 presidential campaign illustrates this point rather well. Candidate Carter said: "I've looked on a lot of women with lust. I've committed adultery in my heart many times." Jimmy Carter confessed to an immoral act in his mind (Scheer 1976).

Definitions of Ethics and Morals

Ethics are values and principles that guide right and wrong behavior. The Golden Rule—do unto others as you would have them do unto you—is an example of an ethical principle that guides behavior. *Morals* are core beliefs about life, humanity, and nature. Beliefs about going to war, executing criminals (capital punishment), abortion, adultery, and lifestyles are moral issues.

A discussion of ethics and morality would be incomplete without considering the matter of where law, promulgated by legitimate public bodies and institutions, fits into the picture. In America, federal and state laws and, at the local level, ordinances enacted by representative governments also address "right" and "wrong" behavior. The recent controversy over same-sex marriage, for example, has been resolved by lawful adjudication that asserts that preventing same-sex marriage violates one's civil rights. In other words, it is right to allow same-sex marriage. Those who view marriage from a moral perspective disagree but, in this case, law supersedes morality in civil affairs. Racial discrimination was once a lawful practice called slavery. Was it morally right? No—but it took a civil war to abolish slavery and, as the decades passed since the dreadful conflict of 1861–1865, even more has been needed to bring racial discrimination to heel. And many Americans would contend that ending racial discrimination remains unfinished work in the second decade of the twenty-first century.

An Ethical Oversight

The intellectual legacy of the great philosophers has spawned a blind spot in our understanding of contemporary ethical behavior. What has been largely overlooked is the *context or environment* in which ethical decisions are made. The scope of questionable decision making grew ever more evident in the mid twentieth century, as the work and play of humans in all walks of life became wholly enmeshed in complex organizations. Social scientists began to study and write about life and morality "in the shadow of organization," as Robert B. Denhardt (1981) puts it. Individual morality became dominated by the prevailing ethos of the organization, leading to the belief that what is right for the organization is right for the individual. The organizational imperative— do whatever is in the best interests of the organization—requires employees to be obedient to the decisions of superiors, to be technically rational, to be good stewards of other people's property, and to be pragmatic, contend W.G. Scott and D.K. Hart (1979, 1989). Above all, "managers must be amoral in order to obtain the most benefits for their organizations" (1989, 34).

Empirical studies also began to focus on the organizational context of (un)ethical decision making.[4] For example, studies of whistleblowers have flourished.[5] One study by Lovell (2003, 201) paints a picture of organizational life in which "the fear of impairing one's future career prospects was a significant factor shaping the muteness of many of the managers about their respective ethical dilemmas." Lovell's research points to the suppressing influence that organizational imperatives can have on moral agency. Suppressed whistleblowing, Lovell contends, is an enduring and troubling phenomenon in modern organizations.

Rosemary O'Leary (2006) adds to this literature with a set of provocative cases about career administrators in state and federal agencies who engaged in what she calls the "ethics of dissent." These seasoned public officials found themselves at odds with their political superiors over significant public policy issues. Rather than resign, all worked behind the scenes to correct what they perceived to be flawed public programs—programs that did not advance the public interest. Most were successful at this form of guerrilla warfare, as she describes it.

Case studies of ethics stress and decision distress also began to appear over the past two decades.[6] Frederickson and Newman (2001), for example, explored the decision by Gloria Flora, a high-ranking manager in the U.S. Forest Service, to resign her position. She "exited with voice" and, according to the investigators, is a moral exemplar. The incident had to do with Flora's judgment that, as the supervisor of a national forest in Nevada, she could no longer carry out her stewardship duties in the face of powerful economic and political pressures to exploit protected federal lands—pressures from interests in mining, timber production, and livestock grazing. Flora's more than 20 years of service with the U.S. Forest Service was terminated with less than three years from being vested in the civil service retirement system. She paid a high price, emotionally and financially, for her moral courage. Frederickson and Newman ask, why would she do this? The answer—because she could not compromise her strong belief to do the "right" thing. "She was motivated to act as she did out of a sense of responsibility" (2001, 360).

Ethics is often regarded as something that cannot be taught or "managed" in the age of high-tech, performance-driven organizations. However, the results of recent studies are casting considerable light on what we know and do not know about ethical behavior in complex organizations. There is, of course, still much more to learn. Nonetheless, a sufficient body of knowledge can be drawn on to learn how to lead and build organizations of integrity.[7]

> In fact, ethics has everything to do with management . . . Managers who fail to provide proper leadership and to institute systems that facilitate ethical conduct share responsibility with those who conceive, execute, and knowingly benefit from corporate misdeeds.
>
> (Paine 1994, 106)

The Ethics–Performance Linkage

Efforts to probe the ethics–performance linkage in public administration began in the early 1990s. Burke and Black (1990), for example, conducted an exploratory study of organizational ethics and productivity by surveying 69 executives and managers, approximately one-third of whom were from the public and nonprofit sectors. Their findings did not demonstrate a conclusive empirical link between ethics and performance but did motivate the authors to recommend that agencies create "a leadership group focused on identifying ethical concerns and productivity measures" (Burke & Black 1990, 132). Bruce (1994) also used survey research to study the ethics of municipal clerks. Municipal clerks, she found, are generally a highly ethical group who feel that city employees are principled and productive. She contended that managers and supervisors have a "substantial influence on employee ethics and, by extension, on organizational performance" (251).

Your author (Menzel 1992, 1993, 1995) has also probed the ethics–performance link. I surveyed different populations—city and county managers in Florida and Texas and city and county employees in two Florida local governments. One study (1993) included the question: "Do ethical climates of public organizations reinforce or detract from organizational values such as efficiency, effectiveness, excellence, quality, and teamwork?" I hypothesized that, as the ethical climate of an organization becomes stronger, the five aforementioned organizational performance values will be strongly supported. My findings led me to accept the hypothesis that an organization's ethical climate has a positive influence on its performance.

Similar results are reported by Berman and West (1997) in their study of the adoption of ethics management strategies. City managers reported that "commitment to workforce effectiveness and the adoption of pay-for-performance policies are associated strongly with ethics manage-ment practices." In addition, the researchers found that "efforts to decrease absenteeism and to adopt a customer-orientation also are significantly asso-ciated with ethics management" (26).

The business community is very much aware of the ethics–performance linkage. Running a business solely on the basis of maximizing profits is no longer the imperative it once was. Calls for a value-based approach to managing high-performance business enterprises leave little doubt about the importance of ethical values for good business. "Ethical dimensions must be in-built in management thinking, management strategy and performance analysis" (Stainer, Stainer, & Gully 1999, 776).

Is the ethics–organizational performance link strong? Do organizations that build and invest in a strong ethical culture get a return on their investment? Unquestionably, although it is difficult to assign a precise dollar amount to a return that is based in part on prevention. How does one attach a monetary value to a behavior that doesn't happen?

Managers as Ethical Leaders

Must managers of public and nonprofit organizations be ethical leaders to have good governance? Perhaps, although it might be argued that if good governance can be achieved with morally mute managers—managers who do not feel a responsibility to promote ethics or morality—then it may be possible to have government that gets the job done efficiently, effectively, and economically. A chilling possibility? Yes. But now consider the question rephrased: If public and nonprofit managers were unethical, would we have good governance? Probably not—perhaps definitely not. Conventional wis-dom suggests that good governance—getting the right things done right—cannot be achieved by men and women who lack ethical or moral values or fail to manage on the basis of those values.

Ethics Management in Practice

Public administration and nonprofit practitioners live with ethical and unethical realities day in and day out. This places them in the unique posi-tion of being able to practice ethics management and, on occasion, to expe-rience the consequences of ethics management. But do they really practice ethics management? And, if they do, how? Gary B. Brumback (1998) offers some advice. There are four key components of ethics management:

Hiring, performance, training, and auditing. He stresses the need to hire the "right" people. But who knows how to hire the right people? Should some kind of ethics screening be conducted? Yes. According to Brumback, hiring authorities should:

1. review background investigation policies and procedures to determine if they are ethical, can be improved, and are used for the right (seductive) jobs;
2. build the agency's reputation for integrity—and then stress that reputation to recruits;
3. not use surreptitious screening and explain the policy to recruits;
4. ask new hires to pledge a commitment to ethics in government in the oath of office. (66)

Once hiring decisions are made, Brumback contends, "factoring ethics into the process of managing performance is the best way to ensure that work objectives are achieved in an ethical manner, and that other on-the-job behaviors are ethical" (1998, 66). Performance evaluations can and should include an ethics dimension. Assertions that "ethics is not performance" or "ethics is too subjective to be measured" are bogus arguments, he believes.

Ethics management should also emphasize training programs. Employees at all ranks are vulnerable to ethics lapses. Thus, a continuous, ongoing program in ethics training amplifies the message that ethics matters. "Above all," Brumback (1998, 68) asserts, "tell people what the preconditions of unethical behavior are, what the bottom line of ethics is, and what the agency and each individual can do to make ethics a work habit."

Another component in managing ethics in public organizations is an audit. An audit, whether based on a survey of employees or an assessment of occupational vulnerability, should be conducted periodically. Stephen Bonczek (1998), a city manager with hands-on experience in Michigan, Texas, and Florida, strongly supports the use of an audit to let employees know the positive as well as the negative effects of their efforts. He also believes that managers should "review with their employees all decisions on ethical issues, asking, what did we do right? What did we not do that we should have done? What should we do in future, similar situations?" (78). He encourages managers to use weekly staff meetings "to review all discussions and decisions for ethical implications" (78). Bonczek fully believes that a strong ethical climate has a positive influence on organizational performance and productivity.

Leading with Integrity

Organizations in difficult times may suffer from the lack of a clear vision for the future and the lack of credible leadership. In roles as a mentor and as the chief executive and adviser to elected and appointed boards and councils, I have found that the commitment to lead with integrity requires the willingness to define and live by clear principles and values in order to build trust and the willingness for others to follow.

(Black, 2001)

Martin P. Black, AICP, ICMA-CM, is the former city manager, Venice, Florida, and General Manager and Chair of the West Villages Improvement District.

Proactive Ethical Risk Taking

The advice offered by these managers is directed at the "how" of ethics management. Others suggest more. Donald G. Zauderer (1994) adds that integrity includes taking risks to oppose unjust acts (don't just go along); communicate truthfully (do not intentionally deceive others); deal fairly (do not provide others with special advantages or disadvantages because of their affiliations or positions); honor agreements (keep your commitments); accept personal responsibility when things go right or wrong; forgive individuals for mistakes or wrongdoing (don't hold grudges or strive to get even); exhibit humility (avoid unbridled ambition and emphasis of rank and status differences); respect the dignity of individuals by giving earned recognition (don't treat employees simply as vehicles for getting the work done); and celebrate the ability and good fortune of others (suppress envy).

The Council for Excellence in Government (1992–1993) urges every individual in government to recognize that public service is a public trust and that he or she must accept two paramount obligations: (1) to serve the public interest, and (2) to perform with integrity. Furthermore, top leaders in public organizations must advocate and exemplify these core values and obligations. Employees' performances, the council asserts, should be evaluated in light of these standards. Leaders should also make every effort to ensure that their organization recruits workers with strong ethical values.

Chris Wye (1994) shares the council's view of the role that top leaders should assume in promoting ethical organizations. "At every level in the organization, but especially at the top," Wye (45) contends, "effective leadership is an essential ingredient for maintaining the highest standards of ethical conduct in an organization." Nonetheless, Wye worries that the present course of action in the United States has been to focus on the "moral minimum," not the "moral maximum." Through the use of and reliance on laws and regulations to restrict certain types of behavior, the line between that which is acceptable and that which is unacceptable has become the default for defining a bare moral minimum. "Shouldn't we," he asks, "spend at least some time encouraging good behavior?"

Managers Speak Out

James S. Bowman's (1977, 1990, 1997 [with Williams]) surveys of public administration practitioners also shed light on the general understanding of what ethics management is and how prevalent it is. When asked by Bowman in 1989 if their agencies had a consistent approach toward dealing with ethical concerns, nearly two-thirds of the surveyed managers said they did not. When he asked the same question in 1997, a smaller (58 percent) yet still-high percentage of respondents replied in the same fashion: "My agency does not have a consistent approach toward dealing with ethical concerns." Do these responses suggest that there is little ethics management in the public sector? Possibly—but not necessarily. Consider the findings reported by Berman, West, and Cava (1994) and Berman and West (1997).

In 1992, Berman and colleagues surveyed more than 1,000 directors of human resource agencies in municipalities with a population over 25,000 in order to find out: (1) what ethics management strategies are employed; (2) how they are implemented; and (3) how effective they are (Berman et al. 1994). Their results confirmed Bowman's findings about the lack of a consistent approach—if consistent means "formal." A minority of cities surveyed reported using formal ethics management strategies while a majority claimed that their cities relied primarily on leadership-based strategies, which are informal. They found four categories of ethics management—two they labeled as formal, one informal, and one a combination of formal–informal.

Formal ethics management strategies involve mandatory employee training, use of ethics as a criterion in the reward structure, and adoption of organizational rules that promote the ethical climate, such as requiring financial disclosure and approval of outside activities.

Informal ethics management strategies involve reliance on role models and positive reinforcement and are behaviorally based (Berman et al. 1994, 189).

Code-based and regulatory-based strategies are two formal strategies used by a large number of cities. Adopting a code of ethics or establishing guidelines for standards of conduct is part of a code-based strategy. Advocates of codes typically presume that codes contribute to a healthy, and therefore higher-performing, organization. Bowman's surveys (1990, 1997 [with Williams]) of practitioner members of the American Society for Public Administration show that the members strongly embrace codes and believe that they have a positive influence on organizational life. Bruce's research (1994) also adds to the believed real-world impact of codes. Her study of members of the International Institute of Municipal Clerks found that clerks "rank a code of conduct as the most powerful way a city can prevent corruption" (29). Using ethics as a criterion in hiring and promotion or requiring approval of outside employment constitutes part of a regulatory-based strategy. Leadership-based strategies, such as demonstrating exemplary moral leadership by senior management, constitute an informal ethics management strategy. Employee-based strategies that incorporate ethics training, protect whistleblowers for valid disclosures, or solicit employees' opinions about ethics constitute a mixed strategy.

Does reliance on an informal strategy, which most cities claim they have, result in ineffective ethics management? Not necessarily. Berman and colleagues' research indicates that moral leadership strategies are more effective than regulatory- or code-based strategies in enabling cities to achieve ethics management objectives, such as avoiding conflicts of interest, reducing the need for whistleblowers, and fostering fairness in job assignments.

Responses to Ethics Failures[8]

Ethics lapses and failures occur; they are part and parcel of contemporary life. When they happen, what else might be done? At the macro level, codification of acceptable behavior in the form of state law or local ordinance is common practice. Many states and cities have opted for ethics laws and regulatory bodies or boards. Megacities like Los Angeles and Chicago, for example, have established ethics commissions to investigate real and alleged cases of wrongdoing. The U.S. government has also taken action, having established the Office of Government Ethics with the Ethics in Government Act of 1978.

These efforts have not gone unnoticed. Several investigators have attempted to assess what difference ethics laws and commissions make in states and communities. R.L. Williams (1996), for example, studied the

Florida Commission on Ethics to assess the agency's effectiveness in training officials, conducting ethics audits, investigating complaints, and encouraging an ethical climate. Based on unstructured interviews with commissioners and archival records of the agency, he concluded that the Florida Commission on Ethics was largely ineffective in all four areas. "Unfortunately," Williams (71) says, "the commission apparently serves more effectively as a punitive agent than as an agent of constructive change."

Your author (Menzel 1996b) also studied the Florida Commission on Ethics, but from a different vantage point—the view from the street. I surveyed persons who had filed ethics complaints (legally referred to as complainants) and public officials who were the objects of complaints (legally referred to as respondents), asking three questions:

1. What is the relationship between how an ethics complaint is handled and citizen trust or distrust in government?
2. Do persons who file ethics complaints have a positive or negative experience? Are those experiences satisfactory and therefore build trust and confidence in government? Or are those experiences unsatisfactory and therefore contribute to the erosion of public trust and confidence in government?
3. What are the outcomes of the ethics complaint making?

The study involved mail surveys of 303 complainants (144 responded) and 555 respondents (161 responded) completed between 1989 and 1992. I found that complainants were much more likely to say they were dissatisfied with the outcome of the complaint they filed than were respondents who were the object of the complaint.

Furthermore, neither complainants nor respondents differentiated process outcomes from substantive outcomes, and both groups seemed to equate how they were treated with how the complaint-making process turned out. I (Menzel 1996a, 80) ultimately concluded that "the ethics complaint-making process in Florida may be widening rather than closing the trust deficit."

Trust Building[9]

Public trust and confidence in government and large businesses in the United States and in some countries abroad are at an all-time low. The reasons are many, with perhaps the two foremost being, first, the perception, if not reality, that leaders—elected and appointed—have lost their way ethically and morally, and second, the commodification of citizenship, that is, the practice of treating citizenship as a product that can be "bought" in some manner. Take, for example, the establishment and growth of walled communities (gated housing subdivisions) or the spreading practice of privately managed communities. Residents in walled and privately managed communities are able to buy a form of commoditized citizenship.

That public trust and confidence in government have diminished because public officials have lost their way ethically and morally is a more controversial matter, as it is freighted with political ideology, moral ambiguity, and social divisiveness. Still, there is evidence that lends credence to this proposition. Consider Menzel's (2009) case study of ethical illiteracy in local governance. The case involved educated, politically astute elected and appointed county officials in a professionally managed local government who found themselves invoking the oft-used claim when there was no other direction to turn—"I didn't do anything unethical, illegal, or immoral." The story turned on the actions of a property appraiser to sell his private property to the county, resulting in the resignations of the county attorney and administrator, the property appraiser forgoing running for a fifth term of office, and a Grand Jury presentment concluding that "the breath of scandal surrounding this affair . . . will have a lasting impact on how the citizens of Pinellas County view its officials and government" (376). Did Pinellas County officials lose their way ethically? So it would seem. Was public trust diminished? Most likely.

There is some evidence that the trust deficit is not as large as we might first surmise. Consider the positive evidence reported by Houston and Harding's (2013–2014) study of public trust in government administrators. Drawing on General Social Survey data, they found that "the trustworthiness of administrators is more positive than what might be generally thought" (53). The link between public trust in civil servants to do their job competently and the trust placed in government more generally, they conclude, must be built on a vision of public service grounded in democratic values. They do not believe that efforts to enhance the competency of government administration alone are sufficient to overcome citizen distrust. Closing the trust deficit between the public and government is a legitimate and needed activity, and one that ethics managers should embrace.

Figuring out how to reduce the trust deficit is no small challenge. However, research by Berman (1996) is suggestive. He sought to find out how much trust there is among local government officials and community leaders, what municipal strategies are employed to increase trust levels, and how socioeconomic conditions may influence perceptions of trust in local government. Berman surveyed city managers and chief administrative officers in all 502 U.S. cities with a population of more than 50,000 to obtain their perceptions of trust levels. He found that "community leaders have only moderate levels of trust in local government" but that cities with a council–manager form of government experience a significantly higher level of trust than do cities with the mayor–council form of government (33).

Leading with Integrity

It's most important today for local government administrators to be guided by ethical principles, honesty and moral standards. I do not recall a time when political rhetoric was so deceiving that news agencies found it necessary to produce "Fact Check" on political pronouncements. In order for citizens to have faith in government, there must be a sense of trust. Local government professionals may foster such trust by actions that are based upon ethical values.

(Edmunds 2011)
former City Manager, Seminole, Florida

Berman identified three principal trust-building strategies—communication, consultation and collaboration, and minimization of wrongdoing. Communication strategies emphasize providing information about the cities' programs and performance. Consultation and collaboration strategies involve engaging community leaders via partnerships, meetings, panels, and so forth. The minimization of wrongdoing strategies emphasizes the adoption of ethics codes, the provision of ethics training, and the like. Strategies vary from community to community, and no single one appears to be more effective than the others. However, there is some evidence that "using a range of strategies by local officials increases trust, even though the impact of individual strategies is modest" (34). Socioeconomic conditions, Berman concludes, influence trust levels. Positive conditions in a community, such as high economic growth and cooperation among local groups, inspire trust in government. "Negative community conditions, such as economic stagnation, low income levels, racial strife and high levels of crime reduce economic and political resources ... for dealing with community problems," contributing to a distrust of government (34).

Democracy requires a degree of trust that we often take for granted . . . it is much harder to build trust than to lose it. But that is our problem in the United States: we have begun to lose trust in our institutions . . . the heritage of trust that has been the basis of our stable democracy is eroding.
(Bellah, Madsen, Tipton, Sullivan, & Swidler 1991, 3)

Many factors can destroy trust in governmental institutions, but none destroys it easier or faster than unethical behavior or blatant corruption by public officials.

Organizational Perspectives on Ethics Management

Theories of organization and governance provide different perspectives on the development of effective ethics management strategies.

Traditional Bureaucratic Theory

Traditional bureaucratic theory, which stresses hierarchy, rules and regulations, standard operating procedures, and work classification, fits comfortably with a compliance-oriented ethics management strategy.[10] Know the rules of acceptable/unacceptable behavior and stay out of trouble, this perspective demands. The bad news is that much of what passes for ethics management is exactly this—compliance-oriented. But, as it is argued throughout the book, this approach is inadequate because it minimizes moral agency.

Transaction-Cost Theory

Transaction-cost theory, which emphasizes decision making under conditions of asymmetrical information exchanges, offers another perspective. Gerald Garvey (1993, 25) describes transaction-cost theory as an effort to reduce "especially the costs of gathering and processing information, as the driving factor in rational human beings' never-ending quest for efficiency." Organizational life is viewed as a series of exchanges within and outside the organization. The principal goal is to minimize transaction costs; that is, strive for greater efficiencies and therefore lower the cost of getting work accomplished. Thus, anything that raises the cost of work in the organization is undesirable, including (1) information that is inadequate or uneven (some organizations have more information than others) and/or (2) corruption or unethical behavior. This view would treat unethical behavior as a cost factor that should be reduced, minimized, or eliminated altogether. Consequently, management must embrace measures that accomplish this goal. Such measures might include "one-shot" ethics inoculations, which require members of the organization to attend an ethics seminar from time to time, or more long-term investments in training.

> One limitation of transaction-cost theory is that it can be very reactive, not proactive. Another limitation is that it may put too much emphasis on an instrumental view of ethics. Thus organizational attention to ethics practices and behaviors is seen as a means to an organizational end—productivity.

Transaction-cost theory draws attention to moral hazards in the workplace. Every occupation contains opportunities that can be corruptible. Police, for example, are always vulnerable to favors and bribes. Planners in public organizations are vulnerable to the influence of developers, including the prospects of post-public employment. Pentagon procurement officers are vulnerable to defense contractors' offers of travel, vacations, and employment. Nonprofit managers are always subject to going along to get along with donors and offering inducements to secure grants. After all, donors are the financial backbone of nonprofits.

Learning Systems

Organizations can be viewed as learning systems that have the capability to adapt to changes in the environment. Peter Senge advances one popular theory in his best-selling book, *The Fifth Discipline: The Art and Practice of the Learning Organization* (1990). A learning organization, Senge advises, is one "where people continually expand their capacity to create the results they truly desire, where new and expansive patterns of thinking are nurtured, where collective aspiration is set free, and where people are continually learning to see the whole together" (3). The learning organization engages members who work as teams to accomplish organizational objectives and, most importantly, to learn from one another. This system's view and thinking put the accent on the whole of the organization, not just the parts. Thus, it offers a long-term view of the organization's well-being that is contrary to the more common emphasis on short-term performance.

A learning theory approach is attractive from an ethics management per-spective for several reasons. First, specific steps taken to promote ethical behavior are not treated as one-shot efforts. For example, ethics training, although directed at specific members of the organization, is viewed as bene-ficial because those who have received the training will influence others. Stated differently, the learning process extends beyond the individuals who are trained. Second, the long-term emphasis of a learning organization would buffer attempts to cut back on, say, ethics training when organiza-tional resources are threatened. Training activities are commonly reduced when organizational budgets are challenged. Despite these positive features of the learning organization, fashioning an effective ethics management strategy is quite challenging. As Mark K. Smith (2001) points out, "while he [Senge] introduces all sorts of broader appreciations and attends to values—his theory is not fully set in a political or moral framework. . . . His approach largely operates at the level of organizational interests."

Networks

Viewing organizations through a networks lens offers another perspective on building organizations of integrity. Stephen Goldsmith and William D. Eggers (2004, 7) point out that "in the twentieth century, hierarchical government bureaucracy was the predominant organizational model used to deliver public services and fulfill public policy goals . . . but its influence is steadily waning." Rather, governments are relying ever more frequently on networks to deliver public goods and services. The growth of third-party government "is trans-forming the public sector from a service provider to a service facilitator" (Goldsmith & Eggers 2004, 10). Outsourcing, contracting, privatization, and the commercialization of public–private partnerships are, as the authors put it, "the new shape of government." Networked governance promises greater speed, flexibility, and responsiveness in meeting the needs and demands of the public. The implications for ethical governance and the development of effective ethics management strategies are difficult to predict with confidence. However, the blurring of public–private–nongovernmental boundaries, as the networked model posits, calls for the development of creative ethics manage-ment strategies.

Organizational Culture

Organizational culture has a long and respectable heritage dating to the organizational theorist Chester Barnard's (1938) famous observations about informal organizations—that is, what happens in organizations is impersonal and not reflected by the organizational chart. In the same era, Mary Parker Follet (1924), a social worker and management consultant, wrote at length about the importance of group relationships in organizations, noting that authority in organizations derives from relationships among its members.

Interest in culture as a conceptual lens for viewing organizational behavior languished for decades after Barnard and Follet drew attention to it. In the 1980s, however, with the publication of popular books such as *In Search of Excellence* (1982) by Thomas J. Peters and Robert H. Waterman, and *Theory Z: How American Business Can Meet the Japanese Challenge* (1981) by William G. Ouchi, there came a renewal of interest in culture as a determining influence in organizations. Values, these scholars argue, must be understood, cultivated, and drawn upon to build high-performing organizations.[11]

Viewing organizational life though values embedded in its culture has much to offer in leading and building organizations of integrity. The ethical culture of the organization then becomes an important subset of values that constitute the overall organizational culture. Managers who have a firm grasp of this culture understand the importance of ethical values and practices in contributing to the effectiveness of the organization and are likely to devote time and energy to building and sustaining an organization of integrity. A culture perspective, therefore, is among the more promising organizational perspectives to consider when devising a successful ethics management strategy.

Governance and the Nonprofit Sector

There are three primary employment sectors (excluding the military) in the United States—nonprofit, for-profit, and public. For-profit firms such as McDonald's or Starbucks or Boeing are incorporated to make a profit from their business that is shared among stockholders or other vested interests. Nonprofit organizations are as proliferate and varied as for-profit organizations but typically have a narrow purpose or mission to advance. Nonprofit resources, however secured (e.g. donations, gifts, contracts), are not shared among stakeholders. The public sector includes governmental and regulatory organizations created by law and funded by tax-generated revenues. All sectors are constrained in some manner by public law, federal and/or state.

In America in 2012, approximately 1.44 million nonprofits, ranging from sports to professional associations to labor unions to chambers of commerce, were registered with the Internal Revenue Service, an increase of 8.6 percent from 2002 (McKeever & Pettijohn, 2014, 2). Charitable nonprofits, as noted above, are typically dedicated to serving a specific clientele with special needs such as health, poverty, homelessness, and so forth.

The nonprofit sector in the United States has a long history, dating to the revolutionary and post-revolutionary eras. Most nonprofit activity in the nineteenth century took place within religious contexts. Between 1900 and 1960, nonprofit organizations grew more rapidly than in the nineteenth century, but their growth was limited by President Roosevelt's New Deal programs that were designed to get aid and employment directly to citizens through government agencies. By 1960 the nonprofit sector of charities, churches, educational institutions and foundations, with some exceptions, grew along with government but were still largely viewed as private-sector operatives.

Much has changed, however, since 1960, with the relationship between many nonprofits and government becoming mutually dependent. While government provides for a public good with legislation or funding, nonprofit organizations are often called on to produce or deliver a public good or service across a spectrum of public wants and needs—shelter and food for homeless people, the revitalization of neighborhoods, after-school activities to comfort and care for latchkey kids, parks and recreation programs for teenagers and seniors, and more. The National Council of Nonprofits (2015a) reports, "the nonprofit sector, as a whole, earns about a third of its total revenue by providing services under written agreements with governments." Put differently, nonprofit agencies and those who manage them are essential actors in local, state, and national governance. Thus, the pursuit of ethical governance necessarily involves initiatives to lead and build nonprofit organizations of integrity.

The transformation of the nonprofit sector in the 1960s, writes David C. Hammack (2002, 1663), was a "quiet revolution." Maybe so, but it was a revolution kindled in large part by President Lyndon B. Johnson's Great Society initiatives that thrust nonprofits into the governance arena. The nonprofit sector was called upon to play a key role in the expansion of the federal government's funding for health care, education, and social services, a role that continues to the present. The devolution of federal programs in tandem with the privatization movement in the 1980s has further propelled nonprofits into the governance process as major service providers. Not all, however, are happy with this transformation. Some critics contend that big government has co-opted charities. "This system," writes James Pierson, President of the William E. Simon Foundation, "has gradually turned much of the not-for-profit sector into a junior partner in administering the welfare state" (2013).

> The Great Society is a place where every child can find knowledge to enrich his mind and to enlarge his talents. It is a place where leisure is a welcome chance to build and reflect, not a feared cause of boredom and restlessness. It is a place where the city of man serves not only the needs of the body and the demands of commerce but the desire for beauty and the hunger for community. It is a place where man can renew contact with nature. It is a place which honors creation for its own sake and for what it adds to the understanding of the race. It is a place where men are more concerned with the quality of their goals than the quantity of their goods.
> —President Lyndon B. Johnson,
> May 22, 1964, Commencement Address, University of Michigan

Evidence of the increasingly significant role played by nonprofits in American governance can also be seen in the growth of nonprofit management education (NME). More than 250 U.S. universities offer courses, certificates, or concentrations in nonprofit management. The University of San Francisco was among the first in 1983 to offer a full-fledged Master's degree in Nonprofit Management. Michael O'Neill (2007, 170s–172s), the program's founder and long-time director, offered his vision of the future of NME:

1. The field is here to stay.
2. Do not expect NME to be standardized any time soon, but "schools and departments of public administration and policy are growing more, not less, interested in NME."
3. There is a strong relationship with public administration and policy that is not likely to diminish in the decades ahead.

Ethics for Nonprofit and Public Managers

So the question must be asked: Are managers in the public and nonprofit sectors more different than alike? While there are certainly differences, there are also similarities. Research on job motivation points to differences, especially between for-profit managers and nonprofit and public managers. The "research literature suggests that public and nonprofit employees are less likely to be motivated by extrinsic factors and more likely to be motivated by intrinsic rewards compared to workers in the for-profit sector" (Lee & Wilkins 2011, 45). Public and nonprofit sector differences, especially in job motivation, are not as sharply drawn. Nor are other differences so prominent, except perhaps in legal environments. Nonprofit organizations are constrained by legal environments that mandate how earnings can be distributed and the purposes they must serve (47). And, while public organizations are also constrained by law, "they are publicly funded to implement the policies adopted by democratically elected officials" (47).

The bottom line is: Do these differences matter when it comes to ethics? The answer is that there are more similarities in ethical worldviews and management philosophies among nonprofit and public managers than there are differences. While managers in the nonprofit and public sectors may find themselves in different situations, they are, as the saying goes, joined at the hip by ethical values and principles.

Ethics are ethics, right—no matter the work or occupation. Ethical principles and values are applicable across domains. Doesn't the Golden Rule, surely an ethical principle, apply to everyone? Wait a minute, you say—aren't there specific ethics for specific professions? Sort of, maybe, yes! Hmmm! This is a bit confusing. Perhaps, but not really, because the professions truly have a foot in both camps—principles and practices. A professional is a person with expertise that can benefit or harm another person. He must know the circumstances or conditions that allow him to apply his expertise in a manner that does no harm. She must also know the practices that are ethical in her profession, practices typically embedded in associational codes of ethics. In the nonprofit sector, for example, fundraising is usually a fact of life. And, fundraising ethics includes, among other things, being a good steward of a donor's rights (revealing the donor's giving history would be unethical). In the governmental world of city managers, it is unethical, according to the International City/County Management Association, for a city manager to change jobs for two years after assuming a position unless there are compelling reasons to do so. Departing a position so quickly after assuming it is thought to be harmful to the community that hired her. So are ethics for nonprofit and government managers different? No, not in kind but "yes" in specific practices.

One other difference that is rapidly fading is the boundary between nonprofit governance and public governance. Research on nonprofit governance has largely focused on the operation of boards of directors, whereas in the public policy and management literature, governance was once equated with government. These distinctions, according to Stone and Ostrower (2007), are no longer accurate. Rather, "at a time when devolution and privatization have made government and nonprofit organizations ever more interdependent, we must question the adequacy of this distinction" (416–417).

While there are differences between nonprofit governance and public governance, the boundaries have indeed blurred. It is worth repeating that nonprofits are essential actors in contemporary governance in the United States and abroad.

Summing Up

Can we talk about managing ethics in the same way we discuss managing budgets, policies, or people? The answer is a resounding "yes!" Indeed, the single act of developing and adopting a code of ethics, as Bowman (1981) documented more than 30 years ago, is managing ethics in the workplace. Thus, ethics management is not a new enterprise; it is an old one. What is new is how we think about it. If we view ethics management as a systematic and consistent effort to promote and advocate for strong ethical organizations, as the American Society for Public Administration (ASPA) Code of Ethics (2006) declares, then there is such a thing as ethics management. Ethics management, however, is not synonymous with "control." *It is not the act of controlling coworkers' behaviors.* Rather, it is the cumulative effect of ethics-building actions taken by managers—actions designed to engender an ethical sensitivity and consciousness that permeates all aspects of getting things done in a public service/nonprofit agency. It is, in short, the promotion and maintenance of a strong ethics culture in the workplace. And, "success in creating a climate for responsible and ethically sound behavior requires continuing effort and a considerable investment of time and resources" (Paine 1994, 112).

Ethics Management Skill Building

Practicum 1.1. A Late Night Surprise!

Dennis, the city manager of a financially strapped municipality, is working uncharacteristically late at night. The offices are empty and quiet. As he is leaving, he notices a sliver of light coming from the door of the new budget director, Susan. He decides to stop in and praise her for her excellent report in which she discovered errors that will save the city millions of dollars, projecting a budget surplus for the first time in years. As he approaches her office, he can see through the gap in the partially opened door that she is in a passionate embrace with Gary, the assistant city manager. The city's employment policy forbids dating between employees, threatening dismissal to those who do.

The city's code of ethics requires Dennis to enforce this policy, yet at the same time he does not want to lose either or both of his valuable employees. It would be difficult, if not impossible, to bring in someone else with their experience and credentials for the amount of money the city can afford to pay in salary.

Discussion Questions

1. What should Dennis do? Should he report Susan and Gary, in accordance with policy? Is it his ethical duty to do so?
2. Should he overlook the situation, believing the city will be best served in the long run? Is this a pragmatic utilitarian approach?
3. Should he speak to each of them and threaten to tell his elected bosses if they don't end the relationship? Would this cause other employees to pay more attention to the city's code of ethics?
4. Does Dennis have any right to interfere in a personal affair between two consenting adults?
5. Is this a management problem? An ethics problem? Both?
6. Can ethics problems be separated from management problems? Why or why not?

Practicum 1.2 Blindsided: What Should You Do?[12]

Suppose you are the administrator of a wealthy, upscale county with a strong record of good governance. In fact, you have been the county administrator for 14 years and have garnered the respect and admiration of the Board of County Commissioners, good government citizen groups, and the local media. You view yourself as a person with high ethical standards and take pride in your organization's performance in getting the job done at an affordable price. You also take pride in your progressive management style, which consists of delegating responsibility to top managers whom you hold accountable.

Your county has a model code of ethics, and you trust your management team to be exemplars of respectability. You have every reason to feel comfortable with the ethical culture that pervades the 2,000-member workforce—until all hell breaks loose! The local newspaper publishes a story about a 55-year-old project manager in the public works department accused of accepting some $15,000 in cruises, hotel stays, gift cards, and other kickbacks from a company whose contract he helped supervise.

As the scandal unfolds, other misdeeds come to light. County supervisors are reported to "piggyback" contracts—that is, opt for the same deal another local government had with a company, thus allowing county administrators to avoid putting contracts out to bid. Procurement managers are said to have practiced "change orders," meaning a contract is bid for specific terms, only to be altered at points along the way (with extra work and pay added). The "change orders" practice would allow favored companies to come in at unrealistically low bids. Topping off the string of procurement problems is the allegation that administrators and supervisors used county-issued credit cards to "break" a payment into several parts in order to stay within a $10,000 purchase limit.

As the county administrator, you are shocked to learn of these practices. You feel as if you have failed personally or been abandoned by the entire management team, in the sense that your business and personal ethics have not been translated into the culture of at least one operation.

Discussion Questions

1. What should you do?
2. Should you start cleaning house by firing a number of managers?
3. Should you write a memo to your top managers admonishing them to "fix the problems or resign"?
4. Should you accept responsibility and resign?
5. How would you "lead with integrity" under these circumstances?

Notes

1. This discussion relies on Menzel (2005a).
2. See Stillman (1999) for an excellent overview of the evolution of public administration practice in the United States.
3. An insightful discussion of philosophical perspectives in administrative ethics is contained in Part II of Cooper (2001). This discussion covers virtue ethics as well as deontological and teleological approaches to administrative ethics.
4. The first serious attempt to bring empirical research to bear on administrative ethics took place in 1991 at Park City, Utah, when H. George Frederickson organized a conference for this purpose. The conference papers were published in Frederickson (1993).
5. See Brewer and Coleman Selden (1998), Folks (2000), Glazer and Glazer (1989), Jos (1989), Miceli and Near (1985), and Perry (1993).
6. This discussion relies on Menzel (2005a).
7. For an in-depth review of the public-service ethics literature, see Menzel (2011).
8. This discussion relies in part on Menzel (2001b).
9. A thorough discussion of trust building is presented in Carnevale (1995).

10. Max Weber is widely recognized as the intellectual father of modern bureaucracy. Weber identified six key characteristics of bureaucracy: (1) official duties are fixed by rules, laws, or administrative regulations; (2) offices are arranged hierarchically, with a clearly ordered system of super- and subordinate relationships; (3) management is based on written documents; (4) management is selected and promoted via the merit principle; (5) the official is a full-time employee; and (6) management follows general rules that are stable and can be learned (Gerth & Mills 1946).

11. For an excellent overview of issues and research on organizational cultures from a sociobehavioral perspective, see Schneider (1990).

12. Based on an actual set of events. See Eckhart (2011).

2

In Pursuit of Ethical Competence

The way to right wrongs is to shine the light of truth upon them.

—Ida B. Wells (1862–1931), African-American
civil rights activist

This chapter examines the what, why, and how of ethical competence. We do so by exploring a wide range of ethical and unethical issues that confront well-intentioned public and nonprofit managers. The issues are large and small and sometimes simple but often complex—almost always difficult to resolve. Outcomes are rarely certain or predictable or knowable. Best "guesstimates" typically dominate the choices at hand. The exploration of ethical competence and an effort to help you become so is approached with a self-assessment of actors in the cases and situations presented. Before we start, however, let's examine what ethical competence is and how it might be pursued.

Ethical Competence

An ethically competent person is not necessarily an ethical leader. However, it is hard to imagine an ethical leader who is also not ethically competent. What then are the skills and qualities needed to become ethically competent? Howard Whitton (2007) identifies six components of ethics competency: (1) having subject matter knowledge of codes and standards; (2) strengthening reasoning skills and the ability to identify difficult ethics situations; (3) strengthening problem-solving skills in situations where ethics standards and codes and various interests must be considered; (4) strengthening the ability to advocate for principled decisions; (5) building self-awareness and consensus-building skills; and (6) strengthening ethics-focused attitudes and commitment to ensure the reliable application of standards (53). "Training and knowledge," Whitton contends, "does not of itself guarantee conforming conduct"; this is why ethics-focused attitudes and commitment are necessary (53).

Another way to define ethical competence is offered by Bowman, West, Berman, and Van Wart (2004). They identify three competencies that managers should possess—moral reasoning, values management, and prudent decision making. They also identify specific ethical skills and competencies, such as having the ability to: (1) engage in principled moral reasoning; (2) recognize ethics-related conflicts; (3) refuse to do something unethical; and (4) apply ethical theory (26). While they do not explicitly define ethical competence, we can presume that it is the possession of these competencies.

Cooper and Menzel (2013) make a clear distinction between competence and competencies. Ethical competence is a state of being with specific competencies such as a commitment to high ethical standards, knowledge of ethics codes and laws, the ability to engage in ethical reasoning, the ability to identify and act on public ethics and values, and the promotion of ethical practices and behavior in our organization (Menzel 2010). Ethical competencies, as indicated in Exhibit 2.1, form a dynamic energy that we can call competence. Furthermore, an ethically competent manager is presumed to have knowledge of the normative foundations of public ethics and a thorough grounding in organization theory and behavior (Cooper & Menzel 2013).

Exhibit 2.1   **Dynamics of Ethical Competence**

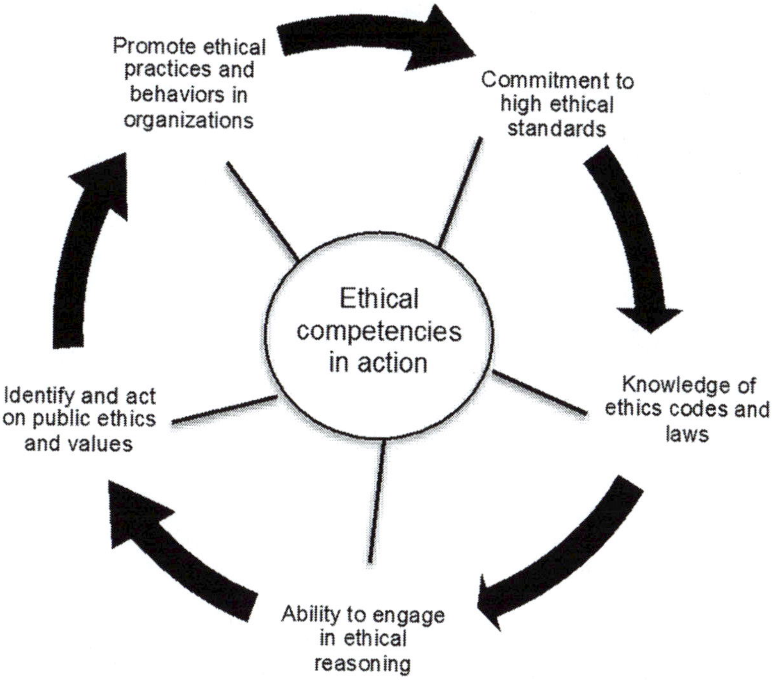

Adapted from Menzel 2010

While the definitions above differ, they share an emphasis on moral reasoning, public service values, and a knowledge–action link. Ethical competence, we could argue, is morality in action.

These definitions are a helpful starting point toward achieving ethical competence, but, you ask—how is competence achieved? And, how do you know if you have become competent? These straightforward, significant questions do not lend themselves to a simple, checklist answer. The pursuit of ethical competence is a foundation building block for ethical leadership, and it is not a one-shot affair. Rather, it is a career-long endeavor, often confounded by missed opportunities, blind alleys, and sometimes, blind spots and other hazards (Bazerman & Tenbrunsel 2011). That being said, let's consider several pathways to becoming ethically competent: Education, common sense, and experience.

Ethical Competence Defined

1. A commitment to high ethical standards of personal and professional behavior
2. Knowledge of relevant ethics codes and laws
3. The ability to engage in ethical reasoning when confronted with challenging ethical situations
4. The ability to identify and act on public ethics and values
5. Commitment to promoting ethical practices and behaviors in organizations

Education, Common Sense, Experience

Competency-based learning is not a new enterprise and may, with some qualification, be said to have roots in vocational education wherein skills are emphasized and tested. We can learn, for example, various welding techniques with instruction and practice but eventually we must demonstrate competence to a teacher or potential employer that we can apply effective and durable welds. Knowledge, of course, is a presumed quantity in this process, while ability is an essential ingredient. Nonetheless, out of this past arrived what is now widespread in many professional occupations, not just vocational work, knowledge, skills, abilities—commonly referred to as KSAs. The acquisition of KSAs in public and nonprofit administration is in vogue. The knowledge component relevant to ethical competence is certainly listed in the definitions offered above and is the domain of formal educational programs at many universities. Training workshops and seminars offered by professional associations also enhance knowledge of codes, standards, and laws. The skills component for achieving ethical competence involves learning how to recognize an ethical issue and, if needed, take preventive action. The ability to reason through an ethical dilemma is also necessary.

Educational institutions and professional associations may be valuable paths on the road to ethical competence but they do not have a monopoly. There are other paths, including common sense and experience. Both are effective teachers that can impart knowledge and wisdom. Still, as the sage Confucius advises: "By three methods we may learn wisdom: First, by reflection, which is noblest; second, by imitation, which is easiest; and third by experience, which is the bitterest" (Confucius n.d.). Experience, for all it offers, can be risky and unforgiving.

Self-reflection

Perhaps the first practical step toward becoming ethically competent is to look inward by conducting a personal ethics audit. Richard Jacobs (2015) contends that public administrators cannot expect to become ethically competent or build an organization of integrity without first taking stock of their state of ethicality. He recommends that the American Society for Public Administration Code of Ethics be drawn on for an ethics audit. More specifically, he poses the following questions, based on the code that we should ask ourselves:

Do and how do I . . .

1. Exercise integrity, courage, compassion, benevolence and optimism?
2. Maintain truthfulness and honesty and not compromise for advancement, honor or personal gain?
3. Resist political, organizational, and personal pressures to compromise ethical integrity and principles and support others who are subject to these pressures?
4. Accept the responsibility and the consequences of my actions?
5. Guard against using public position for personal gain or to advance personal or private interests?
6. Conduct official acts without partisanship or favoritism?
7. Ensure that others receive credit for their work and contributions?

Further, to reduce self-generated subjectivity and assure validity, he suggests that we could ask followers to submit vignettes anonymously from a set of prompts related to a specific principle in the code. For example, Principle 6 calls for members to demonstrate personal integrity. Prompts could include: (1) Describe how I exercise integrity, courage, compassion, benevolence, and optimism. (2) Identify a situation where I was truthful and honest, not compromising for advancement, honor, or personal gain. (3) Relate how I resist political, organizational, and personal pressures to compromise ethical integrity and principles and suppor others subject to these pressures.

Jacobs' call for a personal ethics audit to gain insight into our ethicality is certainly meritorious but also demanding. Still, it has much to promise as a first important step toward becoming ethically competent and acquiring the skills to lead with integrity.

In the nonprofit field, especially for managers who belong to the Association of Fundraising Professionals (AFP), ethical self-examination is a must. Indeed, the AFP has developed an ethics self-assessment tool that enables members to stay focused on ethical behavior. The 14-item online Ethics Assessment Inventory is a voluntary tool designed to provide users with a snapshot of their ethical performance by comparing themselves with peers from across the AFP (2015a). It also allows members to compare the "ethical practices" of their organization with those of other organizations. Finally, a member is asked to define the best ethical practices in the "ideal" organization. The three components—self, the organization the person belongs to, ideal organization—are assessed with each of the 14 items on a five-point scale that ranges from "never" to "always."

Alas, the pursuit of ethical competence can be littered with blind alleys, trap doors, and complicated issues. Are you ready to explore issues that can derail the successful pursuit of ethical competence? Let's start with the usual suspects—bribery, extortion, and graft.

The Usual Suspects

Bribery, extortion, and graft are more than ethical issues. They are typically defined in law as criminal acts with punishment (often incarceration) handed out to the perpetrators. Having said that, the bright line between (un)ethical behavior and behavior that is criminal is rarely that bright. Indeed, the line may be entirely blurred, so much so that it is necessary to go beyond the normal means of determining if suspicious behavior crosses over the line. Such was the case in Hillsborough County, Florida, in the mid-1980s, when three of the five elected commissioners conspired to extort thousands of dollars from developers to rezone land tracts. One ran for office, pledging "to establish good honest government in Hillsborough County" while another promised voters "sound, sober judgment" (Clendinen 1983). The third co-conspirator touted himself as the champion "of the little people." Their extortion racket became known only after a consulting engineer strapped on a Federal Bureau of Investigation (FBI) recording device and, with $15,000 in marked bills, offered the cash to the leader of the cartel. The leader then promptly handed over $5,000 to the other two to vote favorably on a rezoning request. The county administrator also suspected wrongdoing by the commissioners and worked with the FBI to gather evidence. He reportedly brought a stuffed bald eagle to work one day and proudly displayed it in his office for a week. At week's end he told each commissioner that they could have the eagle in their offices for one week at a time. Buried in the eagle was a recording device. You know the rest of the story. Was the county manager a courageous ethics exemplar? So it would seem.

Another jury-determined ethical bright line is the case of former Virginia governor Bob McDonnell (2010–2014). He and his wife traded favors in return for $177,000 in loans, vacations, and gifts from a wealthy family friend who was trying to promote his vitamin supplement business (Steinhauer 2015). McDonnell was pronounced guilty in September 2014 on 11 counts of conspiracy, bribery, and extortion and later sentenced to 2 years in a federal prison. His wife was convicted of nine counts and sentenced to a year and a day in jail. Upon his sentencing, McDonnell said: "I stand before you as a heartbroken and humbled man" (Steinhauer 2015). Ethics management in Virginia?—didn't exist.

Graft—finding a way to enhance one's return on a product or service—is another "no-no." Of course there was a time, now long gone, when a distinction was made between "honest" graft and "dishonest" graft. Honest graft meant taking advantage of insider information to profit oneself. Having knowledge of where a road would be built and then rushing out to buy valuable property adjacent to the road or property that might be developed when access became available was, according to New York State Senator George Washington Plunkett (1842–1924), honest graft. In Plunkett's vernacular: "Ain't it perfectly honest to charge a good price and make a profit on my investment and foresight? Of course, it is. Well, that's honest graft" (Riordon 1963, 3). Dishonest graft in Plunkett's time meant "blackmailing gamblers, saloonkeepers, disorderly people" (Riordon 1963, 3).

Today, graft is, well, graft—making a profit in a dishonest manner, much akin to the butcher adding his thumb to the scales to overcharge you for a steak. Neither government nor nonprofits are exempt from greed-driven graft. Consider the religiously inspired social services nonprofit — the Metropolitan New York Council on Jewish Poverty. The agency, known as Met Council, spends more than $110 million a year on home health care and other services for older people and the poor. Much of the funding comes directly from government contracts. The agency's executive director William E. Rapfogel, with an annual compensation of $400,000, arranged a deal with an insurance broker to pad payments and split the surplus. All total, Rapfogel and his accomplice stole $9 million over a 10-year period. An anonymous whistleblower's tip prompted an internal investigation that uncovered evidence of wrongdoing and led to the dismissal of the executive director. A criminal investigation followed that resulted in a plea agreement whereby Rapfogel would pay $3 million in restitution and receive a 3½–10-year prison sentence (Buettner 2014).

One more interesting aspect about the Met Council scandal should be noted. While some ill-gotten funds were used by Rapfogel to enhance his lifestyle, the insurance firm was directed to make donations to various politicians to benefit Met Council. So the "dark" side of this story, according to *Forbes* columnist Howard Husock, is that nonprofits "have great incentive to curry favor with elected officials but no legal means to do so. Thus, we should not be surprised when an illegal means of doing so comes to light" (Husock 2014).

Next-in-Line Suspects

There are a handful of suspects that, while not criminal, are an endless challenge to achieving ethical competence and building an organization of integrity. First and foremost are *conflicts of interest*. Among the most obvious conflicts for a voting official in government or serving on a nonprofit board can occur when she has a financial stake in the outcome of a vote. While there are typically lawful bans on voting conflicts, the water can still be muddy when an opportunity arises in which the outcome may benefit a friend or family member. Moreover, it is usually up to the board member to recuse herself from a vote that is or could be viewed as a conflict of interest.

Government and nonprofit managers can easily find themselves facing a conflict of interest whenever their decisions can result in an outcome financially favorable to themselves or family members. A city manager who invests in property within his city may rationalize that he is contributing to the city's economic development. And, while that may be true, he is also either ignorant or just plain stupid to make such an investment in the community where his decisions have numerous financial consequences. Of course, most professional ethics code are quite adamant about avoiding this kind of conflict of interest.

Equally sticky is the purchase of goods or services by nonprofits from board members or their companies. The question arises concerning "the real beneficiary of such transactions—the nonprofit or the board member" (Boucher & Hudspeth 2008). A 2008 benchmark study of educational endowments at 767 institutions found that 93 percent have a conflict-of-interest policy while a smaller percentage (22 percent) have a policy that applies to board members. Forty-six percent allow board members to conduct business with the nonprofit. (See Boucher & Hudspeth 2008.)

Appearances Matter

A more troublesome or difficult conflict involves the matter of appearance. Is there a difference between avoiding the appearance of a conflict of interest and a real conflict? Of course there is. Having said that, an appearance standard is finding its way into more codes and practices but it remains very tricky to determine when an appearance is different from reality. Guidelines published by the International City/County Management Association are quite clear about avoiding appearances of impropriety that often arise when real estate is involved. The guidelines state: "Members should not invest or hold any investment, directly or indirectly, in any financial business, commercial, or other private transaction that creates a conflict of interest, in face or appearance, with their official duties" (ICMA 2015).

Yet appearances of wrongdoing happen all too easily. Consider the case of the county administrator in a rapidly growing county with a stellar reputation for getting things done. One day his daughter, a local TV news celebrity, calls and says: "Dad, can you loan me $120,000 to help my husband invest in a condo in the county. We will repay you with interest." Innocent enough? So it seems.

Alas, the plot thickens—it turns out that the daughter's husband has been indicted on 12 federal fraud charges involving two land deals, and it appears that the administrator's money may have been involved in three different real-estate investments that would benefit from the extension of a county road. The administrator claims to have no knowledge of money laundering or any other misdeed.

As the situation evolves further, the county commission decides to order an independent investigation into the administrator's account of the investments to determine whether he is covering something up and may even have lied. The investigation finds that the administrator is not invested in the property owned by the son-in-law. Moreover, the investigation concludes that the administrator did not lie or tell any untruths.

The county commission is relieved but somewhat dismayed. One commissioner says in public:

> Did the administrator lie? No. Did he engage in activities that brought about the appearance of indiscretion? I know he did. He's guilty of that. Actions that reflect poorly on his representation of county government? I find him guilty of that.
>
> (Naplesnews.com 2008)

Another commissioner claims the "board is whitewashing the county manager's involvement." Still another asserts:

> I have determined he has not violated his contract to the point he should be terminated but I beg him to not invest in land in the county again. There should be an ethics requirement added to his employment contract.
>
> (Naplesnews.com 2008)

A fourth commissioner adds: "Is it a sad and pathetic day when we have to amend the county manager's contract to include a requirement that he be ethical?" The board voted unanimously to have the county administrator and the county attorney draft ethics guidelines to include a policy about land investments for county workers.

Exhibit 2.2
BECS Exercise #1

Building Ethical Competence Skills

You are asked to judge the ethical competency of the county administrator in the appearance case using the five components in the definition provided in Chapter 1. Using a scale of 1–5, with 5 representing a high level of ethical competence, assign a value to each actor for each component.

(continued)

Exhibit 2.2 *(continued)*

1. Commitment to high standards of personal and professional behavior
2. Knowledge of relevant ethics codes and laws
3. Ability to engage in ethical reasoning when confronted with challenging ethical situations
4. Ability to identify and act on public service ethics and values
5. Commitment to promoting ethical practices and behaviors

Component

	Low				High	
	1	2	3	4	5	Total
County administrator	___	___	___	___	___	___

As an ethics manager, how would you advise staff members to approach information that may appear to be self-incriminating?

An appearance standard that goes beyond conflicts of interests to include "wrongdoing" is a very high standard and, not surprisingly, difficult to enforce. Still, appearances of wrongdoing, when viewed as real, are real!

Today conflicts of interests have taken on a broader meaning, to include "conflicts of roles and duties—dilemmas in which an individual has obligations to others yet those others have interests that are at odds with one another" (Kennedy 2015, 29). This more encompassing meaning includes conflicting loyalties. It has been a longstanding tenet that, when a person assumes a public post, she will leave behind her partisan commitments. Or, as Thomas Jefferson so eloquently put it: "When a man assumes a public trust he should consider himself a public property." Professional work in government or a nonprofit is expected to put the accent on competence, not political loyalty. Easier said then done—yes! Here may be a case in progress. The Hillsborough County, Florida, environmental commission, a nonpartisan body, hired a new executive director who had twice run for a partisan county office and has been active for years in local Republican circles. Her contract stated that she could not hold political office or engage in any political activity. She objected to the ban, saying it was ambiguous and would hinder her ability to lobby Tallahassee in her capacity as Hillsborough's top environmental official. The commission disagreed, firmly insisting the prohibition on politicking was critical to the agency's integrity (Contorno 2015). Is this case a potential conflict of interest in the making? It certainly has all of the trappings to make it so.

Deception and (Dis)Honesty

Trailing closely behind conflicts of interest as problems for ethics managers are *deception and (dis)honesty*. At first blush one might believe that deception is always bad and honesty is always good. Let's take a closer look at these presumptions. Have you ever played a game in which deception is expected, indeed good? Of course you have. Most certainly we expect deception in sports and war. Of course, deception under these circumstances is not without rules that establish acceptable boundaries to engage in deception. But when deception is practiced that breaks the rules, we think it is bad. Consider the engineer who would search the Internet for hotels near where he was traveling for business. Once he found one to his liking, he would search for a prominent business nearby and, once he found one, he would call the hotel and ask if they had a special rate for that company. He invariably got the discounted rate as hotel clerks rarely asked him to provide evidence that he was a legitimate employee of the nearby business. Is this outright dishonesty? Just bending the rules a bit? Exercising good practical-minded common sense? You decide.

Mark Twain once quipped: "Always do right—this will gratify some and astonish the rest." Might the same thing be said about honesty? Always be honest—this will gratify some and astonish the rest? Perhaps, but this is a somewhat cynical view of humankind. Honesty is regarded by most as a virtue, even though it can be difficult to be honest 24/7. Virtues, Aristotle reminds us, are products of practice, practice, practice! And, if public polling of Americans is reasonably accurate, there is much practice needed, especially among public officials. A Gallup poll (2014) finds that police officers and judges are given respectable marks for honesty and ethics, while members of Congress are viewed as short on both counts.

Deception and dishonesty are often two sides of the same coin and can infuse an organizational culture with disturbing values or cause an ethical numbness. A recent study on lying and dishonesty in the U.S. Army is illustrative. The study "found that many Army officers, after repeated exposure to the overwhelming demands and the associated need to put their honor on the line to verify compliance, have become ethically numb" (Wong & Gerras 2015). Terry Newell (2015a) calls this practice "mutually agreed deception," that is, mandatory workload requirements lead officers to lie about completing the tasks and their superiors silently accept what they know are lies.

Lying and deception are by no means limited to the public and nonprofit sectors. Corporate America is littered with stories and scandals with lying and deception centermost. Even giant transnational corporations have their problems. Volkswagen (VW), the world's largest automobile manufacturer, having surpassed Toyota in mid-2015, was accused by the U.S. Environmental Protection Agency of using software meant to cheat on auto emission tests for diesel vehicles sold in the United States. A *New York Times* editorial proclaimed: "what was Volkswagen thinking?" Apparently, VW wanted desperately to grow its share of the U.S. market. Alas, the "company now faces billions in fines, costly recalls, and possible class action lawsuits and criminal charges" (*New York Times* 2015). And, VW sales have already fallen behind Toyota.

In an effort to determine VW's deception culpability, company executives were hauled before a House committee hearing and asked to explain. VW's chief executive in the United States, Michael Horn, asserted that VW's top management was not aware of the emissions deception. "This was not a corporate decision," Mr. Horn said. "This was something individuals did" (Ivory & Bradsher 2015, B5). He pointed the finger directly at "a couple of software engineers." So, what do we have here—bad apples or a bad barrel? You decide. Wanted: Ethics management at VW!

Gifting

This suspect wears a coat with many colors. When is a gift to a public or nonprofit manager meant as a gesture of good will and when is it meant to be something more, perhaps access or influence? As David Schultz (2010, 165) notes, "In the same way that there are no free lunches, there are no free gifts. Gifts, even if given of one's free will, are not without strings and expectations that they will be reciprocated" (165). There's a story about an elderly woman who had difficulty moving her trash can to the curbside for the city's garbage collection weekly pickup. One morning she was pleasantly surprised to find that a city worker saw she had difficulty getting the can curbside so he moved it for her. So appreciative was she of this kind act that the next week she baked a cake and put it on the garbage can for the worker. He dutifully moved the can curbside. The next week and several weeks that followed she rewarded the worker with more cakes. By the fifth week, the worker, expecting once more to find a cake on the garbage can, when none was offered, refused to move the trash can. Moral of the story—gifts of appreciation can be interpreted as bribes or extortion. Yes, there is no free lunch. What is the ethical problem with gifting, David Schultz asks? "Quite simply, it begins with the problem of reciprocity or indebtedness" (167).

The gifting problem is ever present in the work of public and nonprofit organizations. Thus the ethically competent manager must be able to know how to handle a gifting situation when first, there is no reason to suspect that a gift is given with the intent to influence and, second, it is meant to influence an outcome. Easier said than done! Yes, consequently the prudent course of action is to just say "no, thank you" and, essentially, establish organizational policies that do the same. It is not uncommon, for example, for an appreciative public to shower local officials with seasonal gifts (flowers, candy, sandwiches, turkeys) in which the office policy is to promptly hand gifts over to senior centers, local hospitals, or food banks that help those in need.

> Gifting in professional settings is not always wrong and need not always be prohibited. Workplaces first need to recognize the problem this practice raises in terms of situating personal ethics and behavior in potential conflict with public duties . . . and should adopt policies appropriate to their organizations to address gifting in order to improve ethical service and discourage corruption.
>
> (Schultz 2010, 170)

Overlooked Suspects

Harassment—racial, sexual, gender, and bullying—is an overlooked ethics issue in much of the management literature. Why? Because all are usually defined in law as illegal. Thus the mask of legality becomes a veil that prevents managers from viewing harassment as an ethical issue. But all too often the mask is ripped off when a particularly egregious act becomes public. Such was the case in New York State when the Joint Commission on

Public Ethics determined that state employees needed a hotline that would allow them to report complaints of sexual harassment. The Assembly, New York's legislature, had become a hotbed of allegations involving women staffers sexually harassed by Assemblymen. While the state ethics commission cannot bring criminal charges, it can punish, and has punished, individuals who abuse their position or office. Former Brooklyn Assemblyman Vito Lopez was fined $330,000 after the commission found he sexually harassed eight young female staffers in his office (Lovett 2014). The aggrieved legislative aides filed lawsuits in federal and state court, accusing the 73-year-old Lopez of "instigating unwanted physical contact and sexual advances and peppering them with unsavory comments about their looks and attire" (McKinley 2015). The lawsuits were settled by a $580,000 payment, with the state paying $545,000 and Mr. Lopez paying the remaining $35,000.

Some male legislators in Missouri also seem to have difficulty keeping their distance from female interns and staffers. A state senator and former speaker resigned amid allegations they had harassed interns and exchanged sexual texts with them, prompting the Missouri House speaker to call for annual mandatory sexual-harassment training for lawmakers and staff members (Ballentine 2015).

These cases are highlighted because they not only illustrate the unsavory abuse of public office but suggest that the trail to egregious behavior is likely littered with many subtle unethical instances of harassment that are experienced, but never reported. Sound ethics management, whether in a legislative context or the ordinary workplace, requires sensitivity and vigilance to deter unethical behavior. While training may offer an antidote, it is unlikely to be sufficient absent other options for support. As one of the Missouri interns who claims she was harassed puts it: "sometimes they [victims] just want the support and to be able to talk to somebody about it without worrying that that conversation is going to be released to somebody else" (Ballentine 2015).

Confidentiality and Withholding Information

Nonprofit agencies and public bureaus are repositories of enormous quantities of information (think of the Internal Revenue Service), some publicly accessible but much confidential. Managers and employees are expected to ensure and respect the privacy of clients, donors, and citizens. Nonprofits have an especial fiduciary responsibility to treat a donor with privacy. As stated forthrightly by the Independent Sector, coalition of nonprofits, foundations, and corporate giving programs committed to advancing the common good, in its "Principles for Good Governance and Ethical Practice":

> A charitable organization should respect the privacy of individual donors and, except where disclosure is required by law, should not sell or otherwise make available the names and contact information of its donors without providing them an opportunity at least once a year to opt out of the use of their names.
>
> (Independent Sector 2015)

Withholding information because it is confidential or protects privacy is certainly meritorious and justified but it is not always so easy or straightforward to do. Professional judgment does come into play, so we need to know the boundaries of when withholding information is appropriate and when it is not. There can be an ethical dimension involved.

Consider the case of the city manager in pursuit of a very competitive, high-profile job.[1] During the search process conducted by a reputable consulting search firm he was asked: "If we conducted a thorough background check on you, would we find anything in your background which might embarrass a future employer?" He paused for a moment as his mind flashed back to an allegation that was made about him when he was the city manager of a small community. Two staff members of the community hospital where his wife was terminally ill alleged that he slapped and verbally abused her.

The police investigated the allegation, as did the Department of Children and Family Services (DCF). During the investigation he asserted that the staff members misinterpreted a situation in which his wife was choking and he was helping her. His wife stated to the investigators that he did not abuse her. Neither the police nor the DCF investigation reported that there was any physical evidence (e.g. redness on the face) that he had slapped her. Nonetheless, the investigative report was sent to the State Attorney to determine whether or not to press charges. The State Attorney declined to pursue the matter due to a lack of evidence. Thus the allegation is unsubstantiated.

How should he reply to the question asked by the search firm? Should he or should he not disclose the incident? Let's assume that he reasons that the incident was entirely personal and was found to be unsubstantiated. Therefore, he decides to respond by saying, "There is nothing in my background that would embarrass a future employer."

He receives an invitation to interview. During the interview, he stresses his honesty and high ethical standards. Should he disclose or not disclose the incident to the city's human resources (HR) staff and the city commissioners? Once more, he decides to not disclose information about the incident for the same reason he did not disclose it to the search firm.

The interview goes very well. City commissioners are impressed and decide to offer him a $170,000 job contract. The local newspaper reports the story with the byline—"Ethics and experience bring Jones to the fore."

On the day the contract is to be voted on, city commissioners receive information that he was accused of slapping and verbally abusing his wife in the hospital where she was terminally ill.

The commission decides to call an emergency meeting to discuss the situation. He is invited to appear before the commission and answer their questions.

Should he accept the commission's invitation? He decides "yes" as the air needs to be cleared and he needs the full trust and confidence of his new bosses. During the questioning, he asserts, "I haven't lied. I have not told an untruth." One commissioner asks: "Why didn't you tell us about this allegation?" What should he say?

1. I forgot.
2. I didn't think anyone would find out.
3. You didn't ask me.
4. It was merely an unsubstantiated allegation as my wife and I had a very loving relationship right up to the moment of her death.
5. Withholding information is acceptable under these very personal circumstances.
6. I thought the allegation, although untrue, would place my candidacy in jeopardy if it became public.

Outcome

The commission decides to postpone approving his contract for 2 weeks while they seek more background information about him. Meanwhile, he has withdrawn as a city manager finalist for several other positions and is now worried about ending up without any job.

He muses, "Am I being treated fairly by the city commission? The media? I know I haven't done anything wrong. Why am I being subjected to such scrutiny?"

Investigation Results

A three-member committee, which included one city commissioner, the director of HR, and a representative of the Police Department, was formed and traveled to the community where he had served as the city manager for 4 years. After visiting the community and meeting with former and current town council members, the town manager, the president of the Chamber of Commerce, a police sergeant, and the town attorney, the committee reports, "we have no concerns about his honesty or integrity." One commissioner

---

Exhibit 2.3
BECS Exercise #2

Building Ethical Competence Skills

You are asked to judge the ethical competency of the candidate for the city manager case using the five components in the definition provided in Chapter 1. Using a scale of 1–5, with 5 representing a high level of ethical competence, assign a value to each actor for each component.

1. Commitment to high standards of personal and professional behavior
2. Knowledge of relevant ethics codes and laws
3. Ability to engage in ethical reasoning when confronted with challenging ethical situations
4. Ability to identify and act on public service ethics and values
5. Commitment to promoting ethical practices and behaviors

Component

	Low				High	
	1	2	3	4	5	Total
City manager candidate	___	___	___	___	___	___

As an ethics manager, how would you advise staff members to approach information that may appear to be self-incriminating?

---

sums up his thoughts to the city commission by stating, "He exercised poor judgment as a candidate who sold himself on honesty, integrity and character, but that is not a sufficient reason to not offer a contract. Poor judgment is not an unethical act."

The city commission votes 4–1 to approve his $170,000-a-year contract. "Congratulations," says a commissioner, "we want you here as soon as possible."

Meanwhile, commissioners decide to withhold the final payment to the head hunter until the city attorney determines whether or not they could penalize the firm for not conducting a thorough background investigation.

Advocacy and Lobbying

Nonprofit and government leaders are expected to be strong advocates for their constituents. Charity nonprofits in particular attract many true believers to their cause. Would we want it any other way? Probably not, but the line between advocacy and lobbying for organizational resources and self-aggrandizement is not always so bright. This is the classic ends-become-the-means conundrum. Advocacy can also have a confusing influence on doing the right thing when a person finds herself at odds with an organizational superior. Here is an example.

To Obey or Not to Obey?[2]

Mary is an inspector in the village engineering department and has the responsibility to inspect the sidewalks of residents whose streets are being resurfaced. The village policy is clear—residents who live on streets that are partially resurfaced must pay up to $1,000 per home for their sidewalks to be replaced. But, residents on streets that are fully resurfaced are not required to pay. Mary's job is to determine how much a resident who lives on a partially resurfaced street must pay to replace the sidewalk. Sounds straightforward enough, doesn't it? Not so. Why? Because the technical criteria for determining the difference between a full resurface and a partial resurface are murky. Moreover, as the inspector, Mary has suffered for many years trying to explain the system to residents who are impacted. And, it is her strong belief that the required fee is too great of a burden, particularly as it is not applied in all cases and a large percentage of the residents are retired. After years of expressing her concerns to the director of the engineering department and having them ignored, Mary decides to take the matter directly to the mayor.

The engineering director does not find Mary's conversation with the mayor amusing. Indeed, he becomes quite angry with her for going over his head to the mayor and having his policy decision questioned. He instructs Mary to proceed with collecting money from residents and lobbies the mayor to support the current policy. Mary continues collecting checks and contracts from residents but decide not to cash them or process the contracts because she feel the mayor will rule in her favor. And, she is right. The mayor concludes the system is unfair and resident contributions are eliminated for all sidewalk replacement projects.

Upon hearing the mayor's decision, Mary returns the unprocessed checks and destroys the contracts. The director, not having budgeted for the change, instructs Mary to continue with the old policy for the upcoming construction season and to initiate the new policy the following year. Concerned about losing her job, Mary says that she had not collected any money. Moreover, she feels it would be impossible to collect the money for the upcoming project year as the change in policy had already been announced in the local press.

In the meantime, the director investigates and finds that the money has indeed been collected and subsequently returned. In his opinion, this was contrary to a direct order. Mary admits lying but claims that she had merely followed the wishes of the elected officials. The director gives Mary a pink slip, thus terminating her employment with the village. Mary decides to appeal the decision to the assistant administrator.

The assistant administrator meets privately with Mary and then her supervisor. The assistant administrator, looking for a way out of this awkward situation, informs the supervisor that, while Mary was wrong to disobey him, she acted out of concern for the welfare of elderly citizens. Therefore, he recommends that she be placed on paid leave for 1 week and returned to her position as an inspector.

Exhibit 2.4
BECS Exercise #3

Building Ethical Competence Skills

You are asked to judge the ethical competency of the characters in the village case using the five components in the definition provided in Chapter 1. Using a scale of 1–5, with 5 representing a high level of ethical competence, assign a value to each actor for each component.

(continued)

Exhibit 2.4 *(continued)*

1. Commitment to high standards of personal and professional behavior
2. Knowledge of relevant ethics codes and laws
3. Ability to engage in ethical reasoning when confronted with challenging ethical situations
4. Ability to identify and act on public service ethics and values
5. Commitment to promoting ethical practices and behaviors

	Low				High	
	1	2	3	4	5	Total
Mary	___	___	___	___	___	___
Engineering supervisor	___	___	___	___	___	___
Assistant administrator	___	___	___	___	___	___

Component

As an ethics manager, how would you counsel Mary about her behavior?

Lobbying

Nonprofit and public managers live in an influencing environment day in and day out. They operate on a treadmill that runs two ways simultaneously. They attempt to influence others—boards, staff, and volunteers—and be influenced by others—boards, staff, and volunteers—as well as by those in the interorganizational environment. Such an influencing environment is natural, but can it take on a different hue when we talk about lobbying public officials? Perhaps. "When many people think about nonprofits and lobbying," writes Nayantara Mehta (2009),

> they might think of a relationship like oil and water: they don't mix. There is a widespread perception that nonprofits cannot lobby, or if they do lobby, they are exploiting some kind of legal loophole. The fact is that nonprofits, even 501(c)(3) organizations, which are the most restricted type of nonprofits, may legally lobby.

Further, she contends,

> getting involved in the legislative process and having a say in policy discussions is not just an appropriate role for nonprofits; it is vital. If nonprofits are not speaking on behalf of their often-vulnerable communities, chances are nobody else is either.
>
> (Mehta 2009)

So lobbying, often viewed as plotting and conniving act, is OK in the nonprofit sector? Not necessarily. Some, especially members of public charity organizations, may believe it is an inappropriate activity that can divert resources and distort the organizational mission. Others may view it as blatantly political and distasteful. Regardless of one's taste or distaste for lobbying, we need to take a closer look at the lobbying boundaries set by federal tax law.

Tax-exempt organizations (the IRS identifies 30 types) are described in the IRS Code as "having charitable, religious, educational, scientific, or literary purposes" (Mehta 2009). The best tax treatment allows nonprofits to be exempt from paying federal taxes and donors may deduct their donations from their taxes. No organization that has these tax benefits may support or oppose a candidate for public office—these are 501(c)(3) organizations. Social welfare organizations 501(c)(4), such as the League of Conservation Voters and American Association of Retired People, are also tax-exempt, but contributions to them are not tax-deductible (Mehta 2009). "The tradeoff for this less beneficial tax treatment is that they may engage in unlimited lobbying and also may engage in some partisan political activities (subject to state or federal election law rules)" (Mehta 2009). Having said this, 501(c)(3) public charities are prohibited from engaging in partisan political activities and may not endorse or make contributions to support or oppose a particular candidate or party.

The IRS rules and federal law attempt to put reasonable limits on lobbying, but there are still gray areas. Consider churches and pastors—where might they fit into this picture? Churches are 501(c)(3) organizations and fall within the prohibited zones. But what about pastors? Sarah Jones, writing in *Wall of Separation*, states:

> There's no issue with pastors raising social issues from the pulpit or helping a candidate in a personal capacity. But it's another matter entirely when pastors use church resources to explicitly endorse candidates. The IRS guidelines are in place because pastors are spiritual authorities, and therefore wield incredible influence over their

congregations and communities. Applied to campaigns, that influence can undermine the democratic process and establish a political monopoly.

(Jones 2015)

(Un)Ethical Fundraising

Nonprofit managers, who serve as executive directors, are often expected—indeed required—to raise funds for their organization. Securing funds to advance the mission of a nonprofit is essential. Contracts with governmental bodies can be one source of funds; other sources can be foundations or direct solicitations from individual donors. Regardless of the source, funding sources typically attach strings to how those funds may be used by a nonprofit. Raising and spending funds can become an ethical quagmire without much difficulty. Consequently, it should come as no surprise to learn that the AFP, or Association of Fundraising Professionals, represents 30,000 members in the United States, Canada, Mexico, and China and promotes high ethical standards in the fundraising profession.

The (un)ethical pitfalls in fundraising range across a broad spectrum of issues:

- appearance of impropriety
- stewardship of donors' rights, including donor's giving history
- privacy and security, including gift restrictions and using donations as intended
- tainted money—funds contributed to an organization that may be illegally obtained, say from the sale of illicit drugs, stealing, or white-collar crimes committed by an individual or corporation
- approaching donor prospects for gifts
- honesty and disclosure
- grant seeking and accountability.

Penn State Scandal

This is a story of tragic happenings that tested the ethical competence of all involved in the case of Jerry Sandusky, the convicted child molester who sexually abused ten young boys over a 15-year period and is now serving a prison sentence of 30–60 years. Two nonprofit organizations and, eventually, the government are involved. Penn State is a nonprofit educational institution with an enrollment of 45,000 and a reputation as a national football powerhouse. The Second Mile was a nonprofit organization in Pennsylvania with headquarters in State College, founded by assistant Penn State football coach Jerry Sandusky in 1977. The Second Mile charity served underprivileged and at-risk youth. The group was held out as a "shining example" of charity work when U.S. President George H.W. Bush recognized it as the 294th Point of Light in 1990. Sandusky was football legend Joe Paterno's defensive coordinator for 23 of his 32 years at Penn State.

Why and how a public charity and its leadership turn into a cauldron of darkness is a fascinating story in its own right. However, our interest here is in the actors and action taken—or not—by those with information and knowledge about the behavior of Sandusky that led to the scandal that put Sandusky behind bars and shocked the educational and sports world.

Timeline of Key Events

1994—A boy, identified as victim 7 in the grand jury report, meets Sandusky through the Second Mile at about the age of 10.

1995–1996—Victim 5 meets Sandusky through the Second Mile when he is 7 or 8.

May 3, 1998—Boy assaulted by Sandusky in the locker room and showers at Penn State. Mother reports to university police that Sandusky showered with her son.

May 4–30, 1998—University vice president Gary C. Schultz is informed. His notes of that day say: "Behavior—at best inappropriate@ worst sexual improprieties." Tim Curley, the athletic director, notifies Schultz that he has told Penn State coach Joe Paterno about the incident. In later e-mails: "Anything new in this department? Coach is anxious to know where it stands." Paterno maintained before his death that he didn't know about the incident.

June 1998—A university police detective and a state public welfare caseworker interview Sandusky, who admits hugging victim 6 in the shower, but there was nothing "sexual about it." District attorney Ray Gricar decides there will be no criminal charges.

June 1999—Sandusky retires from Penn State with full access to the campus and football facilities.

Fall 2000—A janitor finds Sandusky in the showers of the football building performing oral sex on a boy. Neither the janitor nor a fellow employee he told about the incident made a report because they were worried about their job security.

February 9, 2001—Mike McQueary, Penn State assistant football coach, hears "rhythmic, slapping sounds" that he believes are related to sexual activity. He later says under oath that he sees Sandusky raping a boy. McQueary leaves and meets with his father and decides to report the incident to Paterno.

February 10, 2001—McQueary reports what he saw to coach Paterno. Paterno tells him: "You did what you had to do. It's my job now to figure out what we want to do." Before he died, Paterno insisted McQueary did not tell him of the extent of the assault—only that McQueary had seen something inappropriate involving Sandusky and a child.

February 11, 2001—Paterno reports the incident to Penn State athletic director Tim Curley and, later, to senior vice president Gary Schultz and university president Graham B. Spanier.

February 25, 2001—Schultz, Spanier, and Curley decide to report the shower incident to the state Department of Public Welfare.

February 27, 2001—Curley informs Schultz and Spanier that he has changed his mind after "talking it over" with Coach Paterno. Instead of reporting the incident, he says they should offer Sandusky "professional help" and tell him to stop bringing guests to the locker room. They do not report the incident.

March 3, 2001—McQueary meets with the athletic director, Tim Curley, and senior vice president for finance and business, Gary Schultz. He tells them he saw Sandusky and the boy engaged in anal sex. Curley and Schultz deny that McQueary told them such an allegation. Instead, they say they had the impression the conduct amounted to "horsing around." Sandusky's locker room keys are confiscated and the incident is reported to the Second Mile, but no law enforcement investigation is launched.

March 5, 2001—Curley tells Sandusky the university is "uncomfortable" with the incident and will report it to his foundation. He tells Sandusky to stop bringing children to the athletic facilities.

August 2001—Sandusky assaults victim 5 in the shower at Penn State.

2005–2006—Sandusky meets the boy identified as victim 1 through the Second Mile. He is 11 or 12 years old.

April 2005—Ray Gricar, the former district attorney who chose not to prosecute Sandusky in 1998, disappears. The circumstances are murky: His car is found abandoned, his laptop is recovered months later in a river without a hard drive, and his body is never found.

Spring 2008—Victim 1 is now a freshman in high school. The boy breaks off contact with Sandusky; the mother calls the boy's high school to report her son had been sexually assaulted and the principal reports the incident to police. In November, Sandusky informs the Second Mile that he is under investigation and is removed from all program activities involving children.

Early 2009—an investigation by the Pennsylvania attorney general begins. A grand jury subpoenas university documents in 2010, but no one tells the board of trustees of the university's potential complicity.

Early 2010—Sandusky steps down from the Second Mile.

2011—Grand jury investigates allegations against Sandusky. On November 4, the grand jury report is released, with Sandusky arraigned on 40 criminal counts. The athletic director Tim Curley and senior vice president for finance and business Gary Schultz are each charged with one count of felony perjury and one count of failure to report abuse allegations. Both step down from their position on November 7. A few days later Paterno announces that he intends to retire at the end of the 2011 football season. Hours later, both president Graham Spanier and coach Paterno are fired by the university board of trustees. McQueary, now a Penn State receivers coach, is placed on indefinite administrative leave.

November 5, 2011—Sandusky is arrested on charges of sexually abusing eight boys over a 15-year period.

November 13, 2011—The chief executive officer of the Second Mile resigns.

November 21, 2011—The board of trustees authorizes an independent inquiry of the school's response to child sex abuse allegation, to be led by former FBI director Louis Freeh.

November 30, 2011—First lawsuit in the scandal is filed on behalf of a child alleged to have been sexually abused by Sandusky.

December 8, 2011—Sandusky posts $250,000 bail, is placed under house arrest, and is required to wear an electronic monitoring device.

December 16, 2011—McQueary testifies he told university officials that he saw Sandusky assaulting a boy in 2001.

January 22, 2012—Coach Joe Paterno dies at the age of 85.

June 11, 2012—Sandusky's trial begins.

June 22, 2012—Sandusky is found guilty of 45 of the 48 remaining counts, after jurors deliberate for almost 21 hours.

July 5, 2012—McQueary learns that his contract has not been renewed.

July 6, 2012—Former Penn State president Graham Spanier tells investigators that he had never been informed of any incident involving Sandusky.

July 12, 2012—The Freeh report is released, accusing the former leaders at Penn State of showing "total and consistent disregard" for child sex abuse victims.

July 23, 2012—The National Collegiate Athletic Association fines Penn State $60 million, bans the football team from postseason play for 4 years, reduces scholarships for 4 years, and vacates the university's football victories from 1998 to 2011.

October 2, 2012—Mike McQueary files a whistleblower lawsuit against Penn State.

October 9, 2012—Sandusky is sentenced to no less than 30 years and no more than 60 years in prison.

November 1, 2012—The Commonwealth of Pennsylvania filed eight charges against former Penn State president Graham Spanier, including perjury and endangering the welfare of a child.

(Sources: CNN Library 2015; Deadspin.com 2015:
New York Times 2015)

Please consider the following facts and statements before you judge the ethical competence of key actors in the Penn State scandal.

University vice president Gary C. Schultz—notes of May 4, 1998, following the mother's allegation that Sandusky assaulted her 11-year-old son read: "Behavior—at best inappropriate@worst sexual improprieties. Is this opening of Pandora's box? Other children?"

Tim Curley, the athletic director, notifies Schultz that he has told Penn State coach Joe Paterno about the 1998 incident—later e-mails: "Anything new in this department? Coach is anxious to know where it stands."

Joe Paterno—maintained before his death that he didn't know about the 1998 incident.

Ray Gricar—the former district attorney who chose not to prosecute Sandusky in 1998 disappears in April 2005. His car is found abandoned, his laptop is recovered months later in a river without a hard drive; his body is never found.

The Freeh report accuses Paterno, the university's former president, and others of deliberately hiding facts about Sandusky's sexually predatory behavior. Spanier repeatedly downplayed the importance of the Sandusky investigation throughout 2010 and 2011.

Exhibit 2.5
BECS Exercise #4

Building Ethical Competence Skills

You are asked to judge the ethical competency of the principal actors in the Penn State case using the five components in the definition provided in Chapter 1. Using a scale of 1–5, with 5 representing a high level of ethical competence, assign a value to each actor for each component.

1. Commitment to high standards of personal and professional behavior
2. Knowledge of relevant ethics codes and laws
3. Ability to engage in ethical reasoning when confronted with challenging ethical situations
4. Ability to identify and act on public service ethics and values
5. Commitment to promoting ethical practices and behaviors

| | Component | | | | | |
| | Low | | | | High | |
	1	2	3	4	5	Total
Joe Paterno	____	____	____	____	____	____
Gary Schultz	____	____	____	____	____	____
Tim Curley	____	____	____	____	____	____
Graham Spanier	____	____	____	____	____	____
Mike McQueary	____	____	____	____	____	____

Questions to ponder:

1. Didn't Joe Paterno do his duty by reporting the 2001 incident to higher university authorities? Did Paterno do anything unethical?
2. Were Schultz and Curley wrong to not report the incident to the police?

(continued)

Exhibit 2.5 *(continued)*

3.   Was president Spanier guilty of a cover-up?
4.   Should the graduate assistant Mike McQueary have kept silent about the 2001 incident? Should he have done more than report it to coach Paterno?

Summing Up

There is no quick or easy path to becoming ethically competent. It can be a long slog through difficult territory; sometimes, as the Penn State case illustrates, becoming ethically competent requires one to do more than follow the chain of command. As coach "Jo Pa" Paterno, as he was called by many, lamented: "In hindsight, I wish I had done more" (Jenkins 2012). Paterno was certainly held out as an ethical role model before the scandal broke. Part of the message here is that aspiring to high ethical standards, even firmly believing that one has achieved high standards, does not mean that one is invulnerable to ethical lapses. Ethical vigilance is required.

This chapter has also illustrated that even the line between criminal behavior and ethical behavior is often blurred and, in worst-case situations, requires an external judgment to be made. Bribery, extortion, graft—conflicts of interest, appearance of impropriety, deception and dishonesty, confidentiality and withholding information—are among the collection of behaviors that managers must deal with in pursuit of ethical competence and building an organization of integrity. And, we have many tools that can be fashioned to overcome improper behavior and foster acceptable behavior in public and nonprofit agencies.

Ethics Management Skill Building

Practicum 2.1 When Interests Collide: Or Do They?

You are the parks and recreation director for the city of Tampaland and are responsible for overseeing the purchase of new playground equipment. The city typically buys new products through a "piggyback contract," which means that another government negotiated the deal and other cities can use the same pricing and terms. This practice was been in place long before you were hired. You decide to place a purchase order for $200,000 in new playground equipment from a business that employs your wife, who was hired by the company to meet with customers, visit parks, and pitch the company's products. City policy requires employees to file written disclosure statements if the employee or a family member benefits from the sale of a product purchased by the city. You do not file a written disclosure statement because you do not perceive this situation to be a conflict of interest.

Discussion Questions

1. Should you have disclosed the fact that the playground equipment company employs your wife?
2. Should you verbally disclose the relationship to the city's chief of staff?
3. Is there a conflict of interest if your spouse works for a firm that does business with the city? Why, or why not?

Practicum 2.2 The Many Hands Problem[3]

The complexities of twenty-first-century organizations wrought by globalization and rapidly changing information and communication technology along with the explosion of social media (e.g., Facebook, Twitter, Instagram, and more) have blurred lines of responsibility and called into question what is right and what is wrong. So many hands making decisions can challenge the ethical health of individuals and organizations, landing all in an unethical swamp. (The case that follows is based on a real case but is presented in an abbreviated format.)

This case involves deception and blunder in a modern, progressive, urban county. The county government has a long history of stability and professionalism. No county commissioner has lost re-election since 1992, and the then popular county administrator's 5-year tenure could turn into a much longer one. After all, his predecessor served with distinction for 22 years. County employees are treated well and enjoy long careers. Yet, it became a county embroiled in controversy and scandal over an insider land deal.

The key actors are the property appraiser, the county administrator, the county attorney, and the members of the elected county commission. One fascinating question threads throughout the story: "How could well-educated, politically smart, and experienced public officials have a collective lapse of ethical judgment?"

The property appraiser was elected nearly 20 years ago and intended to seek re-election, having been re-elected without opposition in 1996, 2000, and 2004. He enjoyed a reputation as a fair, competent public official, described as "a man of high integrity." Thirteen years ago he purchased a beautiful home site for $15,000, a 1.5-acre parcel in the county that he describes as an urban oasis. He tells friends that the site is what the Spaniards must have seen when they first came to Florida.

As the years pass, however, the parcel sits vacant and he reconsiders his plan to build a dream house. He muses, "Perhaps I should put it on the market." And, since his daughter is a new real-estate agent, why not let her handle the listing—$400,000? The land's market value is appraised at $59,400.

Nine months pass and no buyer is in sight. The property appraiser has personal problems too. His 11-year marriage ends in divorce and the $1.2-million house shared with his former wife belongs to her. Consequently, he decides to purchase a $497,000 house, using the money from the sale of the land parcel as a down payment.

Aha! It hits him—why not sell the property to the county? After all, county work crews severely damaged the property when they made flood repairs following the 2004 hurricanes. Surely, he thought, the county commission would be sympathetic to his case and they can legitimately claim that the property would be useful to the county in the event of future flooding. And, he suspects, I can expect fast-track handling of the sale.

The appraiser decides to meet with the county administrator to let him know just how unhappy he is with the damage the county did to his property. He also hires an attorney, who sends a letter to the county administrator suggesting that the county buy the "destroyed" property rather than face a lawsuit about the damage. The letter states:

> While my client is understandably upset about the ruination of his property, he is not vindictive and wishes to resolve this matter in a fair and expeditious manner . . . this letter will serve as a request that the county purchase the subject property so that he can have adequate funds to seek an alternative piece of property with a pastoral setting like the one his subject property previously enjoyed.

The county administrator is a veteran of local government, with more than 25 years' experience as a high-ranking official in a nearby urban county. He has held his current job for 5 years and enjoys a very strong relationship with the county commission. He has acquired a reputation for quality service improvement and adopting innovative approaches to county management.

He is very much aware of the property appraiser's desire to have the county purchase the home site and the property appraiser's strong feelings about the damage the county did to it. In fact, a high-level assistant county administrator visited the site, where he encountered the property appraiser, who "was unbelievably mad—screaming, yelling, cussing." The county administrator is shocked at how upset the property appraiser is and promises to look into the damage. You caution county staff to be very sensitive about the matter, knowing any sign of special treatment given to the property appraiser would raise eyebrows.

He delegates the matter to his assistant county administrator, who is in his first week on the job. The county administrator instructs staff to determine if purchasing the property would be a good acquisition for flood control in the area. The staff return with a positive response. The assistant county administrator instructs staff to proceed with the purchase according to county policy that requires an outside appraisal.

The outside appraiser places a $250,000 price tag on the property but warns that the appraisal does not reflect any water issues (especially flooding, which could devalue the estimate) and recommends that an expert be consulted. The county administrator decides not to seek an expert opinion as he wishes to get the matter resolved quickly and instructs the assistant county administrator to make an offer to the property appraiser of $200,000. The property appraiser counters with $225,000, which the county administrator accepts subject to approval by the county commission.

It is the administrator's practice to discuss all agenda items with each member of the county commission prior to official meetings and this item is no exception. Several commissioners ask about the sale and find the administrator's response satisfactory. A few days later the commission holds its weekly meeting and votes unanimously, with no public discussion, to approve the purchase.

The county attorney enters the situation. She has been with the county more than 25 years and has been the county attorney for 20 years. She enjoys the full trust and confidence of her elected bosses. A former commissioner describes her as "a woman of high integrity and ethics and [who] is always on the side of caution." The property appraiser asks the county attorney to represent him and, as a long-time friend and colleague, she agrees to do so without compensation. She understands that dual representation, representing the property appraiser as a private citizen and the county, is not illegal but could be a slippery slope. She therefore decides to seek a conflict-of-interest waiver that requires the chair of the county commission to sign off. She sends the waiver to the county chair with a cover memo but the memo does not detail the scope of possible work for the property appraiser. The chair signs the waiver. The county attorney does not inform the county administrator or the county commission that she is representing the property appraiser in the sale of the property to the county.

Enter the county commission—by most accounts, the county commission is a collegial group that works as a team with the county administrator and the county attorney. No commissioner judges the purchase of the property appraiser's vacant lot to be a big deal, as the county quite frequently purchases property for flood control. Not all agree—especially the local media.

A newspaper reporter routinely attends county commission meetings and reads each week's agenda carefully. The county's purchase of the property appraiser's property gets his attention because it moved along so fast and was quickly and silently dealt with by the county commission. He suspects insider dealing and begins to ask questions. The more he digs, the more he becomes convinced that the commission was asleep on its ethical watch. The story breaks in the local news and the county scrambles. All seem complicit—the property appraiser, the county administrator, the county attorney, and the county commission.

The local newspaper lambasts the commission for a "conspiracy of silence," calling the commission a "courthouse gang." One columnist claims that the county commission is embarrassingly complacent and deferential and should at least fire the county attorney, who led them astray. Letters to the editor and blog postings are consistently critical of the commission. One writer asserts: "this is only the tip of the iceberg in county corruption." Another writes that this "sort of back-door deal causes residents to distrust the commission . . . a wink and a nod won't do."

The public uproar grows when it becomes known that the county used money from a recent voter-supported referendum called Penny for Prairie County to purchase the vacant lot owned by the property appraiser. A local newspaper editorial calls for the property appraiser to resign and the county commission to fire the county attorney. The property appraiser loudly proclaims his innocence and asks the state attorney to convene a grand jury to investigate the matter. The state attorney rejects the property appraiser's request, but as more details are published in the newspaper, he changes his mind.

The Grand Jury's Findings

The grand jury heard 41 witnesses and reviewed numerous charts and references provided by both the witnesses and both public and private entities. The key findings in the presentment were:

1. There is no evidence that public officials "maliciously abused" their positions.
2. Several officials, including the county commissioners, helped foster the "clear public perception" that the property appraiser received favorable treatment because of his status.
3. Several commissioners were completely unaware that the decision to purchase the property appraiser's property had been preceded by a threat to sue the county.
4. The county attorney's actions were "perplexing and misleading."
5. The normal objective appraisal process was rushed by the county administrator.
6. The county violated the property appraiser's property rights by entering the lot but there was no credible evidence that the work crews were responsible for the devastation claimed by the property appraiser.
7. County officials failed to conduct any public discussion of such a sensitive purchase by a fellow elected official.

The chair of the county commission never imagines that he would be hauled before a grand jury and suspected of going along on an insider land deal. He asserts, "I cannot tell you how disturbed I am to be facing a grand jury because the county attorney failed to disclose information." He decides to raise the matter of what to do with the county attorney. Should the commission fire her? Suspend her with or without pay? Neither until the grand jury finishes its investigation?

The County Administrator's Response to the Grand Jury's Findings

I accept full responsibility for errors or missteps by me and members of my administration in connection with the PA's [property appraiser's] property purchase. I will not address issues surrounding the actions of the county attorney or property appraiser. The following are my initial "after action" conclusions and planned corrective measures within my purview which I intend to discuss with the Board of County Commissioners.

This transaction was expedited in the interest of trying to protect the public from legal liability exposure. I personally should have slowed things down to ensure that greater care was taken with the analysis supporting the decision and that all questions were thoroughly addressed. In the future, the administration should regard legal guidance as just that and exercise more independent judgment on matters such as this.

While I made it a point to alert every commissioner of the individual elected official involved in this transaction (property appraiser) and the rationale for my recommendations, they didn't know as much about the matter as they should have. While there are a myriad of topics I discuss with commissioners regularly, making it difficult to cover all subjects thoroughly, I should have provided more information to the board on this topic. I pledge that this situation will not repeat itself.

The Property Appraiser's Response to the Grand Jury's Findings

"I went through the Grand Jury process and nothing was found there. The presentment was fair but incomplete. It was evident to me that the Grand Jury had been influenced by news media articles about the case and had made up their minds about my guilt. Where did I do something wrong? I fail to see it."

The County Attorney's Response to the Grand Jury's Findings

"I am very pleased that the Grand Jury has completed its work and has determined that no criminal wrongdoing was involved in the County's purchase of the property appraiser's property. It is in everyone's best interest to have a conclusion to this matter. The Grand Jury's recommendations are well taken. I welcomed any fair-minded inquiry into these facts to dispel the many misperceptions reported over several weeks by the local newspaper.

Although I did not provide legal representation to the property appraiser, apparently the Administrator and others perceived that I did. Although my actions were clear, there was apparently confusion and ambiguity surrounding them. I understood my role and intent, but apparently failed in my attempt to explain it clearly to the administrator. Although at all times my conduct was open and ethical, the perception remained that it was not. My only desire was to allow the parties to negotiate between themselves to save the substantial expense of dealing with a well-founded property rights violation. The waiver of conflict letter was consistent with my course of dealing over 20 years as County Attorney in these situations. The Chair has executed such waivers because he or she is the "client," not the county administrator. Pursuant to a protocol which has been in place since before my association with the County Attorney's office 26 years ago, perceived or possible conflict situations are handled on a rather routine basis by presenting a waiver letter to only the Chairman of the Commission. Although the letter implies that I could represent the property appraiser, the purpose of the letter was to advise the Chair that I would not continue to represent Pinellas County, the only client I was representing, if the dispute continued into litigation. Had the matter moved to litigation, the value of the property would have been an obvious issue, and as proof of value, one or both sides of the dispute would refer to the value placed on the parcel by the Property Appraiser in his Official Capacity, thus raising the issue of conflict. The fact of the matter is that the County administration recommended the purchase of the property not because of the legal issues referred to me for opinion, but because the County apparently believed that the land was needed for future flood control activities. The end result is that the county administration acquired the property it said it needed for $25,000 less than its appraised value and the county avoided the costs and expenses related to the inverse condemnation claim which the county probably could not successfully defend against based upon the county's prior actions. This was clearly pointed out in the Presentment returned by the Grand Jury in this matter.

> When terrorists attack, oil spills, banks fail, and other "stuff happens," we naturally look for individuals to blame. But in modern society, the most serious damage is usually done by large organizations including governments. Because many different individuals in an organization contribute in many ways to the decisions and policies, it is difficult even in principle to identify who is responsible for the resets. This difficulty is known as the problem of many hands.
>
> (Thompson 2014)

The County Commission Acts

Recognizing the need to restore public trust and confidence in county government, the county commission fires the county attorney and publicly reprimands the county administrator at the conclusion of a 2-hour meeting. As one commissioner put it, "We've got some sour milk. You smell it and I smell it, and we've got to do something . . . someone has got to pay the price, and that's painful."

In an effort to save her job, the county attorney apologizes for not giving the commission more details on the land transaction but said she expected the county administrator to make that kind of disclosure. She denied doing anything wrong. "I always acted in what I thought was the best interest of the county. I didn't do anything unethical, illegal, or immoral," she said. One commissioner found her claim of innocence annoying and said: "What I am hearing is that everybody else misunderstood her actions."

She is dismissed without cause and entitled to 6 months' severance pay, approximately $97,000.

The County Administrator Acts

Recognizing that his support by the county commission is in jeopardy, the administrator submits his resignation several days later. He states: "This resignation is submitted with no negativity or ill feeling as I am proud of the accomplishments we have achieved together . . . I sincerely believe this course of action is in the best interest of moving the county government forward" (Van Sant, Abel, & Blackwell 2007).

Discussion Questions

1. Why did the county administrator go along with the property appraiser's initial approach to sell the property to the county? Couldn't the administrator simply have told the property appraiser that it was inappropriate to make such a request?
2. Why did the property appraiser ask the county attorney to represent him? Why did she accept? Was her "approval" from the county commission chair to represent the property appraiser above board?
3. Should the county commission accept the administrator's resignation? Why or why not?
4. As an ethics manager, how would you advise the county administrator to strengthen his commitment to high ethical standards?
5. If you were the administrator, how would you have handled the case differently?

Notes

1. This discussion is adapted from Menzel (2010).
2. This discussion is adapted from Menzel (2010).
3. This discussion is adapted from Menzel (2010).

3

Leading With Integrity

It is wrong to use immoral means to attain moral ends [and] it is just as wrong, or even more so, to use moral means to preserve immoral ends.

—Reverend Martin Luther King, Jr., "Letter from Birmingham Jail" 1963

So you want to lead with integrity—who doesn't? Building an organization of integrity requires leading with integrity. But what does it mean to lead with integrity? How is it done? LeRoy F. Harlow (1914–1995), who served as the city manager of five communities in three different states, "walked the talk" with this integrity philosophy—do not fear others or losing your job, just do the right thing . . . and do not do favors. Armed with a B.S. in industrial engineering from Iowa State University and an M.S. in public administration from the University of Minnesota, Harlow moved west to become the first city manager of Sweet Home, Oregon (population 3,300), a war-boom logging and lumbering town that had the local Federal Bureau of Investigation (FBI) reputation as the "toughest town in Oregon" (Harlow 1977, 2).

Sweet Home, Oregon

During the 1980s, Sweet Home experienced a major decline in population and industry as environmental issues forced the closure of sawmills and logging operations. Throughout the 1990s, using grant dollars provided by the federal government, Sweet Home's downtown corridor was revitalized, small businesses were encouraged to relocate there, and assisted-living facilities were built to accommodate a retiring community. The city's population in 2013 was 9,052 (City of Sweet Home, Oregon 2011).

Harlow's early career in Sweet Home was followed by city manager jobs in Albert Lea, Minnesota (a city that enjoyed a reputation as progressive and up and coming); Fargo, North Dakota; Richfield, Minnesota; and Daytona Beach, Florida. In the early 1950s, Harlow characterized the climate in Daytona Beach as beautiful but the "political climate" as "anything but beautiful" (Harlow 1977, 226). In 1954, he left Daytona Beach and spent the next 20 years working as a consultant and adviser from Connecticut to California. An editorial in the *Daytona Beach Morning Journal* (1954) described Harlow as "a dedicated man [who] believes every citizen is entitled to equal treatment and service from their City employees. He performs his duties without fear and without favor."

In this chapter, we explore what it means to lead with integrity by highlighting the careers of public managers like Harlow. We also look at those who have strayed from the walk, since it is sometimes easier to understand "how to lead" by peering through the lens of "how not to lead."

Integrity

In Chapter 1, we described a person of sound moral character as one who possesses *integrity*. When applied to an organization, integrity refers to an environment characterized as wholesome—one in which respect for others transcends self-serving interests. As Lynn S. Paine (1994, 111) notes:

> Organizational integrity is based on the concept of self-governance in accordance with a set of guiding principles . . . The task of ethics management is to define and give life to an organization's guiding values, to create an environment that supports ethically sound behavior, and to instill a sense of shared accountability among employees.

Ethics codes typically call for public service professionals to demonstrate personal integrity that inspires public trust and confidence. Among other things, this means that managers should be truthful and honest with others and not compromise these values for advancement, honor, or personal gain. Moreover, demonstrating personal integrity requires: (1) taking personal responsibility for errors one may commit; (2) recognizing and crediting others for their work and contributions to the organization's mission; (3) guarding against any conflict of interest or its appearance; and (4) being respectful of subordinates, colleagues, and the public. A tall order to be sure, is it not?

Now consider how the International City/County Management Association (ICMA) approaches integrity, which is defined as demonstrating fairness, honesty, and ethical and legal awareness in personal and professional relationships and activities. Stated differently, the ICMA (2015) identifies

three dimensions of integrity—personal, professional, and organizational—
as follows:

1. *Personal integrity*: Demonstrating accountability for personal
    actions; conducting personal relationships and activities fairly and
    honestly.
2. *Professional integrity*: Conducting professional relationships and
    activities fairly, honestly, legally, and in conformance with the
    ICMA Code of Ethics; requires knowledge of administrative ethics
    and, specifically, the ICMA Code of Ethics.
3. *Organizational integrity*: Fostering ethical behavior throughout
    the organization through personal example, management practices,
    and training (requires knowledge of administrative ethics, the abil-
    ity to instill accountability into operations, and the ability to com-
    municate ethical standards and guidelines to others).

The ICMA's commitment to promoting and supporting ethical behavior is unconditional. Nonetheless, the association's extensive code (2,000
words long with a 3,200-word supplementary, "Rules of Procedure for
Enforcement") is sometimes perceived as "a set of rules to comply with."
One friendly critic (Stone 2010) claims that the eight principles of ethical
conduct in Exhibit 3.1 are all that is needed.

Exhibit 3.1
Principles of Ethical Conduct

1. Do my best at work.
2. Avoid conflicts of interest.
3. Speak truth to power.
4. Be a good citizen.
5. Shun any private gain from public employment.
6. Act impartially.
7. Treat others the way I would like to be treated.
8. Report waste, fraud, and corruption.

(Stone 2010)

Is integrity important in the nonprofit sector? Without question. Indeed, integrity—honesty writ large—is a fundamental ethical characteristic that nonprofits need to possess. "Integrity may have different meanings for individuals, but in the context of professional ethics it must mean doing one's job as honestly and as fully in adherence to one's professed principles as possible," writes Thomas H. Jeavons, co-author of *Growing Givers Hearts* (2000) and former general secretary of Philadelphia Yearly Meeting of the Religious Society of Friends (in Ott & Dicke 2012, 86).

J. Patrick Dobel has written extensively about public integrity. At the personal level, he asserts that "integrity covers the wholeness of our life . . . flow[ing] from the process through which individuals balance beliefs, decide on the right action, and then summon the courage and self-control to act upon those decisions" (2009, 10). Administrators, of course, are individuals who are officeholders in public (government/nonprofit) organizations. Consequently, they cannot be classified as "free agents"; the personal integrity of these administrators must be coupled with the obligations of office. Dobel (1999, 21–22) regards public integrity as a set of seven commitments:

1. Be truthfully accountable to relevant authorities and publics.
2. Address the public values of the political regime.
3. Build institutions and procedures to achieve goals.
4. Ensure fair and adequate participation of the relevant stakeholders.
5. Demand competent performance effectiveness in the execution of policy.
6. Work for efficiency in the operation of government.
7. Connect policy and program with the self-interest of the public and stakeholders in such a way that the purposes are not subverted.

These commitments are substantial and demanding, even for the most ethically well-intentioned person. Thus, it is not surprising that when one scans the landscape for individuals who can lead and have led with integrity in private or public organizations, many leaders are encountered who have failed to lead with integrity. Such an outcome is not predestined, however. Men and women who aspire to leadership positions can *learn* to lead with integrity.

Managers as Leaders[1]

Management guru Warren G. Bennis (1993, 88–89) claims that managers and leaders are different kinds of people. Among other things, he asserts:

- "The manager does things right; the leader does the right thing."
- "The manager administers; the leader innovates."
- "The manager relies on control; the leader inspires trust."

But are managers and leaders so different in the twenty-first century? The answer—most likely not! Indeed, public and nonprofit administrators as managers are also expected to be leaders (see Terry 1995).

But there is more. Managers like to say that you must "walk the talk"— that you cannot lead a modern-day organization simply by issuing rules, policies, and standard operating procedures, and controlling things. Former city manager Kim Leinbach (2011) puts it this way: "Leading with integrity boils down to setting an example, practicing what you preach . . . It's not rocket science—it's heart science." Effective leaders must demonstrate through their behavior that they believe what they say. Those who pronounce that their supervisors and street-level workers must adhere to the highest ethical standards must themselves adhere to those same standards. Leaders must be exemplars in their personal and professional lives. Easier said than done? Certainly, but it is essential. Much the same can be said about peer leadership. Middle managers or even the cops on the beat must demonstrate day in and day out their commitment to ethical behavior. Failure to do so can result only in organizations without integrity.

> Lead by example and expect others to follow. Don't forget to regularly read your organization's ethical standards or those of the associations to which you belong—it's a rewarding practice and one that is condu- cive to longevity.
> —Kim Leinbach,
> former City Manager, Temple Terrace, Florida (Leinbach 2011)

Fast-forward to Hillsborough County, Florida, home of the Tampa Bay Buccaneers football team. The county has a long and checkered history of wrongdoing among its elected county commissioners, with three of five commissioners convicted in the mid-1980s of bribery, kickbacks, and extortion. More recently, newly elected commissioners have found themselves awash in free tickets for lush and pricey skybox seating at Buccaneer games. One commissioner explained that he accepted tickets because he couldn't otherwise afford to attend all the community events at which people would like to see him.

This form of unethical, but not illegal, leadership seems to have had a ripple effect on the more than 8,000-member county workforce in Tampa. Consider the 26-year-old after-school program leader for the Hillsborough County Parks and Recreation Department who was arrested for accepting a $150 bribe from an undercover officer. The bribe was offered in exchange for the young man's willingness to falsify the records showing that the undercover officer had performed community service hours at a county facility (Graham 2005). While it isn't clear that the commissioners' behavior motivated this young man to accept a bribe, it is not too much of a stretch to suggest that the example set at the top of the organization does have an influence on the ethical culture of the county workforce.

Elected officeholders can also serve as exemplars. Take the case of Steve Brown, mayor of Peachtree City, Georgia (population 31,580). Brown ran successfully for office on a platform of bringing ethical government to his community but soon found himself before the Peachtree City Ethics Board, accused of violating the city's ethics code. What happened? He faced a situation in which he needed to get his daughter to summer camp and simultaneously negotiate an agreement for a local option sales tax. His assistant volunteered to help and drove his daughter to camp—on city time. The city manager advised the mayor that he might have committed an ethics violation by allowing his assistant to do him a personal favor during work hours. Forty-five minutes later, Brown realized that the city manager could be correct; embarrassed by this ethical lapse, he took out his pen and filed an ethics complaint against himself. After subsequent deliberation by the ethics board, it was determined that no formal reprimand was necessary but that Brown should reimburse the city for the assistant's time away from the office. Mayor Brown readily complied and reimbursed the city $8.94 (Brown 2005).

Another mayor who led with integrity is Pam Iorio, who served as the mayor of Tampa, Florida (2003–2011). When she assumed office the city was engulfed in a housing scandal that eventually landed the city's housing chief and top aide (also girlfriend) in a federal penitentiary. A jury found them guilty of more than 25 counts of conspiracy, wire fraud, and accepting bribes and gratuities. Eight years later she could proudly look back and say that never once in her tenure as mayor was a question raised about the integrity of city employees. "When I became mayor," she explains, "my staff and I not only developed strategic goals but also defined the values of the organization . . . integrity, excellence, teamwork, and respect" (Iorio 2011, 5). "A person without an ethical core cannot be a viable leader," she proclaims in *Straightforward: Ways to Live & Lead* (2011, 4). Pam Iorio walked the talk.

A few years after leaving the mayor's office, Pam Iorio was appointed president and chief executive officer (CEO) of Big Brothers Big Sisters of America. This large nonprofit mentoring organization serves 600,000 children with 338 affiliates in every state and 12 countries abroad. She accepted the position following the resignation of the CEO who, with less than 2 years on the job, found himself the target of a scathing federal audit. The U.S. Justice Department's office of Inspector General said the Big Brothers Big Sisters of America's oversight of millions of dollars of grant money was inadequate; "the organization failed to adequately oversee funding it provided to local affiliate agencies" (Seper 2013). Once again Ms. Iorio was called on to right-size an organization in trouble.

> Some high-level managers exercise ethical leadership by helping subordinates recognize when they (the subordinates) have a lapse in ethical judgment. Here is an example:
>
> > We had an incident whereby a manager hung some of her colleagues out to dry by blaming them for a problem and thereby deflecting her responsibility for a mistake. In counseling with her, I used the GFOA [Government Finance Officers Association] Code of Ethics to explain why her conduct violated a provision in the professional code. She recognized the problem, and there has been no recurrence of unethical behavior.
> >
> > (quoted in Berman & West 2003, 36)

Becoming an Ethical Leader

Why is ethical leadership important? Does this question even need to be asked? The question actually needs to be asked and answered because we too often take it for granted, and it is much too important to ignore. Two obvious, compelling reasons why it is important is that ethical leadership makes a positive difference in organizational performance and builds public trust and confidence in public agencies.

Ethical leadership has three basic ingredients: Being an ethical role model to others, treating people fairly, and actively managing ethics in the organization. Leading with integrity is yet another way of describing ethical leadership. A person with integrity is honest, truthful, and will not compromise his or her values or principles for advancement or personal gain. It means taking personal responsibility for errors we may commit and recognizing and crediting others for their work and contributions to the organization's mission.

But what more do we know about the leadership–ethics link? Is one simply born more or less ethical? James Q. Wilson (1993) argued more than 20 years ago in *The Moral Sense* that all humans are born with a moral sense, an innate quality that enables us to understand and act on the difference between right and wrong. He points to how children at the very earliest age know when they are being treated fairly or unfairly. Still, even if we accept this view, we are not likely to believe that each of us has an ethical autopilot that will prevent us from straying on to the path of wrong behavior. So, there must be more.

Maybe the more has to do with how we were raised. What did we learn from our mother, father, sisters, brothers, friends? Fairness is certainly one of those ethical values that we encountered. It's also likely that we were taught the Golden Rule: To treat others the way we would like to be treated. We may even have had a parent tell us about the importance of human dignity, although maybe not in those exact words. Keep in mind that no one should be treated as a means to another person's end, and each of us is worthy and equal—two pieces of timeless advice from eighteenth-century philosopher Immanuel Kant (1785/1989). Perhaps you learned about virtues such as honesty, courage, benevolence, bravery, patience, respect, trustworthiness, and loyalty and were told to follow your heart. If practiced often enough, so the theory goes, these virtues would become so fully instilled in your being that you would no longer face the dilemmas posed by right and wrong choices. Your "habits of the heart" would help you become a virtuous person, a lofty goal that, however worthy, is never fully attained. Pursuing a life of integrity is just that.

So what might sidetrack best intentions to become an ethical leader?

Beware of Ethical Blind Spots

Can well-intentioned, ethically minded public managers be capable of engaging in unintended unethical behavior? Max H. Bazerman and Ann E. Tenbrunsel, writing in *Blind Spots: Why We Fail to Do What's Right and What to Do About It* (2011), claim that human beings are often blind to their unethical behavior; that is, there is a gap between intended and actual ethical behavior that is caused by conditions and circumstances that bound our ethicality. "Bounded ethicality," they assert, "comes into play when individuals make decisions that harm others and when that harm is inconsistent with these decision makers' conscious beliefs and preferences" (5).

One explanation for ethical blind spots, or gaps between what we should do and actually do, is unawareness. That is, psychologically, "our minds are subject to bounded ethicality or cognitive limitations that can make us una-ware of the moral implications of our decisions" (30). There are "aspects of everyday work life—including goals, rewards, compliance systems, and informal pressures—[that] can contribute to *ethical fading*, a process by which ethical dimensions are eliminated from a decision" (30).

Ethical blind spots can arise for yet another reason—the "want" side of yourself overpowers the "should" side. While the should side dominates pre and post decision making, the "want side often wins at the moment of decision" (66), so Bazerman and Tenbrunsel assert. "The want self describes the side of you that's emotional, affective, impulsive, and hot-headed. In contrast, your should self is rational, cognitive, thoughtful, and cool-headed" (66). Does this description resonate with you?

Rationalization and revisionism are other reasons why we often acquire ethical blind spots. When faced with a potential ethical choice that turns out badly, we are most likely inclined to find a reason, often directed at another person (the boss, for example) or circumstance (the organization), for ration-alizing the behavior. The common refrain, "I didn't do anything unethical" fits easily alongside "the organization made me do it." Or, we might turn into "revisionist historians" so that our unethical actions can be hidden, at least from ourselves (Bazerman & Tenbrunsel 2011, 73).

Avoiding ethical blind spots is not an easy task. Indeed, insofar as there are built-in psychological processes that bias our decisions and how we think about ourselves, and a powerful tendency to want to be ethical no mat-ter what, bounded ethicality is very difficult to recognize and overcome (21).

Beware of the Utilitarian Trap

Without exception, men and women of ambition are thrown into the lion's den of "getting ahead" in the twenty-first century. How, then, is one to make sense of right and wrong? Enter the utilitarian. The mandate to serve the public interest is translated into making decisions that benefit the most peo-ple. As the top executive of a public or nonprofit agency, you might conclude that recommending an across-the-board pay raise to employees is better than a recommendation to increase the pay of a select group of employees based on performance. The organization as whole, you might rationalize, would perform worse with a large number of dissatisfied employees and only a small number of satisfied employees.

Ethics managers must not sacrifice the notion of doing the right thing by trying to satisfy too many people. The utilitarian trap is hazardous, as is the prospect of justifying an unsavory or unethical means to achieve a highly desirable result. The ends do not justify the means when seeking a goal, no matter how attractive that goal may be. This utilitarian trap is Machiavellian.

> Niccolo Machiavelli (1469–1527) was an Italian political philosopher who wrote *The Prince* (1513), a slim volume that advised rulers how to gain power and keep it by any and all means. The term Machiavellian is used to describe a person who is cunning and ruthless in the pursuit of power.

A utilitarian approach is, of course, attractive, because one can calculate—however roughly—possible desirable outcomes. Thus, doing the right thing becomes an exercise in smart, and maybe lucky, calculations. But where and how does one learn to do this? Through common sense? Education? Public executives typically hold master's degrees in business, public administration, or public policy; educational institutions that award these degrees are often committed to teaching students how "to act ethically." Accredited business schools are equally vociferous in this regard, although not everyone feels that such standards make a real difference. One business school graduate put it this way: "We had classes on ethical behavior. But if you are a rotten person going into B-school, you will probably still be a rotten person when you come out" (Bellomo 2005).

The act of projecting right and wrong outcomes to ethics scenarios might seem manipulative and contrived, and it probably is wide of the mark to charge educators with teaching ethics as an exercise in calculation. However, many educators believe that people can learn how to engage in a reasoning process that will more than likely result in a "right" behavior or decision. Terry Cooper, a leading administrative ethics scholar, is the best-known proponent of what he calls "moral reasoning." And, if the popularity of the sixth edition of his book *The Responsible Administrator* (2012) is any indication, the concept has many supporters. At the risk of oversimplifying his argument, Cooper contends that in learning how to resolve an ethical choice, one involving right versus wrong—and sometimes, right versus right—one must develop the skill of moral imagination; that is, have the ability to produce a "movie in our minds" that takes into account the dynamics of the environment in which a choice must be made.

Leadership Styles

Leaders come in all sizes and shapes—as do their styles. Many students of leadership have long been fascinated with how styles, personalities, and leader effectiveness fit together—and sometimes don't fit together. Lasthuizen (2008, 5) points out that there is a lively debate "in organizational science about leadership, its effects, and the type of leadership most likely to maximize employee performance." A secondary and often overlooked aspect of these leadership studies is the effect of ethical leadership on members of the organization as well as on the integrity of the organization as a whole.

Given the wide range of leadership styles—creative, directive, supportive, participative, delegated, achievement-oriented, external, laissez-faire, inspirational, and charismatic, to name several identified by Van Wart (2008)—our interest here is limited to four particular styles: Transactional, transformational, entrepreneurial, and creative. The central question is, how do these styles match up with ethical leadership and the quest to build organizations of integrity? The reader should keep in mind that these leadership styles are ideal types. Whether or not managers can change styles to accommodate different circumstances is an arguable proposition not addressed here.

Transactional Leadership

Have you ever been a member of a public service organization that seems to run smoothly? Most likely you have. Of course, organizations do many different things. Some process the mail and packages and social security checks. Others monitor air and water quality, oversee permits to build shopping centers, and extract minerals from the earth. Still others in the nonprofit sector help those in poverty find a way out or malnourished children receive a hot meal. Still, when an organization is efficient and effective at doing its work, that is, handling routine and sometimes nonroutine tasks, the public and members of the organization benefit. Numerous transactions take place day in and day out in organizations, public and private. And those that are very successful in handling transactions are most likely led by managers who are skillful transaction leaders.

Transactional leaders are able communicators, effective problem solvers, and task-oriented workers. However important these skills are in running the organization, they are not sufficient to ensure the organization is high-performing. What could be missing? A high-performing transactional-led organization must also have leaders who understand and practice fairness, honesty, trust, and transparency. In other words, successful transactional-style leadership is value-driven. This is the key to leading with integrity as a transactional leader.

Transformational Leadership

Values also underpin transformational leaders, who are often described as charismatic, inspirational, motivating visionaries, and sometimes as change agents. Have you ever been on an athletic team? If you have, you know why outstanding coaches can turn a team around when the going gets rough—they are able to motivate and inspire team members to do extraordinary things, including performing at a level that exceeds their ordinary capabilities. "Central to the conceptualization of transformational leadership is the influence that leaders exert on their followers to transcend their own self-interests and incorporate the interest of the organization and society into their goals" (Lasthuizen 2008). In other words, followers buy into the leader's message and feel empowered. The dark side of transformational leadership is that followers can become such true believers in the leader's vision and message that they become "enthusiastic sheep" (Van Wart 2008, 41).

How does one lead with integrity as a transformational leader? Are persuasion and charisma enough? Perhaps in some cases, but most likely there is more. Bernard M. Bass and Paul Steidimeier (1999) state:

> Leaders are authentically transformational when they increase awareness of what is right, good, important, and beautiful . . . when they foster in followers higher moral maturity, and when they move followers to go beyond their self-interests for the good of the group, organization, or society.

No small task, is it?

Organizations in trouble often seek out a transformational leader to make things happen. This "change agent" role has both an upside and a downside. The upside is that the change agent typically has the strong support of the appointing body, and it can be a heady experience to move the organization to a different level. However, due diligence is still required. Consider the case of Al Dunlap, a corporate CEO who enjoyed a reputation as an expert at turning a financially losing enterprise into a profit-making machine. Cutting and slashing staff with impunity earned him the nickname "Chainsaw Al." As he moved from one struggling corporation to another, his record of success grew and caught up with him on his last assignment—to turn around the appliance manufacturer Sunbeam. In 1998, as he was promoting his book *Mean Business: How I Save Bad Companies and Make Good Companies Great* (1997), the Sunbeam Board of Directors—after much anguishing over the firm's financial well-being—decided to fire him. As it turns out, his success with Sunbeam had become suspicious, and rightly so. Under pressure to produce and sustain his reputation, he convinced Sunbeam retailers to receive and hold large inventories of Sunbeam products that on paper looked like sales. This tactic allowed him to claim that the company's bottom line was healthy. Nonetheless, this "bill and hold" approach for barbecue grills and other products amounted to little more than "cooking" the books. Chainsaw Al was shown the door. The Securities and Exchange Commission (SEC) investigated Sunbeam's management, as did the U.S. Justice Department. Dunlap agreed to pay $500,000 to shareholders to settle the SEC's charges. The Justice Department did not file any charges. However, Dunlap was banned from ever serving as an officer of a public company again. He retired to Florida, where he is reported to be living a comfortable life.

Entrepreneurial Leadership

While transformational leadership inspires, entrepreneurial leadership adds value to an organization's product or output. Entrepreneurial leadership is the ability to leverage resources in a manner that "grows" the organization, not necessarily in size but in terms of the return on investment. If this sounds businesslike or market-like, it is. Heightened attention was drawn to entrepreneurial leadership with the publication of David Osborne and Ted Gaebler's best-selling book *Reinventing Government: How the Entrepreneurial Spirit Is Transforming the Public Sector* (1992). The reinvention movement swept across America with added gusto with the publication of *Creating a Government that Works Better and Costs Less: The Report of the National Performance Review* (Gore 1993), led by Vice President Al Gore.

> Ninety-nine percent of people in business just move preexisting pieces abound the board. Entrepreneurs create. If they are very good at what they do . . . they may leave behind something that will continue after they're gone.
> —Peter Barton,
> coauthor of *Not Fade Away* (Barton & Shames 2003)

High among the priorities of the newly elected Clinton administration was the creation of a government that would work better and cost less—so it was claimed. President Clinton launched the National Performance Review in March 1993 with this announcement:

> Our goal is to make the entire federal government both less expensive and more efficient, and to change the culture of our national bureaucracy away from complacency and entitlement toward initiative and empowerment. We intend to redesign, to reinvent, to reinvigorate the entire national government.
>
> (Gore 1993, 1)

Changing the culture of the U.S. federal bureaucracy is widely viewed as a gigantic task with much political risk. Therefore, to do so, government leaders and administrators—so it was assumed—would need to be more risk-oriented and entrepreneurial, hence the moniker *entrepreneurial leadership*. *Customers* became the code word for citizens; *competition and markets* became the central ingredients in the operation of government; and bureaucrats are expected to become *enterprising workers*. Ethical leadership? No one was asked to break the law to make the government work better and cost less. Is this ethical leadership? Hardly.

The reinvention movement in short order evolved into the new public management school with a worldwide following. New public management is defined by the Organisation for Economic Co-operation and Development (OECD) as "a new paradigm which attempts to combine modern management practices with the logic of economics while still retaining core public service values" (OECD 1998, 5). Not surprisingly, entrepreneurial leadership fits comfortably within this new paradigm.

Now, let's consider what it might mean to lead with integrity as an entrepreneurial leader. First, one must be able to balance the powerful and seductive drive to deliver results within the regulatory framework and processes in which the work of the organization takes place. Do you recall the famous quote attributed to legendary Green Bay Packers coach Vince Lombardi: "Winning isn't everything; it's the only thing"? Do you suppose that coach Lombardi meant that anything goes—that the end justifies the means? Not likely. And it is worth remembering the words written by the Reverend Martin Luther King, Jr., in his "Letter from Birmingham Jail": "It is wrong to use immoral means to attain moral ends [and] it is just as wrong, or even more so, to use moral means to preserve immoral ends" (1963).

Second, entrepreneurial leaders surely practice much of what transaction and transformational leaders do—empower followers with a vision while ensuring the work of the organization is conducted in a fair-minded, honest, and transparent manner. In other words, successful entrepreneurs mix and match key qualities of transactional and transformational-style management. Leading with integrity for entrepreneurial managers requires one to incorporate the best features of both leadership styles.

Creative Leadership[2]

Nearly every textbook on leadership describes styles that include transactional, transformational, entrepreneurial, transcendent, and charismatic. But could these not also have a creative dimension? A transactional leader is, by definition, one who is capable of ensuring that organizational members and processes work with minimum friction, thus producing a product or service that is high on quality and low on cost. Would not Henry Ford's amazing success in the development of a factory-assembled affordable Model T qualify him as a transactional and creative leader? Or, how about Steve Jobs' transformational skills and vision that turned Apple into the giant success it is today? Surely he would be regarded as a creative leader as well. Further, consider Bill Gates and Microsoft, or Mark Zuckerberg and Facebook—they unquestionably could be considered entrepreneurial leaders with a creative bent. Then there's Starbucks' CEO Howard Schultz, who built an empire of coffee houses with nearly 20,000 stores worldwide and 300,000 employees in 2014. Who would dispute Schultz's leadership as a creative businessman? U.S. Presidents Ronald Reagan and Bill Clinton shared a strong charismatic leadership quality that could be interpreted as creative as well. So creative leadership, as these examples suggest, is not necessarily a distinct quality. But what is it, if it is not distinct?

Surely creative leadership is something more than having a vision or creating value or attracting followers. One persuasive definition is that creative leadership is "highly relational, grounded in process, utilizes diversity, requires self-reflection and is focused on accomplishing positive change" (Puccini, Mance, & Zacko-Smith 2015, 15). Stated differently, it is the combination of creativity (the ability to generate ideas) with leadership (the ability to execute ideas through the actions of others). Creative leadership is "the ability to deliberately engage one's imagination to define and guide a group towards a novel goal—a direction that is new for the group" (Puccini et al. 2015, 19). It draws together three distinct but interconnected constructs—creativity, leadership, and innovation. The ability to generate and execute innovative ides is what separates creative leaders from non-creative leaders. Traditional leaders tend to execute "tried and true" strategies such as cost cutting or product extensions, but they rarely disrupt their industries or create new product categories. Creative leadership can be considered "an improvisational and experimental art" (Puccini et al. 2015, 17).

This brings us back to the matter of ethical leadership.

Ethical Leadership

Ethical leadership is exemplified by "caring, and principled individuals who make fair and balanced decisions" (Brown & Treviño 2006, 597). They consistently act from moral values and practice what they preach.

As noted earlier, leading with integrity is another way of describing ethical leadership. Acting with integrity, Blustein (1991, 260) writes, is "that quality in man which gives him the courage to hold his own convictions against all influences, against the opinions and desires of others; the courage to remain whole, untouched, to remain true to himself." A person with integrity is honest, truthful, and will not compromise his/her values or principles for advancement, honor, or personal gain. It means taking personal responsibility for errors one may commit and recognizing and crediting others for their work and contributions to the organization's mission.

Creative-Ethical Leadership[3]

Have you become curious about what creative leadership and ethical leadership have in common? Let's begin with motivation. Self-motivation and the capacity to motivate others are common properties of both creative and ethical leadership. As an intrinsic property, self-motivation is essential to being creative and becoming ethically competent. Motivating others is central to creative leadership and an intentional, sometimes unconscious, feature of ethical leadership. While change and innovation are always forces to be reckoned with in creative leadership, they can be confounding influences on ethical leadership. Creative leaders must be able to master complexity to create change and, in a similar manner, ethical leaders face complexity in resolving thorny moral dilemmas. A persuasive argument can be made that ethical leadership shares with creative leadership relational qualities, is grounded in process (ethical reasoning), and requires self-reflection and imagination to produce positive results (Puccini et al. 2015). As Terry Cooper

(2012) reminds us, we must develop a capacity to exercise our moral imagination. While creative leadership, like its more generic form, can be viewed as improvisational, perhaps even as an experimental art, ethical leadership requires us to anticipate desired ethical outcomes while taking into consideration the situation at hand (Heifetz, Grashow, & Linsky 2009). In this sense ethical leadership is improvisational, as it is not determined solely by the situation. There is no place for situational ethics in leading with integrity, and genuine ethical leaders know that.

Leadership Success and Failure

While it might very well seem that successful leaders are people of integrity, there are many cases of successful leaders going astray. Stephen K. Bailey's (1964) dictum that "the higher a person goes on the rungs of power and authority, the more wobbly the ethical ladder" has all too often come true for many.

A Wobbly Ethical Ladder[4]

Consider the case of the administrator of a large urban county in a southern state who climbed the ladder of success over more than 30 years to become the chief executive.[5] What happened? The county established an independent auditor who, among other things, reported that the administrator had given herself and top aides pay raises at a time when the county was experiencing significant fiscal stress, with cutbacks and layoffs occurring. Moreover, the county's 8,000 employees were asked to take on more work to cope with the downsizing, a recipe for low morale and disgruntlement. The county had in place an unwritten policy to reward employees who engaged in innovative cost-saving measures, which included laying off subordinates. One of the administrator's top aides nominated her for a reward in recognition of the decision she made to lay off one of her assistant county administrators. Uncertain that she was eligible to participate in the program, she consulted the county attorney, who told her that she was indeed eligible. And so the county executive ended up accepting (some critics would say "giving") herself a $2,000 salary increase—determined by a set percentage of her $224,000 annual salary—for eliminating someone else's job. However, she failed to seek approval of the salary bump from the county commission, which was unaware of the policy to adjust her salary. The county charter specifically authorizes the commission to set the pay of the administrator.

As events unfolded, including private interchanges between the auditor and individual members of the commission, the administrator began to suspect that the auditor was "out to get her." Consequently, she ordered one of her managers to collect all e-mails involving the auditor, commission, and county attorney relevant to the pay issue. The media began to follow the story and broke the "e-mail snooping" news, as it was called. The administrator admitted that she had collected the e-mail messages but, upon second thought, decided not to read them. The commission's trust in this claim rapidly deteriorated and motivated them to place the administrator, the county attorney, and the auditor on 90 days of paid administrative leave.

As the leave period moved along, the commission struggled with "what to do"—demote the administrator, fire her and the others with or without cause, wait out an investigation by the state law enforcement agency into whether or not e-mail snooping violated the law and then decide what to do, or strike a deal with the administrator to resign. Firing the administrator without cause would let her walk with more than $500,000, according to the terms of her employment contract. Consequently, the commission and the administrator (through their lawyers) attempted to work out a settlement. As the suspension approached its end, the administrator became more determined to find an arrangement that would let her receive $550,000 or more in severance and benefits. In the meantime, there was considerable stress and distress reported in the media about the ill effects that the situation was having on employee morale, job performance, and the public's negative perception of the imbroglio. The story ends with the auditor losing his job, the administrator fired unceremoniously with cause, and the county attorney reinstated.

This case is replete with ethical breaches, most of which are obvious. Perhaps a less obvious but nonetheless egregious breach was the utter disregard for doing what was believed to be in the best interests of the community, and, of course, the consequent erosion of public trust and confidence in county government caused by the incident. While it was clearly in the best financial interests of the administrator to stay the course, did she also have an obligation to put the community interest ahead of her personal and professional interests? It would seem so. However, it is fair to say that she felt strongly that she had been victimized, especially by the auditor's reports and behavior. Her sense of fair treatment and justice was at stake along with her professional reputation; with more than three decades of county employment under her belt, she was well known in the community and had established ties with many municipal leaders and businesspeople.

The administrator in this case was held in high regard during her 6-year tenure as chief executive and many years as human resources director and assistant county administrator. She had gained respect and a solid reputation for promoting professional behavior among managers and employees. And, although she was a longstanding member of several public service professional associations that advocate high standards of ethical behavior, it was still her responsibility to do the right thing. "Of course, the reach and impact of professional associations and university programs are limited," writes Professor Robert D. Herman, who received the 2010 Distinguished Achievement and Leadership in Nonprofit and Voluntary Action Research award. Herman adds, "a commitment to high ethical conduct cannot be imposed by professional associations or academic courses. Such a commitment must come from those who are attracted to participate . . . in the charitable sector" (cited in Pettey 2013, 364).

This story points to two important conclusions: (1) experienced administrators can develop "ethical blind spots" that tarnish a long, successful career; and (2) the achievement of ethical competence is a lifelong pursuit that is never quite reached. This is not to suggest that the *pursuit of ethical competence* is fruitless or that one is hopelessly doomed to failure. Rather, it is to suggest that the journey is challenging, but so very important.

Exemplary Leadership

No matter how wobbly the ethical ladder may become, some leaders are able to keep climbing. One such person was the former U.S. attorney general Elliot Richardson (1920–2000). Richardson became an iconic figure in U.S. history for refusing the order from President Richard M. Nixon to fire Archibald M. Cox, the special Watergate prosecutor who was determined to obtain tape recordings made surreptitiously in the White House. On October 20, 1973, attorney general Richardson resigned rather than fire Cox. His second in command, William D. Ruckelshaus, also refused to fire Mr. Cox and resigned. This set of events came to be called the Saturday Night Massacre. Richardson's stand was "widely lauded as a special moment of integrity and rectitude that secured him a place in the nation's history" (Lewis 2000). In *Reflections of a Radical Moderate*, a book published several years before his death, Richardson wrote: "The more I thought about it the clearer it seemed to me that public confidence in the investigation would depend on its being independent not only in fact, but in appearance" (Richardson 1996).

Although it is not always recognized as such, the appearance standard is a very high ethical standard—one that often slips to the sidelines when an ethical choice has to be made. Mr. Richardson understood the significance of the appearance standard and had the willpower and courage to abide by it. This is leading with integrity, is it not?

Another well-known contemporary figure widely acclaimed for leading with integrity was the American soldier, diplomat, and Nobel Peace Prize recipient George C. Marshall (1880–1959). Lauded for his role as army chief of staff during World War II and later as U.S. secretary of state, he is also remembered as the architect of the Marshall Plan, a postwar strategy for rebuilding and modernizing Europe. Throughout his career and life, Marshall demonstrated exceptional courage, placed the public interest before his self-interest, and earned a sterling reputation for always telling the truth. In addition, he refused to seek special treatment for his family or friends, showed consistent dedication for the welfare of others (especially the citizen-soldier), "demanded a high level of ethical conduct from everyone with whom he worked, and conducted himself in a manner that set a clear model for others to emulate" (Pops 2006, 176). "George Marshall," remarked former secretary of state Colin L. Powell, "did not crave power or glory . . . and never confused honor with pride" (George C. Marshall Foundation 2003).

George Catlett Marshall

People not only thought he was telling them the truth, he did tell them the truth. He always told me the truth when I was President of the United States.

—Harry S. Truman (Mosley 1982, 401)

A third notable leader with integrity was Elmer B. Staats (1914–2011), who was appointed to a 15-year term as head of the General Accounting Office (GAO) by President Lyndon B. Johnson in 1966. (The GAO was renamed the U.S. Government Accountability Office in 2004.) Prior to his role as the comptroller general of the GAO—a role he singlehandedly redefined—Staats served with distinction at the Bureau of the Budget and the National Security Agency over the course of three decades. He earned his bachelor's degree in 1935 from McPherson College, Kansas, a master's degree in political science and economics from the University of Kansas the next year, and a doctoral degree in political economy from the University of Minnesota in 1939.

The GAO was established in 1921 as an independent agency charged with informing Congress on matters of government finance and effectiveness and serving as a check of president powers (Frederickson 1992, 218). The GAO routinely dealt with issues of fraud, waste, and criminal behavior. By 1968, the agency was heavily involved in performance auditing (conducting program evaluations).

Elmer Staats viewed his job and those who served in government as "fixing, improving, and making things work better." He assumed that civil servants meant well, were hard-working and, for the most part, virtuous. Indeed, he "expected generally virtuous practices on the part of most bureaucrats" (Frederickson 1992, 225). Still, he recognized that "there is no foolproof way that you can avoid a situation where a program gets into serious trouble where fraud and waste may be involved" (223).

Leading with integrity was serious business for Elmer Staats. He was quoted as saying:

> The Comptroller General must be above reproach, cleaner than Caesar's wife. The bottom line is that the agency doesn't do anything that it wouldn't want to see in the *Washington Post* the next morning. The perception of unethical practices is almost as damaging as are actual unethical practices . . . The main thing . . . is to make the whole organization conscious of the role that it plays, that it has to be in a position where the GAO can't be damaged by any successful charge of unethical practices.
>
> (Frederickson 1992, 235–236)

Fraud, waste, and corruption have been and are all too commonplace in America. Blowing the whistle on those who defraud the public, however, is not done easily or without consequence. Consider the case of Marie Ragghianti (1942–), who served for 14 months as the chair of the Tennessee Board of Pardons and Paroles until being fired by governor Ray Blanton on August 3, 1977. She was accused of "gross improprieties . . . as well as demoralizing the corrections department and crippling its procedures" (Hejka-Ekins 1992, 304). Her real "crime"—she refused to acquiesce to corruption in the governor's office, where clemencies were exchanged for bribes.

I would rather try and fail than fail to try.
—Marie Ragghianti, cited in Cooper and Wright (1992)

It wasn't long before Ragghianti began to understand the scope of corruption at her doorstep and realized that it was not something she could combat on her own. She sought help from outside the governor's office. After contacting the FBI, she agreed to testify secretly to a grand jury investigating the bribery incidents. She then experienced "organizational retaliation for her failure to support the administration" (310). Though feeling badgered and bullied, Ragghianti refused to go along with the governor to cover up the bribery incidents. She "told the governor that she had done nothing wrong and would not resign" (311). The scandal finally broke when three top staffers with the governor's office were arrested and indicted on bribery and extortion charges. The FBI investigation revealed that over 600 pardons and clemencies had been issued during governor Blanton's tenure (316). Although never formally charged in the scandal, he was eventually indicted on charges of selling liquor licenses, then convicted and sentenced to federal prison (Wikipedia 2011b). Marie Ragghianti was a public servant who led with integrity. Is it not so?

Exemplary leadership sometimes requires one to make very difficult choices between two rights rather than a right or wrong. Hiram Bingham IV (1903–1988), a 34-year-old American career foreign service officer assigned to the U.S. Consulate in Marseilles, France, in 1937, was faced with a "right or right" dilemma when the French government surrendered in June 1940 to Adolf Hitler's forces. Hiram's duties were to issue visas for those seeking to enter the United States. The Vichy French puppet government launched a roundup of Jewish refugees who would be sent to Nazi concentration death camps. Consequently, many refugees sought travel visas to the United States. Not yet at war, the American government wanted to maintain good relations with the new Vichy government in France and refused most requests for visas. The State Department issued instructions that diplomats should follow "the laws with which the United States maintains friendly relations" (Wikipedia 2015). The lines of people outside the Marseilles' consulate pleading for help grew longer day after day. "On his own authority, he began issuing what would eventually total more than 2,000 travel visas and fake passports" (Newell 2015b). In May 1941, following complaints by German and French officials, Hiram was removed from his post and transferred to Lisbon, Portugal, and later to Argentina. Frustrated with his stalled career and the failure of the State Department to investigate his reports that Nazi assets and war criminals were being given safe harbor in Argentina, Bingham resigned in protest in 1946 (Lee 2015). Did Hiram Bingham exercise exemplary and courageous leadership at the risk of losing his job and compromising his career by issuing visas on his own authority and pressing the State Department to investigate in Argentina? So it would seem. More than six decades later (June 27, 2002), he was recognized by then secretary of state Colin Powell with a "courageous diplomat" award posthumously presented to his children (Lee 2015; Newell 2015b).

Now that you know something about ethical leadership, are you ready to start building an ethical culture in your organization?

Building an Ethical Culture

Creating and sustaining an ethical workplace take many hands and much time. It is not that public and nonprofit organizations are staffed with unethical workers; over the years, though, many fall prey to a series of false assumptions about the role and place of ethics in their agencies. So, the manager who wants to build ethics into the organizational culture must first dismiss the following false assumptions.

Ethical Values Are Personal and Are Not Expressed Within the Organization

Part of the mythology of working in the public sector is that employees should not act on their values and beliefs because to do so would undermine their ability to be fair and impartial. In other words, it is OK to have personal values and ethics, but do not bring them to the workplace! This approach will breed ethical complacency and eventually contribute to ethical lapses within an organization.

Ethical People Always Act Ethically Regardless of What Goes On in the Organization

To suppose that ethical people will not experience ethical lapses is a false assumption. Recruiting ethical people is certainly an important first step, but it is not sufficient to ensure that ethical government will result. Employees with sound ethical intentions still need support and reinforcement in the workplace.

Ethics Discussions in the Workplace Contribute Little, if Anything, to Productivity, Good Morale, or Problem Solving

Many managers may believe that it is nice to talk about ethics in the workplace but that such talk matters little when it comes to getting the job done.

This is another false assumption. Indeed, time devoted to ethics discussions or formal training might be viewed as a major distraction from time that could be devoted to providing services in a more cost-effective fashion. Growing empirical evidence shows a significant correlation between the presence of a strong ethical climate and the emphasis the organization places on values such as efficiency, effectiveness, quality, excellence, and teamwork.

It is important for managers to develop strategies that encourage dialogue on issues with ethical implications and to provide an approach toward establishing an ethical workplace. The creation of a shared value system based on principles requires meaningful and serious dialogue through an inclusive, not an exclusive, process. The involvement of employees in training and development seminars that allow for questions and confrontations will give individuals the confidence needed to take action, resolve problems, and raise productivity.

Ethics Cannot Be Learned, Taught, or Even Discussed in Any Meaningful Way

There is a widespread myth that ethics is acquired in one's youth, and therefore, any effort to teach or learn about ethics as an adult is fruitless. A corollary is that one can learn ethics only through the crucible of personal experiences. These views reduce ethics to whatever values and life experiences workers bring to the workplace and are hardly reassuring to managers who wish to build ethics into their organizational culture.

Neither ethical persons nor workplaces are entirely products of past experiences, whether personal or organizational in nature. This "naturalist" view of how an ethical sense is acquired or transmitted must be rejected. Rather, ethical behavior must be viewed as learned behavior that can be relearned and modified, if needed.

Ethical behavior is learned behavior, and managers can build organizational processes and strategies that contribute to this learning effort. Initiatives such as placing ethics stories in newsletters and training, for example, might not transform unethical employees into good organizational citizens, but they can facilitate decisions that reflect organizational values and purpose. When training is successful, employees become aware of choices and have the knowledge and resources to choose and carry out the right choices.

Creating and Distributing a Written Ethics Policy Eliminates Any Further Responsibility of the Organization or Its Leaders

False! While it is important to have guidelines and to provide them to employees, this action alone will fall short of guiding behavior and can do little to change it (when such change is needed). Building ethics into the organizational culture does not occur in a single shot. It is a continuous process that finds expression in many ways. A written statement of principles is an important beginning point, and no organization should be without one. Equally valuable, however, are the moral cues sent out by members of top management. Managers who do not "walk the ethical talk" will soon experience a credibility gap that employees will see as hypocrisy—"do as I say, not as I do."

Appearing to Do Wrong and Actually Doing Wrong Are Different Matters

While true from a factual perspective, this claim is inconsequential when it comes to building ethics into the organizational culture. The belief that a person's ethics should be judged not by appearance but by facts does not reflect the power of perception. Appearing to do wrong when we have done nothing wrong may have the same negative impact as actually doing wrong. The appearance of impropriety erodes employee and public trust in public agencies and weakens the principles of accountability. It may, for example, be legal for a manager to invest in a business that does business with her agency, but she will have difficulty convincing a skeptical public and workforce that she is not using her position for personal gain. The appearance of impropriety is inescapable, regardless of the reality. Appearances matter!

Practical Wisdom

Beyond dismissing these false assumptions, managers should rely on both formal and informal ethics management strategies to strengthen their agencies' ethical environment. They do not need to run through a daily checklist to achieve an ethical workplace. No algorithm or methodology will cultivate an ethical culture. Still, the literature reviewed here suggests that managers should take a systemic and comprehensive approach to fostering ethics in the workplace. Evidence collected to date points to the need to incorporate a wide range of ethical practices into the total fabric of an agency. Doing so is likely to have a lasting imprint on ethical life in the organization. Moreover, managers are likely to enjoy the benefits of a sustained ethical workplace by encouraging employees to participate in professional associations, finding creative ways for ethical behavior to be rewarded, establishing an ethics conscience within their organizations, adopting a code of ethics or statement of principles, providing for ethics training or dialogue, and "walking the talk."

Organizations of integrity are places where human beings carry out their daily duties with pride and respect for others. Practitioners whose viewpoints were examined in this chapter embrace this view. Character, integrity, accountability, moral competency, and exemplary behavior are words that one finds threaded throughout the practitioner literature. The U.S. GAO exemplifies these core values in practice. If you visit Washington, D.C., as former comptroller general David M. Walker points out, you can see three core values etched over the entrance to the GAO's headquarters—accountability, integrity, and reliability.

Ethical governance is not an oxymoron. Ethical workplaces can be found in many governmental and nonprofit agencies. Yet, one size does not fit all. So, how do organizational leaders and professional managers know which size to pick? Perhaps the advice that President John F. Kennedy offered is helpful: The ultimate answer to ethical problems in government is honest people in a good ethical environment. Honest people can certainly contribute to an ethical workplace, but more is needed—a strong ethical environment. The components of such an environment include exemplary ethical leadership, a community that cares about its least advantaged citizens, and a management profession that values integrity and demands high standards of performance.

But how does one create a strong ethical environment? The starting point may be from the manager's bookshelf. But as helpful as that might be, it is not sufficient. Rather, a strong ethical culture is built and maintained the same way a new house is built—stick by stick, nail by nail, day by day—with continuous care, competence, and attentiveness required to sustain the enterprise. Ethical governance cannot be created with the wave of a wand or the application of a magic elixir. Without a strong infusion of ethical leadership and management in organizations, good government is not likely to exist. Government officials and appointed nonprofit managers can—indeed must—do everything within their power and imagination to build and sustain ethical organizations.

Summing Up

Leading with integrity is not easy; indeed, it can be downright difficult. Oh, you say, I've always been a person with high ethical standards. Have you?

Do you think of yourself as more ethical than your boss? Your fellow employees? The person sitting next to you? Your author has evidence drawn from many educational and training sessions that most of us perceive ourselves to be more ethical than those we work with, supervise, or the bosses who run any given organization. There is good news in the desire, at least, to feel as if our ethical standards are higher than those of other people. The bad news? A sense of ethical superiority is a potential trapdoor through which one can plummet in the quest to lead with integrity. How so—authenticity. Followers must genuinely believe that what you say and do is authentic. Contrived authenticity with respect to your ethics will doom you as a leader. You may be able to change and adapt your leadership style to fit varying organizational roles and workplace cultures, but you cannot do the same with your ethical standards and the perception of those standards by others.

> Ethics has everything to do with management ... Ethics is as much an organizational as a personal issue. Managers who fail to provide proper leadership and to institute systems that facilitate ethical conduct share responsibility with those who conceive, execute, and knowingly benefit from corporate misdeeds.
> —Lynn Sharp Paine (1994), Harvard Business School

As this discussion of leadership styles makes clear, one can lead with integrity no matter the style—charismatic, transactional, transformational, or entrepreneurial. One goal of this chapter was to show that people can learn to lead with integrity, although it is not simply a matter of reading a leadership classic or taking a course. Nor does one have to be a "born leader"—whatever that may be. Rather, motivated individuals must practice, practice, practice in much the same way one aspires to lead a virtuous life rooted in honesty, benevolence, compassion, and fairness.

In its fullest sense, "leading with integrity" includes moral leadership that, as Linda A. Hill (2006, 267) puts it, "is more than avoiding ethical wrongdoing; it is about making a positive difference in others' lives and in our communities." No wobbly ladder here. Stephen K. Bailey (1964, 236) reminds us that "the essential moral qualities of the ethical public servant are: (1) optimism; (2) courage; and (3) fairness tempered by charity."

Are you ready to take a close look at the tools in the ethics manager's box to build an organization of integrity? Ready, set, go—Chapter 4 is up next.

Ethics Management Skill Building

Practicum 3.1 Moral Management?

Assume that you are the top elected official of a county constitutional office, such as the clerk or property appraiser. As part of your campaign to become elected, you promise that you will hold employees of the organization to a code of conduct that will not jeopardize the credibility and integrity of the office. A week after you take office, you learn that several married employees are engaging in extra-marital intimate behavior that offends your sense of morality and is causing disruption in the agency.

The agency's written policy is quite clear. It states:

> Agency personnel, whether married or single, shall not develop an association with another member whom they know or should have known is married to another person. Married members also shall not develop an association with agency members who are single. Excluded from this are members who are separated and residing apart from their spouse, or those who have legally filed for divorce. For the purpose of this policy, "association" means residing with, dating, or entering into any intimate relationship with.

Discussion Questions

1. What do you do? Do you turn your head and hope the situation disappears? Is this solution in the best interest of the organization?
2. Are you obligated to enforce the agency's written policy?
3. Do you call the employees to your office and have a conversation about adultery?
4. Do you consider revising the agency's written standard of conduct?
5. What changes would you make in the existing policy?

Practicum 3.2 Office Romance 101—Do? Don't? Maybe?

Romantic relationships in the workplace can be complicated. Consider this case.

Rob, an elected county constitutional officer who is widely regarded as bringing expertise and competence to his office, and Carolyn, his human resources director, have had an on-and-off romantic relationship that suddenly became newsworthy when Carolyn filed an Equal Employment Opportunity Commission (EEOC) complaint against Rob, charging sexual harassment. She claims that he e-mailed her pornographic images and links to porn sites, and in conversation asked for sexual advances that she rejected. Rob's wife discovered the relationship and insisted that he move Carolyn to a suburban office, which he did.

Some background—Rob and Carolyn had been dating for years when both were single. When they broke up, Rob started dating his now wife. He hired Carolyn, with whom he had worked at a local bank before he was elected to office, as a training technician in the agency. She received a series of promotions afterward, ultimately overseeing human resources and community services.

In response to Carolyn's complaint, Rob admits that he had sent the pornographic e-mails, and it was a personal mistake for him to be involved with a woman he once dated in a consensual and mutual relationship. Rob contends the whole matter is private and has nothing to do with his competence in conducting the work of his office.

Discussion Questions

1. If you were a member of the EEOC deliberation body, would you find "for or against" Carolyn's complaint?
2. If you were Rob and the EEOC rules in your favor (i.e., dismisses the complaint), would you fire Carolyn?
3. If you were Carolyn and the EEOC dismisses the complaint and Rob fires you, would you bring a lawsuit?
4. If you were Rob's wife, what would you do?
5. If you were a voter, what would you do if Rob stands for reelection?

This case is based on a true story. If you want to find some answers to these questions, see the *Tampa Bay Times*, May 24 and 25, July 4, 2012. Also visit http://www.tampabay.com/news/politics/woman-considers-wrongful-termination-suit-against-rob-turner-who-sent-her/1232813. The answers may surprise you.

Notes

1. See Van Wart (2011) for an in-depth review of administrative leadership.
2. This discussion draws on Menzel (2015a).
3. This discussion draws on Menzel (2015a).
4. This discussion draws on Cooper and Menzel (2013).
5. This case is drawn from newspaper accounts published in the *Tampa Tribune* and *St. Petersburg Times* in March–June 2010.

4

Tools for Building Organizations of Integrity

Management is doing things right; leadership is doing the right things.

—Peter F. Drucker (2004)

What are the tools available to public and nonprofit managers to build and sustain organizations that promote ethical behaviors and practices? How well do they work? Are some more effective than others? These are the critical questions addressed in this chapter. Ethics management tools range from soft, even symbolic, measures to more concrete measures such as ethics audits and training. No single tool will suffice to build an organization of integrity. Rather, effective ethics management requires a comprehensive approach with top-down and bottom-up commitments.

Let's begin by taking a look at a widely used tool—ethics training—its value, scope, and type.

An Ounce of Prevention—Ethics Training

Ethics training was a cottage industry a short while ago, but no longer. It is now a growing enterprise in both private and public sectors. There is scarcely a large American corporation that does not conduct ethics training. And governments at all levels in the United States are spending taxpayers' dollars for ethics training. Ethics training is typically different from ethics education in the approaches taken and the emphasis given to laws, rules, and regulations. Normative ethics theories such as utilitarianism, principle or duty-based ethics, and virtue theory are unlikely to be discussed in ethics training. Even the concept of "moral reasoning" is unlikely to be addressed directly, although some training employs moral-reasoning exercises.

Compliance Training

One model dominates ethics training—the compliance model. It is designed to regulate employees' conduct. As Carol W. Lewis (1991, 9) notes, this model is "a largely prescriptive, coercive, punitive, and even threatening route . . . to spur obedience to minimum standards and legal prohibitions." Harvard professor Lynn S. Paine (1994, 106) adds that the goal of a compliance-based ethics program is "to prevent, detect, and punish legal violations." This model emphasizes training in what the law says, what the rules mean, and what one needs to do to stay out of trouble. Ethics officer Alan Johnson (2011a) of Palm Beach County, Florida, describes ethics training programs as stressing "awareness and compliance among officials and public employees, and to a lesser extent, vendors and service providers to the public entity."

Law is the touchstone of public organizations. Thus, it is not surprising that the compliance model is so prominent (Exhibit 4.1). Nor is it surprising that many public officials feel more comfortable about ethics when it involves understanding the law and following it.

Integrity Model

An alternative model is the integrity model, which fosters:

> an awareness of a public service ethos, ethical standards and values, plus a process of moral reasoning to inspire exemplary actions or

Exhibit 4.1   Deterring Unethical Behavior With a Compliance Approach

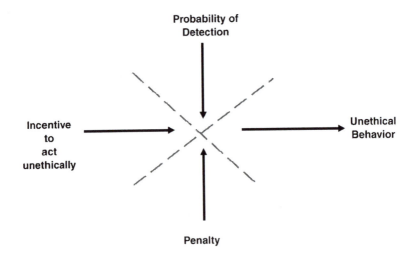

ethical conduct. The emphasis is on the promotion of moral character with self-responsibility and moral autonomy as essential components.

(Hejka-Ekins 2001, 83)

Hallmarks of an Effective Integrity Strategy

- The guiding values and commitments make sense and are clearly communicated.
- Organizational leaders are personally committed, credible, and willing to take action on the values they espouse.
- The espoused values are integrated into the normal channels of management decision making and are reflected in the organization's critical activities.
- The organization's systems and structures support and reinforce its values.
- Managers throughout the organization have the decision-making skills, knowledge, and competencies needed to make ethically sound decisions on a day-to-day basis.

(adapted from Paine 1994)

While there is much to be said for adopting the integrity model, perhaps a more realistic expectation is to combine the two models into what Carol Lewis (1991) calls the "fusion" model. Other ethics experts who recommend a fusion approach are Grosenick (1995) and Truelson (1991). Truelson further argues that the fusion model should blend with the organizational culture; that is, ethics training should both influence and be influenced by the organizational culture, thus fostering a genuine and deep-seated culture of organizational integrity.

Scope and Type of Training

The cliché that "too much is not enough" may be an apt characterization of the size and scope of ethics strategies needed in the public and nonprofit sectors. At the same time, there are two overlooked issues that sometimes sideline the adoption of an effective strategy: the failure of managers to (1) appreciate and understand what it means to manage ethics in their organization, and (2) given the day-to-day demands of getting the job done, be willing to devote time and energy to put ethics management strategies in place.

Should formal or informal ethics management strategies be adopted? What is the best strategy to adopt? The answer is: "no single size fits all." Rather, managers need to adopt strategies—formal or informal—that fit their organization. A survey by West and Berman (2004, 189–206) found that two of every three cities provide ethics training, with new employees the targets of the most training. Some cities (four out of every ten) report that managers are also trained. Most cities, however, do not require ethics training.

Municipal training typically focuses on the city's ethics code and/or the state's ethics law. Issues and topics include: (1) knowing what a conflict of interest is; (2) understanding what "having financial interests" means in a day-to-day, practical sense; (3) emphasizing the meaning of personal honesty; (4) describing how to make an ethics complaint; and (5) explaining due process. However, some cities go beyond these topics to include how to decide if an act is unethical, cope with an ethical dilemma, evaluate ethical choices, and understand the importance of transparency.

Live instruction, as opposed to computer-simulated or web-based instruction, is the most common method employed by ethics trainers. This method includes the use of hypothetical scenarios, realistic case materials, role playing, and lecturing. Web-based or other electronic means for delivering ethics instruction is used in fewer than ten of every 100 cities, although there is every indication that this statistic is growing (West & Berman 2004). A more recent survey would surely show much more online training.

The most notable changes reported in their study were: Adopting a standard of conduct (up 27 percent since 1994), monitoring adherence to a code of ethics (up 26.5 percent), and requiring familiarity with the city's code of ethics (up 24.5 percent). Also noteworthy is the fact that more cities were using ethics as a criterion in hiring and promotion and mandating ethics training for all employees. More cities were also making counselors available for assistance in dealing with ethical issues.

There is considerable variation among the states in the provision of ethics training, with 41 state ethics commissions offering some type of training. Ethics training may take the form of in-person seminars or online modules or be little more than a link to an ethics guide or slide presentation. Interactive online ethics training is not widespread but is growing. A web-based training course was brought online in New York in late 2003. The course covers the fundamentals of the state's ethics laws. "Those who complete the course successfully can print out a certificate. At least two agencies have used the course as the basis for their own online training programs," comments Walter C. Ayres, director of public information, New York State Commission on Public Integrity (Ayres 2005; Washburn 2011).

State ethics training is mostly compliance-oriented. And, in some instances, the training consists of little more than a superficial effort to inoculate employees against errant behavior. Illinois is a prime example. The state of Illinois is among the newer entrants into the ethics-training field and has put in place web-based training aimed at all state employees, including state college and university faculty and staff. All were trained soon after the law went into effect in 2004, and by law must be retrained annually. While it may be premature to judge the effectiveness of this "inoculation" style of training, it is unlikely to do more than increase awareness of the "do's" and "don'ts" in the state's ethics law.

State professional associations such as the Florida City and County Management Association (FCCMA) also provide ethics training. Indeed, the FCMMA adopted a policy in 2013 that all members, except those in the corporate category, are required to take at a minimum 4 hours of ethics training each fiscal year. The FCCMA board of directors, by consensus, concluded that mandatory ethics training for all members within the profession will help members focus on a subject area that becomes more complicated as technology advances while also giving the Association a standard when public, media and private-sector inquiries are made (FCCMA 2015).

At the federal level, the U.S. Office of Government Ethics (OGE) is the primary provider of ethics training and education materials for agencies and departments located in the executive branch. The OGE web site (https://www2.oge.gov; also see https://www.youtube.com/user/OGEInstitute) contains an impressive collection of training materials that the education division, a unit with seven specialists, has developed. The materials are provided in multiple formats (instructor-led, web-based, and videotapes) and cover a variety of topics to enable agency ethics officials to meet their training needs. Examples of the web-based training materials are modules dealing with the "misuse of position," "gifts between employees," "working with contractors," and "gifts from outside sources" (OGE Institute for Ethics in Government 2016). Other government sites with computer- and web-based ethics training are identified as well. These include the U.S. Departments of Agriculture, Defense, Interior, Justice, and Treasury and the National Institutes of Health.

Since 1978, when the OGE was established, the executive branch of the federal government has certainly conducted a major effort to raise the ethical bar and encourage federal employees to do the right thing. Still, ethical lapses occur, as evidenced by the U.S. Air Force–Boeing air tanker scandal in 2003. This scandal involved a high-level senior civil servant, Darlene Druyun, the chief acquisition official with the Air Force, who collaborated with high-ranking Boeing executives to secure jobs for her daughter, her son in law, and herself in exchange for an Air Force contract to lease tankers from Boeing for a whopping $23 billion! The scandal landed Druyun in jail for 9 months for violating conflict-of-interest laws. Boeing's chief financial officer, Michael M. Sears, also received jail time after he pleaded guilty to a conflict-of-interest charge for negotiating with Druyun over a Boeing job before she retired in 2002. At that time, Druyun was responsible for overseeing Pentagon contracts with Boeing (Merle 2004).

This single instance does not condemn the federal government's entire ethics education and training initiatives, but it does cast some doubt on its effectiveness at the highest levels, especially in the field of contract management.

Does Training Make a Difference?

Probably. But if the question is asked: "Does ethics training prevent unethical behavior?" the answer could be the question: "How is evidence gathered about something that doesn't happen—no wrongdoing?" Yet one can find plausible evidence of a link between the absence of ethics training and the occurrence of wrongdoing. Consider the case of Sarasota County, located on Florida's Gulf Coast, with a population of 369,765 in 2009. Upscale and professionally managed for 14 years by a highly regarded administrator, the county experienced an ethical meltdown in 2011 when a mid-level manager was arrested on charges he accepted illegal gifts from a sewer repair firm. Subsequent investigations into procurement policies and practices unearthed a wide-ranging pattern of credit card abuse, contract specification deception, and bundling small jobs together for one bid that opened the door for collusion and corruption (Brady 2011).

Did the county fail to have sound ethics policies in place? What had the county done to prepare its 2,000-plus employees for ethical challenges? The answers to these questions came in part with a report issued by the National Institute of Governmental Purchasing (NIGP). "Ethics and integrity do not stop at the procurement organization's doorway," the report noted (Brady 2011). Indeed, the report revealed that the county's human resources department published ethics guidelines "that are all encompassing and apply to all county employees, elected officials, appointees and family members [but] the county lacks an ethics training program." Nor did the county have an Intranet web link to its standards of conduct. Did unethical behavior flourish in Sarasota County as a result of too little attention paid to implementing ethics education and training programs? As the NIGP report notes: "Ethics policies are not easy to follow and encompass policies not normally encountered during the course of work."

Another explanation of ethics failure in Sarasota County was the business attitude embraced by the management team. Running a government like a business can lead to a mindset that goes something like this—if we invest $1 in ethics training, what is the dollar return on our investment? The answer, of course, is anybody's guess. How is a return on investment calculated for unethical behavior that doesn't occur because of sound ethics management? Is it any wonder that ethics problems are abundant in this managerial environment?

Value Added by Training

The steady growth in ethics training offers *prima facie* evidence of its effectiveness in discouraging unethical behavior and encouraging ethical behavior. Still, there is intense debate about the content, style, frequency, and effectiveness of training. The minimalist approach consistent with compliance training aims at preventing unethical behavior by removing ignorance (I didn't know I did something wrong) and, insofar as possible, minimizing mistakes. The presumption is that employees who understand ethics rules and laws are less likely to commit an unethical act, especially out of ignorance. A more robust approach, the integrity model, seeks to provide employees with the decision tools to sort through ethical dilemmas and motivate individuals to aspire to higher ethical standards.

While it may seem a nearly impossible task to demonstrate that ethics training motivates "good" behavior and prevents "bad" behavior, there is a growing body of evidence that training makes a positive difference. Consider the survey data gathered from eight communities by the Shared Ethics Advisory Commission of Northwest Indiana. Established in 2005 by an interlocal agreement, the commission regards training as the heart of its mission and conducts training on a regularly scheduled basis. Consequently, in 2009 and 2012 the Commission launched an ethics survey of the members' employees "to get an indication of whether our ethics training is making a difference," states commission president Cal Bellamy (2015). Of the 1285 full-time employees, 565 (44 percent) completed the survey. The 2012 survey results compared the aggregate and individual community responses of employees who had received training with those who had not. The aggregate results are shown in Exhibit 4.2.

Exhibit 4.2

Ethics Training Survey, Shared Ethics Advisory Commission of Northwest Indiana, 2012

Question	(n = 155)	Untrained (410)
1. Percent aware of the ethics code	78	43
2. Percent saying ethics training is important or very important	67	67
3. Percent who witnessed unethical behavior in the last 12 months	38	49
4. Percent who know how to report unethical behavior	77	41
5. Percent who asked for advice on ethics	22	18
6. Percent who have reported unethical behavior	21	23
7. Percent who would report such behavior	83	77
8. Percent who felt corrective action would be taken	72	53

A study of ethics training among municipal police also confirms the value added of training. Wyatt-Nichol and Franks (2009–2010) surveyed 34 chiefs of police in 100 U.S. cities with populations ranging from 100,000 to 500,000 to identify the "frequency and administrating of ethics training, content and instructional strategies, and perceptions of the value of training" (44). They found that police chiefs strongly endorse the value of training, indicating that it reinforces written policies, promotes discussion of ethical issues, and helps officers recognize ethical issues as they arise. The chiefs also believe ethics instruction reduces infractions among officers and encourages officers to be more willing to report unethical behavior.

Yet another study (West & Berman 2004) of 195 U.S. cities with populations of 50,000 and greater examined statistically the correlates between the 16 elements of ethics management and three important organizational variables—organizational culture, labor–management relations, and employee productivity. Cities that offer ethics training claimed improvements in their organizational culture, better labor–management relations, and higher employee productivity. West and Berman also found positive correlations between leadership strategies and improvements in the organizational culture, better labor–management relations, and higher employee productivity. Code-based strategies, those that stress adopting a code and monitoring adherence to it, are much less likely to be associated with these three organizational variables.

Perhaps the study with the most compelling results about ethics training is a survey of 161 managers in a large U.S. state government agency. It was hypothesized that ethical leadership: (1) increases the willingness of public-sector employees to report ethical problems to management; (2) strengthens the organizational commitment of employees; and (3) reduces the frequency of absenteeism (Hassan, Wright, & Yukl, 2014, 335–336). Ethical leadership was defined as "being a role model for others, treating people fairly, and actively managing ethics in the organization" (Hassan et al., 334). All hypotheses were supported by the statistical findings.

So does ethics training deter unethical behavior and foster ethical behavior? The answer would seem to be a resounding "yes." But there are some naysayers. Annabel Beerel, president and chief executive officer (CEO) of the New England Women's Leadership Institute and former Master of Business Administration business professor, claims that ethics training doesn't work because it focuses on catching "bad" people. She adds:

> Most ethics training is heavily based on the stories, dilemmas or actions of other people, and minimal emphasis is placed on the moral dilemmas the students or the professionals are personally facing. As a result, discussions are an abstraction. People seem more interested in how and why people were caught than in the real-life emotional wrestling that results in misconduct.

What's needed is ethics education that advances the spirit of learning and wisdom, not catching "bad" people (Beerel 2014).

Next up are ethics codes as a management tool.

Ethics Codes

The conventional wisdom is that codes deter unethical acts, especially by motivated, well-intended public servants. Those who want to be ethical find a code helpful, but those who are unethical will be so regardless of whether a code is adopted. Of course, the motivation for adopting a code is all too often a scandal or a publicized set of unethical acts. Let's take a look at a set of codes with an eye toward deciding whether or not the conventional wisdom is amiss.

Professional Association Codes

Professional association codes can be very helpful to public and nonprofit managers. Nearly all professional organizations have an ethics code. Indeed, an association that does not have a code is viewed as lacking legitimacy with no claim to members who call themselves professional.

Governmental Associations[1]

Public managers typically belong to one or more associations. Municipal managers typically belong to the International City/County Management Association (ICMA), an organization that quickly adopted a code for its members 7 years after its founding in 1914. The American Society for Public Administration (ASPA), founded in 1939, is the professional home for students interested in a public management career, academics who teach in public affairs programs, and local, state, and federal administrators. ASPA, however, due to its diverse membership, did not adopt a code of ethics until 1984.

Other associations that are professional homes for governmental subfields include the American Public Works Association, the International Public Management Association for Human Resources (IPMA-HR), and the Government Finance Officers Association. Not every professional association has a formal code of ethics; the IPMA-HR, for example, has a statement of principles and values. Neil Reichenberg, executive director of IPMA-HR, says that they don't have a code because a code requires an enforcement mechanism and "we don't want to do that" (2015).

Two professional codes that receive considerable attention from public managers are the ASPA code and the ICMA code. The ASPA code emphasizes aspirational values such as "uphold the law" and "serve the public" (Exhibit 4.3). The ICMA code is a mix of aspirational values and practical wisdom. While it admonishes managers to "be dedicated to the highest ideals of honor and integrity" to merit the respect of elected officials, employees, and the public, the code and accompanying guidelines offer specific directives about (in)appropriate behavior. For example, it is inappropriate behavior for a member to endorse commercial products. Guidelines for Tenet 12 state that: "Members should not endorse commercial products or services by agreeing to use their photograph, endorsement, or quotation in paid or other commercial advertisements, whether or not for compensation" (ICMA 2015).

Exhibit 4.3
American Society for Public Administration (ASPA)
Code of Ethics (Revised March 2013)

Since 1984, ASPA has promoted a commitment to high standards of ethical practice by public servants. The Code of Ethics presents the key principles that public servants should advance, and its educational and review activities support the ethical behavior of members and hold them accountable for adhering to these principles. In its current strategic plan, ASPA's first goal is to "advocate strong, effective and ethical public governance."

ASPA Code of Ethics

The American Society for Public Administration (ASPA) advances the science, art, and practice of public administration. The Society affirms its responsibility to develop the spirit of responsible professionalism within its membership and to increase awareness and commitment to ethical principles and standards among all those who work in public service in all sectors. To this end, we, the members of the Society, commit ourselves to uphold the following principles:

1. Advance the public interest. Promote the interests of the public and put service to the public above service to oneself.
2. Uphold the constitution and the law. Respect and support government constitutions and laws, while seeking to improve laws and policies to promote the public good.
3. Promote democratic participation. Inform the public and encourage active engagement in governance. Be open, transparent and responsive, and respect and assist all persons in their dealings with public organizations.
4. Strengthen social equity. Treat all persons with fairness, justice, and equality and respect individual differences, rights, and freedoms. Promote affirmative action and other initiatives to reduce unfairness, injustice, and inequality in society.

(continued)

Exhibit 4.3 *(continued)*

5. Fully inform and advise. Provide accurate, honest, comprehensive, and timely information and advice to elected and appointed officials and governing board members, and to staff members in your organization.

6. Demonstrate personal integrity. Adhere to the highest standards of conduct to inspire public confidence and trust in public service.

7. Promote ethical organizations: Strive to attain the highest standards of ethics, stewardship, and public service in organizations that serve the public.

8. Advance professional excellence: Strengthen personal capabilities to act competently and ethically and encourage the professional development of others.

A separate document contains practices that serve as a guide to behavior for members of ASPA in carrying out its principles.

Members of ASPA commit themselves to support the Code of Ethics and may be sanctioned for their failure and refusal to uphold the Code.

Leading with Integrity

As a member of various professional associations, my actions are subject to multiple codes of ethics. Some, such as the ICMA [International City/County Management Association] Code of Ethics, provide fairly explicit interpretations that allow easy reference on a variety of situations. ICMA supplements those written guidelines by providing its members personal guidance on individual issues.

Given the challenges that city and county managers routinely face, specific guidelines and personal guidance to members are understandable.

—Eric Johnson,
Assistant County Administrator,
Hillsborough County, Florida (2011)

Nonprofit Associations

The National Council of Nonprofits encourages all nonprofits to craft an appropriate "statement of values" or "code of ethics" (2015b). Among national associations with codes for their members are the Association of Fundraising Professionals (AFP), the Independent Sector, and the National Council of Nonprofit Associations.

Codes in the nonprofit sector have proliferated over the past several decades corresponding in part to the rapid growth of nonprofits as service providers and often partners with a governmental agency. The Independent Sector has compiled a list of 100 standards, codes, and principles adopted by state and regional organizations and by organizations in the arts, culture, humanities, health, human services, education, and more. Among subfields in human resources with practitioners in nonprofits and government organizations, the National Association of Social Workers (NASW) has adopted a widely respected code of ethics to help social workers sort through a myriad of issues involving protecting the privacy of clients, providing appropriate professional services in public emergencies, and avoiding conflicts of interest. "NASW also uses the code to review and adjudicate ethics complaints filed against NASW members and assess members' ethical competence," asserts Rhode Island College professor Frederic G. Reamer (2013, 169) whose research has addressed a wide range of human service issues. NASW members who are found in violation of the code can be and are sanctioned.

State Associations

State professional associations such as the Florida City/County Management Association and the Utah Nonprofits Association are also advocates of codes and standards of ethics. The Standard of Ethics for Nonprofit Organizations in Utah is quite comprehensive, with standards that cover mission, governance, financial and legal accountability, fundraising, communications, human resources, information management, public policy advocacy, and evaluation. The Utah Association's membership includes organizations and individuals. Organizational members are expected to file an annual affirmation statement to indicate they meet standards or are working to meet standards (Utah Nonprofit Association 2015). Patty Shreve, operations director for the Utah Association, notes that the standards are not enforced, as the Utah Nonprofit Association is not a policing or an accrediting organization. Rather, "we offer our Standards of Ethics to our member organizations as a metric to guide and measure their growth" (2015). Nonprofits in Utah, she adds, are monitored by the Utah State Division of Consumer Protection where complaints can be handled.

Code Enforcement

Must an effective professional code be enforced? And, if so, how should it be done? The ICMA certainly advocates and practices enforcement, although it is done in a very careful, deliberative manner. The ICMA goes to great lengths to ensure that allegations of wrongdoing are investigated while at the same time ensuring fairness and confidentiality. Managers who violate the code can be reprimanded and even expelled from ICMA. An expulsion can sideline a promising career.

The ICMA's sanctions vary according to the severity of the violation. A *private censure* is issued if the violation is relatively minor. This takes the form of a letter sent to the member, the state association, and the person who made the complaint, that the member has been found to violate the code, the ICMA disapproves of such conduct, and if repeated in the future, there may be cause for more serious sanctions. A *public censure* is a notification to the member, complainant, state association, and news media that a violation took place and that the ICMA strongly disapproves of such conduct. Additionally, a notification is sent to the local governing body to "protect the public against unethical conduct in local government." The next level of seriousness is a *revocation* of the member's privileges. Finally, the most severe sanction is a *prohibition* against reinstatement of membership. In other words, the member is expelled permanently (ICMA 2016).

The permanent expulsion of a member from the ICMA occurs only under the most compelling and clearly warranted circumstances. In December 2010, for example, the ICMA executive board took such action against Robert Rizzo, the former city manager of Bell, California. Bell's citizens voted in 2011 to recall the mayor and four other council members (Gorman 2011). That same year, the former city manager was indicted and charged with more than 50 counts of fraud, falsification of records, and conflicts of interest. He pleaded not guilty (Dobuzinskis 2011).

The board found that Mr. Rizzo personally benefited from misuse of city funds; failed in his fiduciary responsibility to ensure that public funds were legally and properly used for the public's benefit; did not fully and accurately disclose his compensation in a transparent manner; and failed in his obligation to ensure that city matters were transparent and fully communicated to the council and public (ICMA 2016).

The ICMA has been in the forefront of promoting ethics management. One study of ethical code violations by ICMA members makes it clear that ICMA encourages city managers to live and work more by aspirational, virtue-based tenets than by deontological or act-based tenets (Eskridge, French, & McThomas, 2012). City managers who view their ethics and the ethics of those around them mostly in terms of rules or consequences are likely to fall far short of managing ethically or fostering a strong ethical culture.

As noted, the NASW code of ethics is enforced, with alleged violations investigated and sanctions levied when appropriate. As with the ICMA, care and due diligence are taken to ensure that a member's due process is respected. Sanctions may include "public notification, such as the notification of state licensing or regulatory boards, employers and others, if violators fail or refuse to take corrective action" (National Association of Social Workers 2015).

The AFP enforcement procedures for its code of ethical principles and standards are as extensive (16 pages) as those of the ICMA. The AFP states it "is intolerant of practices that threaten the integrity and reputation of the fundraising profession." The enforcement procedures, the claim is made, are designed to eliminate unethical behavior, not mete out punishment (AFP 2015b). The investigative procedure followed by the AFP starts with a description of what an ethics complaint is and who has standing to lodge a complaint. The next step is to establish the factual sufficiency of the complaint to determine if the complaint warrants further investigation. If an investigation is warranted, a formal hearing may be called to determine if the member has violated the code. If a violation has occurred, the next step is to decide on an appropriate disciplinary action. Procedures for conducting the hearing involve full and fair disclosure, and a 30-day notice in which the accused member may obtain counsel and prepare a defense. A member found to be in violation of the code may be:

1. reprimanded
2. censured
3. suspended, or
4. have membership revoked—that bars a member from permanently participating in any AFP-sanctioned activity at any level.

Members found in violation of the code may appeal the decision if there is evidence that enforcement procedures were not followed properly or there are material errors of fact. Twelve individuals have been expelled from the AFP since these procedures were adopted in 1992.

Exhibit 4.4   **Association of Fundraising Professionals Enforcement Process for Alleged Violations of Ethics Code (Simplified)**

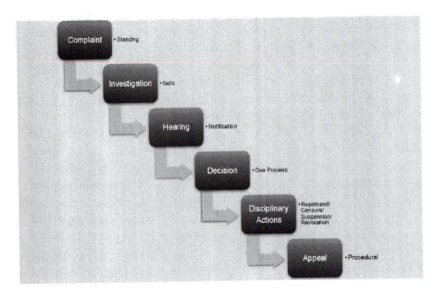

How Do Managers Use a Code?

Some exhort members of the organization to adhere to a professional code by encouraging them to join associations such as the AFP or ASPA or ICMA or the Government Finance Officers Association. Others demonstrate through their own behavior that they walk the talk. Still others go so far as to require subordinates to endorse their code publicly. For example, here is what one city manager claims: "I require managers to sign their professional codes and to hang them on their office wall, and I list the values that are most important to me on a plaque on my wall, as well" (Berman & West 2003, 36).

Leading with Integrity

In roles as a mentor and as the chief executive and advisor to elected and appointed boards and councils, I have found that the commitment to lead with integrity requires the willingness to define and live by clear principles and values in order to build trust and the willingness for others to follow.

> Relying upon the expertise and advice of others requires the ability to also admit one's own mistakes and limitations and to seek and accept the thoughts and ideas of others. Having the flexibility to reach identified goals through a variety of paths can help build that trust and the credibility needed for sustained success.
> —Martin P. Black,
> AICP, ICMA-CM, former city manager, Venice, Florida;
> General Manager and Chair of the West Villages
> Improvement District (Black 2011)

Requiring members of the organization to sign and display a code does not always produce desirable results. Consider an example from the private sector—the Boeing Company. Boeing suffered a string of corporate scandals in the early 2000s that motivated the company to bring former CEO Harry C. Stonecipher out of retirement to restore Boeing's reputation. One of his first steps was to require Boeing's top managers and 160,000 employees to sign the company's code of ethical conduct. He also signed the code. Alas, he was forced to resign a mere 15 months after taking the wheel because of a sexual tryst with a female executive officer. The board of directors concluded that, while a personal consensual affair is a private matter, Stonecipher's extramarital affair had become a management and public relations issue severe enough to dismiss him. The chairman of the board, Louis E. Platt, said that having an affair in and of itself was not a violation of Boeing's code of conduct (Wayne 2005). However, the one-page code states that "employees will not engage in conduct or activity that may raise questions as to the company's honesty, impartiality, or reputation or otherwise cause embarrassment to the company" (Boeing Company 2015). The code further states that integrity must underlie all company relationships, including those with and among employees. Mr. Stonecipher's actions, Platt asserted, embarrassed Boeing and compromised his "ability to lead going forward" (Wayne 2005).

Local-government codes of ethics are often covered by state statutes or incorporated in local ordinances—but not always. Pinellas County, Florida, for example, adopted a "statement of ethics" (Exhibit 4.5) that emphasizes the aspirational values of right behavior rather than the "follow the rules or else" mentality that many law-derived codes espouse.

Many local governments do not have stand-alone codes. The typical rationale is that the state's ethics laws cover employees, so it is not

---

Exhibit 4.5
Pinellas County Statement of Ethics

We, the employees of Pinellas County, as providers of public service, and, in order to inspire confidence and trust, are committed to the highest standards of personal integrity, honesty and competence.

To this end we will:

- Provide open and accessible government, giving courteous, responsive service to all citizens equally.
- Accept only authorized compensation for the performance of our duties and respectfully decline any offers of gifts or gratuities from those with whom we do business.
- Disclose or report any actual or perceived conflicts of interest.
- Comply with all laws and regulations applicable to the County and impartially apply them to everyone.
- Neither apply nor accept improper influences, favoritism and personal bias.
- Use County funds and resources efficiently, including materials, equipment and our time.
- Respect and protect the privileged information to which we have access in the course of our duties, never using it to stir controversy, to harm others or for private gain.

(Pinellas County, Florida n.d.)

---

necessary to have a local code, although this is not always the case. New York's ethics laws, for example, do not cover local governments. Adopting a code can be a struggle for small communities, where there is often an understanding that friends and neighbors are or should always be ethical in dealing with each other. Yet, the struggle can be hard for other reasons. Consider the case of North Mankato, Minnesota (population 13,394 in 2010). One member of city council urged her colleagues to adopt a "Statement of Values to promote and maintain the highest standards of conduct among elected officials, managers and employees of the city" (Fischenich 2012). The values consisted of a lengthy list developed by the League of Minnesota Cities (2012).

Not so fast, her colleagues replied. After surveying the statement of values, one council member commented: "God is the only one I know of who could do all this stuff. And I wish he was on the council." To which the council member added: "to me, this [referring to the list of values] is wishful thinking." The city attorney in turn asked the usual lawyerly question: "Is this a 'gotcha' kind of thing?" (Fischenich 2012).

Local governments that draft a local code often find the drafting process as important as the final product itself. Mountain View, California, for example, developed a code from the "bottom up," a process that involved more than 150 employees from all city departments (Duggan & Woodhouse 2011). Former city manager Kevin Duggan and deputy city manager Kevin Woodhouse assert that a bottom-up approach "can proceed successfully and efficiently alongside all of the other priority demands of an organization" (2011, 10). Of course, if a code is not viewed as a living document, it may become little more than a nicely framed ornament that adorns an office wall.

Why Codes Succeed or Fail

How can a code be more than words on a piece of paper? Administrators, especially at the highest organizational level, must demonstrate their commitment to the values and principles contained in the code. One approach toward doing this is for top managers to conduct special sessions on the code, including sessions for newly hired employees. A study of employees in one high-tech organization found that sessions delivered on the ethical code of conduct by high-ranking executives had an enduring impact (Adam & Rachman-Moore 2004). Such sessions can "leave an unforgettable impression about the importance assigned to ethics in the workplace" (2004, 239).

Codes should be regarded as living documents that are integrated into the fabric of the organizational culture. Ethics managers who take pride in their professional code of ethics by displaying it in the work environment are taking an important step in cultivating an ethical culture.

Still, hard evidence that a code of ethics deters unethical behavior and encourages ethical behavior is difficult to find in the scholarly literature. Studies along these lines have been carried out primarily in the field of business administration, and the results are mixed. Nonetheless, the fact that nearly nine of every ten Fortune Global 200 companies have a business code of ethics certainly suggests that top management believes codes make a difference. A recent study by Muel Kaptein (2011) examines several factors thought important in determining the impact of a code on unethical behavior. His research assessed: (1) the presence of a code; (2) the content of the code; the (3) frequency and (4) quality of the communication activities surrounding the code; and (5) the extent to which senior management as well as local management were committed to the code. The study sample consisted of 3,075 adults working for organizations in the United States that employ at least 200 people.

Which of the five factors identified above mattered the most? The mere presence of a code absent the other four factors was insignificant in deterring unethical behavior. Similar results were found when the frequency of communication was added to the model. The results changed dramatically, however, when the other three factors are added to the model. The one factor that had the greatest impact on reducing unethical behavior in the workplace was the suffusion of the code's values by senior and local management throughout the organization. In other words, the effort and commitment by top management to embed the code in the organization's culture were major factors in building an organization of integrity.

Another way to assess a code's effectiveness is offered by Stuart C. Gilman (2005), a practitioner-scholar who has written extensively on this subject. Here are his explanations for why some codes succeed and others fail: Successful codes must have clear behavior objectives. The behaviors you want to encourage and discourage should be spelled out. Successful codes must fit with the mission of the agency: a tax collection agency, for example, must be respectful but firm. "They must demand honesty from not only public servants but from the public as well" (61). Codes that are successful must have pragmatic goals; codes that promise too much are not likely to succeed. Codes that promise to end corruption are promising too much—nothing will end corruption, Gilman asserts. We can only hope to control it so it has the least impact on citizens. Finally, successful codes must be supported by feedback. "Aggregate data such as the number of administrative actions taken or successful prosecutions not only helps administrators understand the effect of their program, but it also provides insights as to changes or necessary resource reallocations that might be necessary" (63).

Exhibit 4.6 contains a code of ethics for the city employees of Mountain View, California. You can "test" Gilman's recommendations by answering the following questions: (1) Does the code have clear behavior objectives? (2) Does it fit well with the city's mission statement? (3) Does the code have pragmatic goals? (4) Does the code promise too much/too little?

Exhibit 4.6
City of Mountain View, California,
Employee Code of Ethics

As a City employee, I will be guided by prudent judgment and personal responsibility, whether serving the public or working with colleagues, and my decisions and actions will be made according to the following ethical principles:

- I will uphold the City's policies in a transparent and consistent manner at all times.
- I will make unbiased decisions and use my authority fairly and responsibly.
- I will act with honesty and be an advocate for an environment that promotes public trust.
- I will not use City resources or my position for personal gain.
- I will be mindful of how my actions may be perceived by others and avoid conflicts of interest.

These ethical principles serve as guidance and work in concert with:

The City's Mission Statement

The City of Mountain View provides quality services and facilities that meet the needs of a caring and diverse community in a financially responsible manner.

The City's Organizational Values

Provide exceptional service, act with integrity and treat others with respect.

Source: http://www.mountainview.gov/google/default.asp?q=code+
of+ethics (accessed September 11, 2015).

Most codes fail because they raise unrealistic expectations or try to control too much. Codes that require excessive reporting and tracking can produce cynicism within the organization and among the public. The pursuit of absolute integrity can be a fool's quest if the result is organizational ineffectiveness. A shift in political leadership can also bring a working code to its knees. "It is not uncommon for new political leaders to either de-emphasize ethics programs or to criticize them as being ineffective" (Gilman 2005, 65). Finally, codes can fail if there is no commitment to public service or they simply become out of date. Changes in technology, the legal structure, or the organizational culture often necessitate a re-examination of the code of ethics.

Oaths

Oaths signed by employees are also used to encourage ethical behavior and can be a key element in an integrity or fusion model. Oaths are challenging to adopt because they are difficult to frame in a manner that public officials find agreeable. Public service oaths such as those shown in Exhibit 4.7 are widely used in the federal government, and some states and local governments have developed their own version of an oath. Consider the oath for the Unified Government of Wyandotte County and Kansas City, Kansas. It requires elected and appointed officials, including employees on the front lines of service delivery, to swear (with their signature) that they will support the U.S. Constitution and the State of Kansas's Constitution and abide by the provisions of the code of ethics of the unified government.

Exhibit 4.7
Public Service Oaths

U.S. Presidential Oath of Office

Since George Washington first said the words on April 30, 1789, as prompted by Robert Livingston, chancellor of the state of New York, every president of the United States has repeated the following simple presidential oath of office as part of the inauguration ceremony:

(continued)

Exhibit 4.7 *(continued)*

I do solemnly swear [or affirm] that I will faithfully execute the office of president of the United States, and will to the best of my ability, preserve, protect and defend the Constitution of the United States.

(Constitution of the United States 1787, Article II, Section 1)

U.S. Senator Oath of Office

I do solemnly swear [or affirm] that I will support and defend the Constitution of the United States against all enemies, foreign and domestic; that I will bear true faith and allegiance to the same; that I take this obligation freely, without any mental reservation or purpose of evasion; and that I will well and faithfully discharge the duties of the office on which I am about to enter: So help me, God.

(U.S. Senate 1884)

The Athenian Oath

The Athenian oath was recited by the citizens of Athens, Greece, over 2,000 years ago. It is frequently referenced by civic leaders in modern times as a timeless code of civic responsibility.

We will never bring disgrace on this our city by an act of dishonesty or cowardice. We will fight for the ideals and sacred things of the city both alone and with many. We will revere and obey the city's laws, and will do our best to incite a like reverence and respect in those above us who are prone to annul them or set them at naught. We will strive unceasingly to quicken the public's sense of civic duty. Thus, in all these ways, we will transmit this city not only, not less, but greater and more beautiful than it was transmitted to us.

(National League of Cities 2010)

Salt Lake County, Utah, adopted an ethics ordinance and oath in 2004 in response to several scandals (Exhibit 4.8). Notice that the oath applies to all persons employed by the county, including elected and nonelected officials. Notice also that all officials and employees are required only to "read and review" the oath—nothing more.

Exhibit 4.8
Salt Lake County, Utah, Code of Ordinances:
County Ethics Code

Ethics Statement

All county elected officials, appointed officers, deputies and employees, in the employment of Salt Lake County, before commencing the duties of their respective offices, shall read and review the following ethics statement:

Employees of Salt Lake County support, obey and defend the Constitution of the United States, the Constitution of the State of Utah, the laws of the State of Utah, and the ordinances of Salt Lake County, to the best of their abilities and will always strive to meet the highest ethical standards implicit in their employment and in the furtherance of the best public interest.

(Salt Lake County, Utah 2011)

Some scholars believe that oaths have lost much of their value in the modern age. Stephen L. Carter (1997, 108), for example, claims,

> In the cynicism of our age, nobody assumes that simply because an individual swears by God to tell the truth that the person is telling the truth. . . . An oath . . . is seen as a silly little formality, like the stamping of a passport.

It might be recalled that President Bill Clinton was impeached by the House of Representatives in 1998 largely because of lying under oath. (A trial in the Senate did not convict him of the charges.) Other scholars take a different view of oaths. Gilman (2006) puts it this way:

I take a slightly less cynical view of oaths and their impact. I have been in a position to really watch them work, and work the way they are supposed to. To suggest this occurs all of the time would be silly. But I have watched the mighty fall, most notably Mr. Edwin Meese III, former U.S. Attorney General in the Reagan Administration, and Mr. John Sununu, former White House Chief of Staff under President George H.W. Bush, because of ethics violations. Each was ultimately allowed to resign because the violations were tied to their oath of office.

Oaths, especially those tied to a code of ethics, are not common in state and local governance. John A. Rohr, a highly respected ethicist, takes strong objection to this oversight. He contends it is the oath of office that defines the public servant as a professional (see Exhibit 4.9 for an example). In his classic *To Run a Constitution: The Legitimacy of the Administrative State* (1986, 192), Rohr asserts:

> The oath to uphold the Constitution can then be seen not simply as a pledge to obey but also as an initiation into a community of disciplined discourse, aimed at discovering, renewing, adapting, and applying the fundamental principles that support our public order. The task is to see the oath more as an act of civility than submission.

Exhibit 4.9
Oath of Office for Employment in the U.S. Postal Service

Before entering upon their duties and before receiving any salary, all officers and employees of the Postal Service shall take and subscribe the following oath or affirmation:

I, _____, do solemnly swear [or affirm] that I will support and defend the Constitution of the United States against all enemies, foreign and domestic; that I will bear true faith and allegiance to the same; that I take this obligation freely, without any mental reservation or purpose of evasion; and that I will well and faithfully discharge the duties of the office on which I am about to enter.

(U.S. Department of Justice 2005)

LeRoy F. Harlow (1914–1995), an ethics exemplar you met in Chapter 3, believed an oath is far more than words on a piece of paper or uttered during a swearing-in ceremony. In *Servants of All* (1981), he contends that "all elected, appointed, or employed public servants, whether full-time or part-time," should be required to take an oath of honor. The result "may reestablish character in the public service [and] may divert and lessen the stream of governmental corruption that has come close to inundating us all" (323). Harlow readily admitted that no sworn oath would stop a public officeholder bent on violating the public trust; nonetheless, an oath may be the moral crutch that many leaders and followers who straddle the ethical fence may need to strengthen their "resolve to perform their duties regardless of personal consequence" (323). Although Harlow's comments were made over 30 years ago, they still resonate loudly today. Is it not so?

A Public Servant's Oath of Honor

I hereby swear [or affirm] that during my service with [name of agency] I will not [or I did not] lie, cheat, steal, or illegally favor one citizen or group of citizens over another (nor tolerate any public officer or employee who does).

(Harlow 1981, 322)

The point here is that oaths provide officials with the legitimacy and empowerment to carry out their duties in a manner that is both ethically and morally sound. This approach contrasts significantly with the "follow-the-rules" method that many codes become when transformed into law-like documents.

Ethics Audits

A proactive tool for building organizations of integrity is the ethics audit. Although not widely employed, an ethics audit can be a very useful tool. It has been described as an "appraisal activity, the purpose being to determine if changes need to be made in the climate, environment, codes, and the enforcement of ethics policies" (Wiley 1995). An ethics audit is not an accounting or financial management audit. By way of example, the New York State comptroller completed an audit of the accounting and expenditures of a Long Island school district and found that the former district superintendent and the assistant superintendent for business had, over 8 years, plundered the district's treasury of $11.2 million (Lambert 2005). This affluent school district had a stellar record for graduating students who went on to top universities. Perhaps this is the reason why the school board, the treasurer, and the external accounting firm hired by the school district failed to exercise adequate oversight. Failed oversight is, in itself, unethical.

Scope of Audit

What should be the scope of an ethics audit? Should all members of the organization be included? Should behavior and attitudes be covered? Should legal compliance be included? These are among the central questions that quickly surface when considering an ethics audit. Carole L. Jurkiewicz and Glen M. Vogel (2015) recommend a wide scope for inclusion in an audit to include three key areas: Cultural values, organizational governance, and legal compliance (40). An ethical organization is characterized by a set of moral norms (García-Marzá 2005). Among the values one would assess in an ethics audit are: Respect, transparency, problem solving (i.e. ethical dilemmas are regularly addressed in meetings and responses to alleged wrongdoing handled in a timely manner and with respect and openness), equity, fairness, dignity, and discipline (Jurkiewicz & Vogel 2015, 41–42). Organizational governance involves power, responsibility, accountability, relationships, and transparency by those who govern the organization. "Good organizational governance requires, among other things: Trustworthiness, accountability and transparency, fair, impartial, and unbiased operation and management" (43). Legal compliance includes, but is not limited to: (1) nondiscriminatory treatment of employees and applicants; (2) financial reporting and proper internal controls; (3) environmental sensitivity to ensure compliance with all environmental laws and regulations; and (4) compliance with ethical codes relevant to a specific profession or industry.

The scope recommended by Jurkiewicz and Vogel is substantial. Is it not? Frederic G. Reamer (2007), who argues that an ethics audit should focus on what is currently considered to be essential or core ethical issues in a profession, recommends a more limited scope. An ethics audit, Reamer asserts, allows an assessment of the adequacy of an organization's ethics-related practices, policies, and procedures.

Ethics Audit Process, According to Frederic G. Reamer

1. Establish an ethics audit committee with members who have demonstrated interest in the agency's ethics policies, practices, and procedures.
2. The audit committee should identify specific ethics related to focus but, in some settings, the committee may want to conduct a comprehensive audit.
3. The audit committee should decide what kind of information it will need, e.g., documents and relevant codes.
4. Once data are gathered, the committee should assess each issue with respect to relevant agency policies and procedures staffers follow.
5. Once the audit is completed, steps should be taken to make use of its findings.
6. The committee should identify which staff will be responsible for the various tasks and establish a timetable for completion of each, and a mechanism to follow up on each task to ensure its completion and monitor its implementation.
7. The committee should document the complete audit process to demonstrate its good-faith effort to assess ethics-related policies and procedures.

(http://www.socialworktoday.com/archive/EoEJan Feb07.shtml, accessed July 7, 2015)

Ethics Audit Process

The National Council of Nonprofits (2015c) recommends that a comprehensive ethics audit should be conducted every 3–5 years, with more frequent periodic reviews to review written guidelines or the soundness of training or preventive assistance programs.

Good advice no doubt but—ethics audits are not commonplace? Why? There are several reasons. First, it can be threatening if presented as an effort to root out wrongdoing; furthermore, when done for the first time, it raises anxiety levels and questions about why it is needed. After all, don't most public employees believe they are ethical and work in an ethical organization? Perhaps. Second, audits are uncommon because they need to be comprehensive in both the information solicited and the members of the organization covered. It can be challenging in terms of the time and effort required, which, in turn, places a demand on the agency's budget. Third, employees and managers may not be convinced of the confidentiality of the audit, especially in states with strong laws that require public officials to conduct all business in an open, transparent manner, sometimes referred to as in the "sunshine." The reasons for not carrying out an audit should be weighed carefully in light of the organizational payoffs they provide: Increased productivity, greater worker satisfaction, lower turnover rates of personnel, and the building of public trust and confidence in the agency.

There are other important reasons to conduct an ethics audit. First, it can identify gaps in policies and procedures, including gaps in the need to increase awareness of areas of potential ethical risk (McAuliffe 2002). Second, another plus for conducting an audit occurs if the agency contracts with an outside party, such as a university institute, to carry it out. An internal, agency-conducted audit is automatically suspect and unlikely to be viewed as trustworthy by employees. A more transparent, university-conducted audit benefits agency officials through "ethical conversations, opportunity for critical reflection, and the support that could be offered to staff with no professional qualifications" (4).

An ethics audit might also include an assessment of occupational risk or vulnerability. Some organizational work is inherently vulnerable to ethical abuse, if not criminal wrongdoing; for example, work that involves the handling and processing of finances, purchasing and contracting, conducting inspections, and enforcing rules and regulations is high-risk, especially for workers whose ethical compass is subpar in the first place. A systematic assessment of the ethical risk factor of work is a necessary first step in putting into place appropriate accountability and transparency mechanisms. It is also a valuable step in identifying ethical training priorities.

When Serious Wrongdoing Turns Up

An ethics audit may discover serious incidents of wrongdoing, especially when interviews rather than mail surveys are employed to collect information about the ethics climate. If these incidents are of sufficient scale and severity to be potentially criminal in nature, such as that in the Long Island school district, what are the auditors to do? The answer is straightforward: They must report their suspicions and findings to the appropriate authorities. However, the line between criminal acts and unethical acts is sometimes difficult to discern. Auditors must be convinced that an unethical act has a very high probability of being unlawful while at the same time being very careful to not assume the role of a prosecutor.

Although objectivity is at a premium in conducting an audit, administrators "must recognize that an assessment of this nature involves considerable subjective judgment" (Reamer 2000, 364). Nonetheless, an ethics audit, whether done by a third party such as a consultant or university, is a valuable tool that can be drawn on to foster integrity in the workplace.

Human Resources Management

Personnel decisions—hiring, evaluating, promoting, and firing—are essential features of all organizations. Should the ethical behavior of an employee be considered in these decisions? Should only "honest" people be hired? Promoted? Hiring and promoting honest people is no easy task. How does an agency know if a person is honest? Should a lie-detector test be used? Or an integrity test? Or a fitness-of-character test? And, even if we could determine if a person is honest or of high moral character, can we presume that these qualities will persist over the years of employment? Not necessarily, given what we know about the moral challenges facing individuals in complex, modern organizations of the twenty-first century.

Stephen J. Bonczek, a city manager with many years' experience in different localities and states—Michigan, Florida, Texas, and Pennsylvania—is a strong advocate of raising the ethical awareness of employees through hiring, evaluation, and promotion. He is equally adamant about installing an ethical consciousness in the organization through the use of codes, audits, committees, and weekly staff meetings. He claims,

> It is advantageous to use weekly staff meetings to review all discussions and decisions for ethical implications. When a potential problem is identified, a staff member can be assigned to clarify the issue and develop a strategy for resolving it at the next meeting.
>
> (Bonczek 1998, 78)

Hiring Practices

Screening of a job applicant for her ethical judgment is, of course, challenging. One approach that can be taken during the interview is to ask the candidate to respond to hypothetical situations. Here are several examples. Mary Jane Hirt, the former city manager of two Pittsburgh communities, recommends this scenario:

You are the assistant manager in a community and have just been informed by a council member that council intended to fire the town manager at the next public meeting. The council member asked whether you are interested in being considered for the manager's position. What is your response? Do you warn the manager that s/he is about to be fired?

(Hirt 2003)

Ann Hess with the City of Boston asks a specific question during the interview process by posing a hypothetical situation. "When I interview staff for the City Council (one staff; fourteen bosses), I try to gauge an applicant's understanding of the need to be confidential while respecting divergent interests across bosses" (Hess 2003). She presents the candidate with this scenario:

You as a central staff member are asked to compile some research for one councilor. Another councilor comes to you with a request for information on the same issue, but the councilor has a different position on the issue. Part I: How do you comply with each person's request? Part II: The first councilor comes back to you and asks who else is working on the issue and what else you have produced for them. What do you say?

I usually give the applicant 5 minutes to draft some informal comments and responses and then we talk about it. I look for how they come to the decision—while there's no specific right answer, better candidates will discuss wanting to know level of confidentiality in advance, providing both sides of the story to both councilors with focus on the particular position they are advocating, the inability to disclose who else they are doing research for, and how they present that fact to the requesting councilor with respect and understanding.

Scenarios like these can be helpful in screening job applicants, but more probing may be needed as well. To query applicants about their personal lives—have you ever stolen anything, lied, cheated?—can be a tricky matter. Of course, there is also the possibility of prying too deeply into individuals' private affairs when taking this approach. Considerable care and caution need to be exercised.

Annual Evaluations

Putting an ethics component into human resources management is a daunting task but one that many managers find useful. While it's challenging to incorporate an ethics criterion into evaluation, it would not be difficult to require employees to complete an ethics education or training course before being promoted. Mayor Steve Brown (2005), of Peachtree City, Georgia, urges local governments to "create a study course on ethics that has to be completed in order to be eligible for promotion." The U.S. Department of Defense (DoD) Acquisition Workforce requires ethics training annually but does not mandate it as a condition for promotion. As Keith McAllister (2005) notes,

> To be a DoD Program Manager or Contracting Officer, one must be certified to an appropriate level. Certification as a Program Manager includes a series of formal classes (continuous learning credit) . . . The DoD spends significant public resources annually. It is imperative that those resources be used in a manner consistent with public expectations and trust—hence the embedded ethics training.

One approach that might be taken to incorporate an ethics component in an employee's annual evaluation is to place a checkbox on the evaluation form. The checkbox could read: "Employee treats others with respect and dignity." As simplistic as this solution might be, it would certainly make every employee sensitive to the fact that he or she will be held ethically accountable once a year. And, if multiplied over hundreds or perhaps thousands of employees, what a difference it could make.

Ethics Counselors

Another tool for ethics management is the ethics counselor. An example is a clinical psychologist working as a federal employee in a U.S. Department of Veterans Affairs Medical Center. She is chairperson of the hospital ethics committee and coordinator of the employee assistance program (EAP). Her committee members function as consultants when people confront dilemmas and wish to discuss them. Issues like these reach her as an EAP counselor when someone is attempting to resolve an ethical issue between a superior and a subordinate; for example, the person may come to her to discuss the incident and seek advice. A Veterans Affairs-wide National Center for Ethics in Health Care provides formal and informal consultation, as well. If the psychologist has a thorny issue come up in the Hospital Ethics Advisory

Committee and wishes to get an outside perspective, she can call the National Center to get ethics advice.

The Department of Veterans Affairs Medical Center also has a monthly hotline teleconference where issues are discussed (for example, the Pope's declaration on patients in a persistent vegetative state, or whether gifts or meals provided by vendors can be accepted by service providers). Most of these issues deal with clinical or organizational ethics, and the consultants represent a variety of disciplines, including medicine, nursing, social work, psychology, law, and chaplaincy (West 2005).

Human resources management can be drawn on to promote ethics and integrity in governance. This discussion has demonstrated the many possibilities that lend themselves to this task. The failure by officials to include human resources management in their ethics management arsenal will limit the ability of the most dedicated, well-intentioned leader to build an organization of integrity.

Hotlines

The most famous hotline in history connects the red phones in Washington, D.C., and Moscow, a Cold War relic perhaps. Fortunately, the Washington–Moscow hotline has had little use. Not so with other hotlines in widespread use in many organizations and governments. Tracking down fraud and waste is not an easy task, but fraud hotlines can be crucial in solving such cases. Ethics hotlines are typically dedicated to allegations involving violations of an ethics code. Sometimes, however, the same line is used for both purposes—tracking fraud and code violations. Consider the cases of Jacksonville and Palm Beach County, Florida.

Jacksonville

In August 2007, Mayor John Peyton directed the city's ethics officer to implement a confidential telephone hotline for the discovery of waste, fraud, and ethics violations. Later in the year, the city council authorized the ethics commission to receive hotline calls for reporting offenses under the local ethics code. A single telephone hotline number was used for all calls.

The results for the period August 2007–May 2011 show that 395 calls were made, with 59 cases opened for further review and all but six closed. Many calls (30 percent) involved citizen education, as some complaints were based on a misunderstanding of the law or the facts. The ethics officer was able to clear up these issues quickly. Other calls came from city employees concerned about hiring relatives or allegations about employees receiving gifts (for example, football tickets). The ethics officer, Carla Miller (2011), feels strongly that the educational benefits of hotlines are significant, as is the prospect of deterring intentional or unintentional wrongdoing by city employees.

Local Government Ethics Hotline Effectiveness

- Anonymity for the caller.
- Documentation for oversight and transparency.
- Well-trained staff who can distinguish various legal and ethical issues and put them in a local context.
- Effective working relationship between the ethics office and other bodies such as the General Counsel and the Inspector General.
- Dedicated line that is not part of the city phone system.
- Fairness in handling complaints made about employees and elected officials.
- 24/7/365 access.

(C. Miller 2011)

Setting up a hotline is not without fiscal cost. In the case of Jacksonville, however, the ethics officer estimates that the cost savings far outweighed her $75,000 yearly part-time salary. She says the city saved somewhere between $579,483 and $938,527 as a result of the withdrawal and rebidding of several contracts (C. Miller 2011).

Palm Beach County

Ethics reform in Palm Beach County, launched in 2010, included the establishment of an ethics hotline and the use of e-mail to receive and process attributed and anonymous information. Alan Johnson, Palm Beach's ethics officer, views the value of an ethics hotline as going far beyond investigating tips and allegations of government wrongdoing. He contends,

> Training programs stress awareness and compliance among officials and public employees, and to a lesser extent, vendors and service providers to the public entity. Outreach is a critical step in the ethics process and includes the publication and maintenance of a viable hotline.

(Johnson 2011b)

The Value of a Hotline

Regardless of the number of legally sufficient referrals through the hotline, it serves as a safety valve for public discontent with government. Whether it's a call regarding a rude employee, or allegations of significant abuse in public contracts or procurement, it provides an avenue that the citizen or public employee can turn to.

During office hours, our hotline is answered by a member of our staff. After hours, the caller can leave a message. We acknowledge receipt of all hotline calls that are identified. On many occasions, even if the facts do not allege an ethics code violation, we can refer the caller to an appropriate agency to handle their concerns.

Sometimes just "blowing a little steam" has a beneficial effect on the caller. In these cases, there is a palpable benefit to the public regardless of the outcome. While an ethics hotline is important, it serves as only one cog in the wheel of an effective program created to foster an increase in ethics awareness and compliance.

—Alan Johnson (2011b),
Ethics Officer, Palm Beach County

Summing Up

Public and nonprofit administrators must use all the ethics management tools available to them to put into place a comprehensive and integrated program. Still, it is reasonable to ask whether some tools are more effective than others. One study of a private-sector organization provides help in answering this question. Adam and Rachman-Moore (2004) examined several methods used to implement a code of conduct. Among others, they assessed three tools discussed in this chapter—managerial leadership, the means of enforcement, and ethics training. What did they find? First, they found that training was more important than either managerial leadership or the means of enforcement. Second, the surprise finding was that the means of enforcement—that is, signing an oath, providing performance evaluations, and so forth—were the least important in influencing employees "to behave in accordance with organizational ethical rules." This result is contrary to the "common view that organizational enforcement mechanisms are of prime importance as control mechanisms and are considered to effectively impact on the conduct of employees" (Adam & Rachman-Moore 2004, 238).

As this chapter has shown, many tools can be drawn on to cultivate an ethical culture in public organizations. However, no one tool is the single most effective. Ethics managers must use all the tools at their disposal.

Ethics Management Skill Building[2]

Practicum 4.1. Ethics and Performance Evaluations

Your city workforce has been experiencing a rash of ethical lapses. It seems as if nearly everyone, from the janitorial staff to the department managers to the deputy directors, has had an ethics miscue over the past year. As the director of human resources, you feel strongly that it is time to put an ethics component in the annual evaluation of hourly workers and managerial/professional employees. You realize, of course, that your boss must agree, and you begin to think about how you will make the case to evaluate the ethical behavior of employees.

Why not collect information from cities like yours to identify what others are doing? After a few weeks of telephone calls and e-mails, you discover that very little is being done, but you do find one municipality that has an ethics component in the annual evaluation of the city manager, the city clerk, and the city attorney. The evaluation instrument asks the evaluator to rate the city manager/clerk/attorney as "excellent," "fully satisfactory," "satisfactory," or "unsatisfactory" in response to the statement: "Conducts self in accordance with the ethical standards of the office of Charter Officer."

Disappointed by what you learn, you decide to form a committee to draft language that could be placed on the form to evaluate professional/management personnel. You decide to do the same thing with the hourly employees' evaluation language, but at a later date. The committee takes their assignment to heart and produces the following set of evaluative statements:

1. Demonstrates an ethical approach in the discharge of duties.
2. Displays ethical behavior—promotes an environment that is open, fair, tolerant, trustful, and respectful. Values public interest over self-interest and is accountable.
3. Clearly understands and communicates ethical practices, policies, and goals relevant to the community.
4. Shows respect for the views of others, takes pride in work products, places public interest over own self-interest.
5. Demonstrates integrity in all aspects of work.

6. Adheres to the city's ethics code.
7. Demonstrates a clear ability to identify, evaluate, and resolve issues related to ethics.
8. Demonstrates sound ethical judgment and encourages ethical behavior in others.
9. Complies with rules and laws defined by city personnel manual and professional standards and conducts self with integrity while avoiding undue influence.
10. Displays proper attitude toward organizational transparency and has sufficient knowledge of city's ethical standards.
11. Demonstrates ethical judgment as defined by the city code of ethics or applicable professional standards.

Discussion Questions

1. Which of these 11 statements do you like the best? The least? Why?
2. Rank three of the 11 evaluative statements as your first, second, and third choices, with the first being the most important.
3. Would the list differ in any significant manner for hourly employees?
4. In forming the committee to draft language that will appear on the performance evaluation, what should be the key criteria for membership?
5. Do you anticipate resistance from the workforce about including an ethics component in the annual evaluation? Why or why not?
6. Do you believe that the ethical performance of an employee can be evaluated fairly and accurately? Why or why not?
7. What do you say to persuade your boss that the city should place your preferred statement on the annual performance evaluation form for managerial/professional staff?

Practicum 4.2. Ethics Training for the Trainer

Your urban county government has nearly 10,000 employees who are responsible for streets, sewers, water, solid waste pickup and disposal, and an array of social services such as assisting homeless people and curbing drug abuse. As the head of the county's Division of Training, it is your job to provide a range of training exercises that fits the needs of a diverse workforce.

Some training, for example, helps frontline employees deal with angry people. Other training involves following proper procedures when a citizen complains about an employee or a public service.

The county administrator, who recently attended an ethics program conducted by her professional association, returned with a great deal of enthusiasm for establishing a comprehensive ethics training program for all 10,000 county employees. Recognizing that the training division does not have trainers with this expertise but knowing that you have a strong background in this area, she asks you to put into place a "train the trainer" initiative.

You immediately call your staff of six trainers together to discuss the situation. The staff are somewhat uncertain and uneasy about taking on this responsibility. In fact, one of your trainers pipes up and says, "Adults can't be taught ethics. People learn ethics from their mother or father or church or wherever. It's a waste of county time and money to take this on. You should go back to the county administrator and respectfully tell her to forget it."

Discussion Questions

1. How would you respond to your staff member? Would you tell him he's totally off base—that acquiring ethics is a lifelong endeavor?
2. If you and the staff agree with the trainer who spoke up, how would you approach the county administrator? Would you say that the training staff feel strongly that a countywide ethics training program will not be successful? Or, would you tell her that the training staff do not feel that they can teach adults ethics, but will go through the motions anyway?
3. Would you say to the administrator that we could teach compliance with ethics ordinances and state law but nothing more? How would you defend this assertion?

Notes

1. Some material in this chapter is drawn from Menzel (2005b).
2. For a broad overview of professional associations that serve public administrators, see Haynes and Gazley (2011).

5

State and Local Ethics Management Environments

Do the right thing. It will gratify some people and astonish the rest.

—Mark Twain, 1835–1910 (Twain n.d.a)

Public and nonprofit agencies and those who manage them are constrained by history, culture, custom, laws, and rules. This chapter focuses on state and local ethics management environments; the two chapters that follow explore the U.S. national and international environments.

Watchdogs Are Everywhere

Roaming about ethics management environments are what can be labeled ethics watchdogs—for-profit and nonprofit organizations whose mission is to keep track of unethical or suspicious happenings. Probably foremost among the for-profit watchdogs are newspapers and radio and television stations. Citizens, of course, can become watchdogs and many do in some communities. Stories of the little old ladies with sneakers abound. Both the media and community activists can be quite aggressive in calling attention to untoward behavior by governmental and nonprofit officials.

There is no shortage of energetic watchdogs in American states and localities. In Florida, for example, the Center for Investigative Reporting focuses on corruption, waste, and miscarriages of justice. Another nonprofit, Integrity Florida, advertises itself as "a nonpartisan, nonprofit research institute and government watchdog whose mission is to promote integrity in government and expose public corruption" (Integrity Florida 2015). Citizens for Responsibility and Ethics in Washington (CREW) monitor both national and state organizations. CREW's stated mission is to promote ethics and accountability by targeting officials who, in their judgment, sacrifice the common good to special interests. Another ethical watchdog is the Center for Public Integrity, a nonpartisan, nonprofit investigative news organization founded in 1989. The Center draws on the tools of investigative journalism to reveal "abuses of power, corruption and betrayal of public trust by powerful public and private institutions," according to the mission statement posted on its website.

Let's take a close look at efforts by American states to foster ethical behavior and discourage wrongdoing.

American States

The American states have taken a number of measures to strengthen ethics and integrity in governance, although there is considerable variation among them. Some states do a great deal; others do very little. New York passed the first major ethics law in 1954. Other states have moved more slowly in launching ethics reform initiatives, with many doing so in the 1970s on the heels of the Watergate scandal. In this section we will take a wide-lens view of ethics management in the American states by focusing on the executive, legislative, and judiciary branches of government.

Ethics Laws

The Better Government Association, a Chicago-based civic watchdog group, compiles a 50-state Integrity Index (Exhibit 5.1) based on the extent to which the states have adopted laws dealing with freedom of information, whistleblowing, open meetings, and financial conflicts of interest. In 2013, five states—Rhode Island (1st), New Jersey (2nd), Illinois (3rd), Nebraska (4th), and California (5th)—received the best overall scores, while Montana (50th), Wyoming (49th), Michigan (48th), South Dakota (47th), and Idaho (46th) were ranked the bottom five. Some states performed better than others in specific categories. Arkansas, Kentucky, Nevada, and Vermont, for example, were ranked higher on freedom of information than the best overall state Rhode Island. The reader should keep in mind that the Integrity Index is based on the strength of laws in four areas; it does not measure ethical or unethical behavior. For example, while Arkansas (80.6 percent) enjoys the highest score for freedom of information, there are no assurances that the law is not broken consistently (Better Government Association 2013).

Exhibit 5.1

Better Government Integrity Index, 2013
(states ranked from highest to lowest)

The 2013 index contains laws in four areas: freedom of information, open meetings, whistleblower protection, and conflicts of interest.

State	2013	State	2013
Rhode Island	1	Oklahoma	26
New Jersey	2	North Dakota	27
Illinois	3	Arizona	28
Nebraska	4	Minnesota	29
California	5	Maryland	30
Louisiana	6	Oregon	31
Texas	7	Mississippi	32
Washington	8	New Mexico	33
Kentucky	9	Kansas	34
Arkansas	10	Alaska	35
New Hampshire	11	Wisconsin	36
West Virginia	12	Colorado	37
Hawaii	13	Florida	38
North Carolina	14	Maine	39
Massachusetts	15	Ohio	40
Pennsylvania	16	Delaware	41
Indiana	17	South Carolina	42
Nevada	18	Vermont	43
Iowa	19	Tennessee	44
Virginia	20	Alabama	45
Missouri	22	Idaho	46
Utah	22	South Dakota	47
New York	23	Michigan	48
Connecticut	24	Wyoming	49
Georgia	25	Montana	50

As suggested, states differ widely in the content and coverage of ethics laws, although all states provide some protection from retaliation for employees who blow the whistle on government fraud, waste, or abuse of power. All 50 states also require lobbyists to file disclosure reports that identify persons seeking to influence legislation, as well as the expenditures made by lobbyists. Gift restrictions on legislators vary substantially. "A variety of approaches are used in the 50 states, including restrictions, outright prohibitions, and exemptions to those limits and prohibitions" (National Conference of State Legislatures 2015).

Restrictions on campaign finance contribution are in place in 37 states, with 27 states placing restrictions on the contributions that legislators can receive from lobbyists. Restrictions on former legislators from lobbying are in place in 26 states, with 19 states restricting former legislators from lobbying for 1 year after leaving office and six states imposing a 2-year ban on this revolving door. Twenty-eight states prohibit legislators from receiving honoraria if offered in connection with a legislator's official duties. However, among those 28 states 19 allow legislators to accept an honorarium for services performed in relation to their private profession or occupation. A lawyer-legislator, for example, can receive an honorarium for a speaking engagement at a university law school.

Ethics Commissions

The principal agency for overseeing a state's ethics laws is a commission or board. These boards generally act as regulatory watchdogs, although some critics contend their state ethics commission is a "toothless" watchdog. Forty-one states have an ethics commission or board that administers and enforces ethics codes and rules for public officials, state employees, and lobbyists. The 8 states that do not have ethics commissions are Arizona, Idaho, New Mexico, North Dakota, South Dakota, Vermont, Virginia, and Wyoming. Ethical oversight, however, can be provided through other state agencies such as the Office of the Secretary of State or Office of Attorney General or a legislative ethics committee. Hawaii was the first state to establish an ethics commission, in 1968. The commissions vary enormously in size and capacity, with some states (for example, Montana) having a single commissioner and other states (such as West Virginia) having 12 commissioners. State ethics laws typically cover local-government employees, although not all do. These agencies can issue advisory opinions, provide training and information regarding the state's ethics laws, and adjudicate allegations of unethical behavior. The more powerful agencies can initiate investigations, subpoena witnesses, and levy civil fines. Decisions reached by ethics commissions are subject to judicial review.

Altogether, the 50 states reflect a patchwork of boards, commissions, and laws. There is little coherence overall but the question still must be asked . . .

How Effective Are State Ethics Laws and Regulatory Bodies?

It is not easy to determine. Moreover, the legalistic and rule-driven approach taken by most states emphasizes ethics management as a legal process; thus, training, for example, turns mostly around interpretations of the law—what the law says and what can happen to those who break the law. And, of course, state ethics regulatory commissions and agencies are mindful of the need for due process in all rulings.

Among the handful of studies that have attempted to assess the effectiveness of state ethics laws and agencies is Smith's (2003) study of Connecticut, Florida, and New York. These states have established commissions that, as ethics watchdogs, take as their primary mission the enforcement of ethics laws. All were created as a result of scandal, with the Connecticut and Florida ethics commissions established in 1978 and 1977, respectively. The New York State ethics commission was created in 1987. All issue advisory opinions, provide training, and conduct investigations, although the Florida commission cannot initiate investigations on its own, nor can it directly levy civil penalties; it can recommend penalties but needs an executive order to implement a recommendation. Smith concludes, "ethics commissions play a positive role in the states" (293). "Enforcement actions," he asserts, "send a message to violators or would-be violators to be mindful of ethics transgressions" and therefore function as an effective deterrent.

A growing chorus of critics contends that ethics laws and regulatory agencies need to be empowered with adequate funding, greater operating autonomy, and vigorous enforcement authority. Mackenzie (2002) claims that the enactment of numerous ethics laws and ordinances—federal, state, and local—has tried to make government scandal-proof, but there is little evidence that this approach has succeeded. Indeed, he goes so far as to suggest, "some ethics deregulation will improve the overall quality of the public service and of government performance with no discernible impact on public integrity" (164–165).

Perhaps the most comprehensive examination of state laws and practices is the State Integrity Investigations compiled by the Center for Public Integrity in 2012 and 2015. These studies measured corruption risk in all 50 states across 13–14 categories. The corruption risk indicators allowed each state to be graded (from A to F = failure) and they draw a distinction between "in law" indicators, which simply judge whether a law exists, and "in practice" indicators, which assess whether or not the laws are properly enforced (Center for Public Integrity 2015). The latter is considered an "enforcement gap." So how did the states' grades turn out? The answer—not well. In fact, the 2015 report found that no state earned an A grade and only three states—Alaska, California, and Connecticut—scored higher than D+. Eleven states—Delaware, Kansas, Louisiana, Maine, Michigan, Nevada, Oklahoma, Oregon, Pennsylvania, South Dakota, and Wyoming—received Fs.

Not surprisingly, enforcement gaps vary considerably across the states. Four states—Kentucky, North Carolina, Ohio, and Texas—had alarmingly wide gaps in 2012. A handful of states—Idaho, Montana, Nebraska, South Dakota, Vermont, and Virginia—had no enforcement gaps. Indeed, these states had a negative enforcement gap, meaning "those states are actually providing more enforcement and transparency than their laws require" (Majorsky 2015).

Two other issues are frequently mentioned as hampering the effectiveness of ethics commissions. One is whether the agency is truly independent. That is, the budgets as well as the proceedings are free of political interference. "Elected officials," asserts Jonathan Rauh, "face the problem of an appointed ethics commission with the ability to censure or otherwise harm them" (Rauh 2015, 99). Craig McDonald, director of the nonprofit watchdog group Texans for Public Justice, states bluntly: "It has to be independent, or it doesn't work so well" (Ginley 2012). The State Integrity Investigation conducted by the Center for Public Integrity reports that only eight states achieved perfect scores for having a commission that maintains protection from political interference (Ginley 2012).

The other issue is the ease or difficulty of filing an ethics complaint against a public official. All states with a commission allow anyone to file a complaint, although there are qualifications in some states. In Texas, for example, an individual must be a resident or own real property in the state. In Ohio, only individuals with "factual knowledge" may file a complaint (National Conference of State Legislatures 2013). Florida is much more welcoming; anyone may file a complaint, no matter the source.

> In many states, a complex mix of legislative committees, stand-alone commissions and law enforcement agencies police the ethics laws. And more often than not, the State Integrity Investigation shows, those entities are underfunded, subject to political interference or are simply unable or unwilling to initiate investigations and issue sanctions when rules are broken. Or at least that's as far as the public can tell: many of these bodies operate largely in secret.
>
> (Kusnetz 2015)

Are state ethics commissions "toothless tigers," as the *Austin Statesman* editorial (2012) called the Texas ethics commission? Since its creation in 1992, "the ethics commission has not referred a single ethics investigation to prosecutors and has mostly levied relatively small fines for failure to properly file financial disclosure statements and other similar paperwork."

Let's take a closer look at ethics management in one state—Illinois—that has had more than its share of unethical problems.

The Case of Illinois: Race to the Top or Bottom?

Illinois, reeling from the double whammy of the past two governors—George Ryan and Rod Blagojevich, both driven from office—has been battered by ethical scandals and official misdeeds for many years. The result: A steady decline in public trust and confidence in state government. Nonetheless, efforts to strengthen the ethics infrastructure were launched more than a decade ago when the legislature passed and governor Jim Edgar signed into law the State Gift Ban Act of 1998. The act banned the giving and receiving of gifts to and by officials and employees of all government entities in Illinois. It also: (1) contained significant political campaign disclosure requirements for identifying who gives how much to whom; (2) required all local government entities to pass "gift ban" ordinances consistent with state law; and (3) called for the establishment of seven separate statewide ethics commissions. Two years after its passage, following much maneuvering and considerable legal challenge, Will County circuit judge Thomas Ewert threw out the law, ruling it was so vague and filled with so many exemptions that it was unenforceable. Thus, Illinois became lawless to prevent abuses in gifts given to and received by public officials.

A Shoebox Mystery

Illinois secretary of state Paul T. Powell (1902–1970) was an undefeated politician for 42 years who never earned more than $30,000 a year. Yet, upon his death, he left an estate worth more than $2 million ($12.2 million in 2016 dollars), including $800,000 ($4.8 million in 2016 dollars) of it in bills packed into shoeboxes, briefcases, and strongboxes in the closet of his hotel suite in Springfield. His philosophy of a successful politician: "There's only one thing worse than a defeated politician, and that's a broke one" (*Time* 1971).

This condition was finally brought to an end with the 2002 election of the reform-minded Democratic governor of Illinois, Rod Blagojevich. He issued Executive Order 3 in January 2003 to create the Office of Inspector General (OIG). The OIG's power and duties were expanded to include jurisdiction over all state agencies, with the exception of the attorney general, the secretary of state, the comptroller, and the treasurer. As an independent agency reporting directly to the governor, the OIG has subpoena power and is authorized to investigate complaints of fraud, abuse, or misconduct. When the OIG reports a finding of wrongdoing, disciplinary action is then recommended to the governor and the appropriate agency director. If the recommended disciplinary action is not taken, the OIG can forward the finding to the newly established Executive Ethics Commission for a ruling.

Illinois took another step in strengthening its ethics infrastructure on December 9, 2003, when the legislature enacted and the governor signed into law the State Officials and Employees Ethics Act (Public Act 93–0617). The law provides for both civil and criminal penalties, with fines of up to $10,000 and/or 1 year in prison for some violations. Key provisions of this legislation include the following:

- The establishment of the executive ethics commission, a body of nine commissioners appointed by the state constitutional officers and the governor. No more than five commissioners can be of the same party. The commission receives complaints, conducts administrative hearings, prepares and publishes guides regarding the ethics laws, issues subpoenas, and makes rulings and recommendations in disciplinary cases. The commission has jurisdiction over the employees and officers of the executive branch of government (Illinois Attorney General 2010).
- Legislators and constitutional officers are forbidden from using public money to pay for billboards, bumper stickers, and other paraphernalia bearing their name or image. These practices have been widely used by public officeholders to gain greater name recognition.
- State employees are banned for 1 year after leaving the state payroll from taking jobs with companies about which they made regulatory, licensing, or contracting decisions.

A 2014 survey of 500 state of Illinois executive branch employees found that:

1. the majority of survey respondents are familiar with the State Officials and Employees Ethics Act;
2. 80 percent report they are aware of officials in their offices whose job responsibilities include providing advice to employees on ethical issues;

3. 89 percent said they receive ethics training annually, most often via computer-based methods;
4. more survey respondents report a willingness to seek ethics advice than a nonwillingness.

Source: 2014 Illinois Executive Employee Ethics Survey http://www.illinois.gov/eec/Documents/Ethics%20Survey%20Agencies%20Under%20the%20Governor.pdf (accessed September 16, 2015).

- State workers are prohibited from soliciting political contributions on state property and from performing political work—another widespread abuse in years past.
- Units of local government—including park districts, municipalities, special-purpose districts, school districts, and community colleges—are required to adopt an ordinance or resolution that is no less restrictive than the act.
- Unpaid advisers to the governor and other state officials must file economic disclosure statements if they act on behalf of the officials.
- Perks such as golf outings and tennis matches paid for by lobbyists are not permitted, but lobbyists may spend up to $75 per day per official for drink and food, provided they are consumed on the premises from which they were purchased, prepared, or catered.
- Ethics training for all state employees and constitutional officers is required annually.
- Lobbyists are required to register with the secretary of state, and the law broadened the definition of a lobbyist.

Have these provisions and others put Illinois on the path to integrity and sound ethics management? So it might seem. Among other things, a 24-hour ethics hotline has been established by the office of the executive inspector general, and more than 3,000 calls have been received. Nearly 1,800 complaints have been received, with more than 500 investigated and closed. Eighty-five instances of wrongdoing have been found, with recommendations made for disciplinary action. Additionally, the commission helped train approximately 150,000 state officers and employees on ethics rules in fiscal year 2010.

While these steps suggest that Illinois is in the race to the top of effective ethical reform, the Blagojevich impeachment and his subsequent removal from office sent the state into a tailspin. Pat Quinn moved into the governor's chair on January 30, 2009, and wasted little time in attempting to resolve a "crisis of integrity" by issuing Executive Order No. 1, reconstituting the Illinois Reform Commission (IRC) as an independent advisory body. The IRC was charged with evaluating existing Illinois law and the operational practices of the state from the perspective of ethics in government. Two months later, the IRC put forward a series of reform proposals covering campaign finance, procurement, enforcement, and transparency. Was the race to the top on again? Yes! Has Illinois arrived? No, but the Illinois Executive Ethics Commission (IEEC) was strengthened significantly.

The general assembly enacted legislation in 2010 that "expanded the transparency and oversight of the disciplinary process of State employees who behave unethically on the job" and gave the IEEC new "authority to oversee the purchase of goods and services procured by State agencies under the control of the Governor and State universities" (IEEC 2011b). State employee investigation reports containing serious, confirmed ethical misbehavior are now made available to the public. And, as of October 8, 2015, 127 such employee investigation reports were on the commission's web site (http://www.illinois.gov/eec/Pages/disciplinary_decisions.aspx). In procurement oversight, the commission "appointed Procurement Compliance Monitors for each State agency . . . to ensure that laws, rules and best practices are followed by state employees" (IEEC 2011a, 3). Despite these promising developments, Illinois' ethics enforcement agencies received an "F" in the 2015 State Integrity Investigation conducted by the Center for Public Integrity, largely because they did not have an independently allocated budget.

Ethics management in the state of Illinois is progressing in a manner similar to that of most other states. In all likelihood, it has deterred willful acts of wrongdoing by public officials and government employees. However, it is not possible to know how many or what kinds of unethical behavior have been prevented. Nor is it possible to assess the consequences of the online ethics-training program. Many training programs in both the private and public sector are people-to-people, hands-on experiences. The approach taken by Illinois is clearly reaching a large number of government managers and workers, but the effectiveness of online training remains unknown.

Is Illinois in a race to the top or the bottom? Is ethics management in the American states moving forward? Are fines sufficient penalties for sound ethics management? You decide.

Governors

The ethics problems facing state governments are not insignificant and all too often cross over into the criminal domain. Perhaps the poster child for unethical governors is John G. Rowland. He was the youngest governor in Connecticut history when elected to office in 1994 at age 37. In March 2005 he was sentenced to 1 year and 1 day in federal prison for accepting $107,000 in gifts from people doing business with the state and not paying taxes on them. Mr. Rowland resigned in July 2003, halfway through his third term in office. After serving his sentence, he returned to his old ways and was convicted in September 2014 of obstructing justice, conspiracy, and falsifying documents in violations of campaign finance laws for services he provided to a Republican candidate for Congress in 2012. In March 2015, he was sentenced to 30 months in prison. Apparently, former governor Rowland was not rehabilitated by his last prison term (Hussey & Santora 2015).

In Illinois in 2001, Republican governor George Ryan chose not to seek reelection after one term in office as a result of the "licenses-for-sale" scandal. The scandal involved bribes paid to state officials to issue commercial drivers' licenses. The bribe money was laundered into governor Ryan's 1998 campaign for governor. Federal investigators brought indictments against 79 persons and secured convictions for 75 of them, including Ryan. After a lengthy, complex trial lasting more than 5 months, the former governor was found guilty of 18 felony charges that ranged from racketeering conspiracy to mail fraud, tax fraud, and making false statements to the Federal Bureau of Investigation (FBI) (Davey & Ruethling 2006). Former governor Ryan was released from the federal penitentiary in Terra Haute, Indiana, on July 4, 2013.

Perhaps the most sensational, highly publicized case involving gubernatorial corruption belongs to Illinois Democrat Rod Blagojevich (discussed earlier) who succeeded George Ryan in 2002. Mr. Blagojevich, the first Democrat to win the Illinois governor's seat in 25 years, campaigned on a platform of government reform, including ethics reform (yes, you read that right). Seven years later (2009), he became the first governor in Illinois to be impeached (House vote 114–1) and removed (Senate vote 59–0) from office for abuse of power and corruption. Most controversial was his effort to "sell" the U.S. Senate seat once held by President Obama.

I'm going to keep this Senate option for me a real possibility, you know, and therefore I can drive a hard bargain. You hear what I'm saying. And if I don't get what I want and I'm not satisfied with it, then I'll just take the Senate seat myself.
—Former Illinois governor Rod R. Blagojevich (Davey 2008)

Following his removal from office, Mr. Blagojevich was indicted by a federal grand jury on racketeering and charged with 16 felonies, including racketeering conspiracy, wire fraud, extortion conspiracy, attempted extortion, and making false statements to federal agents. The trial in the summer of 2010 resulted in a hung jury on 23 out of 24 counts against him, with a single guilty finding of lying to federal agents. Federal prosecutors called for a second trial in May–June 2011; this time, Mr. Blagojevich was not so fortunate. He was convicted on 17 of 20 counts, including the charge that he conspired to sell the U.S. Senate seat held by Barack Obama. The jury forewoman, a retired church employee from the Chicago suburbs, put it this way: "There's a lot of bargaining that goes on behind the scenes . . . but I think in the instances when it is someone representing the people, it crosses the line." After about 6 weeks of testimony, she added, "I told my husband that if he was running for politics, he would probably have to find a new wife" (Davey & Fitzsimmons 2011).

Not every governor who has ethics lapses is subject to criminal proceedings. Former governor Bob Taft (Republican) of Ohio failed to report 52 gifts, including golf outings, hockey tickets, and meals, on his annual financial disclosure reports from 1998 to 2004. The gifts amounted to nearly $6,000. Under Ohio law, gifts worth more than $75 must be reported. Governor Taft admitted that he had failed to disclose the gifts. A judge ordered him to pay $4,000 in fines and write a letter of apology to the people of Ohio (Dao 2005). Another governor, James McGreevey (Democrat: New Jersey), was forced out of office in 2004 as a result of an adulterous affair with a former aide, a man who was given special employment consideration by the governor as an adviser to the New Jersey Office of Homeland Security.

New York's former governor, David A. Paterson, found himself on a wobbly ethical ladder when he, two members of his staff, his son, and his son's friend attended the first game of the 2009 World Series at Yankee Stadium. An investigation by the New York Commission on Public Integrity found reasonable evidence that he had misused his official position to solicit and secure free tickets. The governor testified that he attended the World Series game in his official capacity and always intended to pay for the tickets of his son and his son's friend. Subsequent testimony by his staff refuted the governor's testimony. Furthermore, information from e-mail exchanges, along with an independent handwriting expert's assessment of a check written to cover the cost of the tickets, led the commission to conclude that the governor had given false testimony and knew that his conduct was unlawful. On December 20, 2010, the Commission levied a fine of $62,125, which included $2,125 for the value of the tickets and $60,000 for violating several provisions of the state's Public Officers Law. Michael Cherkasky, the chairman of the commission, wrote: "The moral and ethical tone of any organization is set at the top. Unfortunately the Governor set a totally inappropriate tone by his dishonest and unethical conduct" (Scott 2010).

One governor who set the moral and ethical tone of his administration on day one was Florida's Charlie Crist. Upon taking office in January 2007, Governor Crist issued Executive Order Number 07–01.

An Excerpt From Former Florida Governor Charlie Crist's Executive Order 07–01

I hereby direct the immediate adoption and implementation of a Code of Ethics by the Office of the Governor. This Code of Ethics applies to all employees within the Office of the Governor, as well as the secretaries, deputy secretaries, and chiefs of staff of all executive agencies under my purview.

I further direct the immediate adoption and implementation of a Code of Personal Responsibility by the Office of the Governor. The Code of Personal Responsibility applies to all employees within the Office of the Governor and sets forth clear standards and procedures regarding appropriate conduct in the workplace (State of Florida 2007).

Legislators

Members of the 50 state legislatures, like governors and members of Congress, are subject to ethical lapses. Indeed, some critics assert that legislative ethics is an oxymoron. Certainly, there is no shortage of lobbyists in Tallahassee, Albany, Springfield, or Sacramento—all seeking to influence lawmakers legally but all too often unethically. Campaign contributions flow freely from the clients of lobbyists, and conflicts of interest are a constant peril. Most efforts to curb unethical behavior among state legislators in the pre-Watergate period focused on enacting anti-bribery laws.

States began tightening their ethics laws following the Watergate scandal, an ethical meltdown that drove a sitting president from office. "Eleven states that had not enacted any laws regulating legislative conflicts of interest before 1972 took decisive action during the short period from 1973 to 1976" (Rosenson 2005, 91). Other states—North Carolina and Texas—strengthened their bribery statutes, and still others—California, Minnesota, and Wisconsin—added financial disclosure to their ethical restrictions. Eight states, including Florida and Kansas, set up independent ethics commissions to monitor legislators' financial disclosures and investigate allegations of wrongdoing (91). By 1996, three dozen states had taken steps to strengthen their legislative ethics laws.

A handful of states have been aggressive in enacting restrictive ethics laws. Beth A. Rosenson, writing in *The Shadowlands of Conduct: Ethics and State Politics* (2005), points to California, New Jersey, and Illinois as placing "substantive restrictions on legislators' activities, including limits on lawyer-legislators' appearances before state agencies, limits on gifts, limits on legislators becoming lobbyists after leaving office, and mandatory financial disclosure" (65). And in 2005, the Republican-controlled Florida legislature enacted what is probably the most restrictive gift law in the nation: Effective January 1, 2006, "no lobbyist or principal shall make, directly or indirectly, and no member or employee of the Legislature shall knowingly accept, directly or indirectly, any expenditure" (Section 112.313 of the Florida Statutes).

The devil, of course, is always in the detail. Consequently, the legislative leadership drafted "Interim Lobbying Guidelines for the House and Senate" (Lee & Bense 2006). The guidelines advise that, among other things, a legislator cannot accept a subscription to a newspaper or periodical that is paid for by a lobbyist or a client, free health screening by an association that is a principal, payment for travel expenses to deliver a speech, or a drink at a bar without verifying that the person picking up the tab is not a lobbyist or a client of one. The law does permit a lobbyist or principal to buy a legislator a meal if the legislator "contemporaneously provides equal or greater consideration." So, if a lobbyist puts out $50 for a legislator's dinner but the legislator buys a $75 bottle of wine, all is well.

The law exempts political fundraising. A legislator can accept food or drink paid for by a lobbyist or principal who sponsors a fundraising event. Moreover, the law does not prohibit expenditures made by lobbyists or principals to influence legislative action through oral or written communication.

A standing legislative ethics committee typically handles investigations of alleged ethics violations by members of a state legislature. Every state except Colorado and Connecticut has a standing legislative ethics committee. In Colorado and Connecticut, the speaker of the House and the Senate president appoint a committee when a complaint is lodged against a lawmaker (Rosenson 2005, 114). Ethics commissions in states where they exist may also be involved if the complaint alleges a violation of state law.

Judiciary

State judges are not subject to the U.S. Code of Conduct, but each state has a judicial commission that deals with complaints of judicial misconduct, with most commissions established in the past 30 years (Wex Articles n.d.). Judicial commissions typically have the power to sanction a judge and to require a judge to retire or resign. Commission findings are almost always appealable to state courts.

State judges are selected in a variety of ways—partisan election, nonpartisan election, appointment and then reelection on a ballot that permits citizens to vote to retain or not retain the judge, and merit selection by appointment or with a commission. Eight states (including Illinois and Kansas) select judges through partisan elections, 13 (including California and Florida) choose judges through nonpartisan election, 15 states (including Massachusetts and Utah) use merit selection with a nominating committee, nine states (including South Carolina) choose judges through merit selection combined with other methods, and two states (New Jersey and Virginia) authorize the governor and/or legislature to select judges (Public Broadcasting Service 2005).

The kaleidoscope of selection methods and accountability mechanisms poses its own ethical challenges in the states. Consider the case of Judge John Renke III, a Florida circuit court judge. In 2002, then-candidate Renke defeated two others vying for a seat on the Pasco-Pinellas circuit court. The election was very competitive, with Renke accused of nine counts of campaign misconduct. The Florida Judicial Qualifications Commission heard the case in 2005 and ruled that Renke brought disrepute to the judiciary as a result of his misconduct. The misconduct included an illegal contribution of $95,800 from his father. The commission recommended a public reprimand and a $40,000 fine, but not removal from office. Evidence collected by the commission indicated that Judge Renke had done an excellent job as a circuit court judge, presiding mostly over domestic cases (Jenkins 2005).

The Florida Supreme Court concluded that the Judicial Qualifications Commission-recommended sanctions were not severe enough for the violations documented. Consequently, the court ruled that Judge Renke be removed from the bench. "He is presently unfit to hold office and . . . removal from the bench is the only appropriate sanction in this case" (The Supreme Court of Florida 2006, 1).

Judges who break the law pose a special challenge for judicial ethics. Ohio Supreme Court justice Alice Robie Resnick, for example, was convicted of drunken driving and therefore charged with violating the state's judicial code of conduct. Canon 2 of the Ohio code states: "A Judge Shall Respect and Comply with the Law and Shall Act at All Times in a Manner That Promotes Public Confidence in the Integrity and Impartiality of the Judiciary" (The Supreme Court of Ohio 1997). A 13-member panel of state appellate judges heard her case and decided that Justice Resnick had indeed violated Canon 2. The panel publicly reprimanded her for professional misconduct. No other discipline, such as suspending her law license or removing her from the bench, was recommended.

Some states are especially lax about judges receiving gifts and favors. In Pennsylvania, for example, judges (including those holding the highest posts) can receive gifts as long as they are reported. Exceptions are judges at the grassroots level. Neither Philadelphia's traffic court judges nor Pennsylvania's 546 magisterial district judges are allowed to accept gifts and favors. Much criticism has been directed at Pennsylvania's former Chief Justice Ronald Castille, who received and reported gifts of dinners, event tickets, golf outings, and plane rides from law firms and businessmen (*New York Times* 2010a). No evidence, however, has surfaced to indicate that Justice Castille has shown favoritism in his decisions. Should disclosure be the final say? Does the acceptance of gifts and favors, regardless of who gave them to whom or when, create a public perception of biased judicial decision making?

Another Pennsylvania Supreme Court Justice J. Michael Eakin has ethics problems of another nature. He was suspended from the bench in 2015 by the Pennsylvania Court of Judicial Discipline because his behavior has "tainted the Pennsylvania judiciary in the eyes of the public" (Couloumbis 2015). What did he do to earn a suspension? He sent and received offensive e-mail messages with images of naked women and denigrating jokes about minorities, women, and others. At a hearing, Justice Eakin apologized for the messages, claiming he never intended for them to be made public. The messages were sent on his private e-mail account but were captured on government servers when the messages, that were exchanged with a friend in the state Attorney General's Office, used his work e-mail. A formal trial is scheduled to determine Justice Eakin's guilt or innocence (Couloumbis 2015).

Ethics Management in the Local Environment

The U.S. Census Bureau reports that there are 19,492 cities and villages in the United States and 3,033 counties (U.S. Census Bureau 2009). Cities and counties are legal artifacts of the states; local governments have no U.S. constitutional standing in the same manner as states do. State laws and constitutions set their powers and authority of local governments—cities, counties, and special districts. Counties do not exist in every state; Rhode Island and Connecticut do not have counties. In 48 states, however, America's 3,000-plus counties occupy an unusual niche in the American federal system. They are a hybrid government, with both state- and local-government characteristics. They have responsibility for many state functions, such as maintaining vital records on births and deaths, marriage and divorce, property transactions, taxation, and so forth. At the same time, counties, especially the more urban counties, provide numerous services such as public safety, emergency medical services, solid-waste collection and disposal, road repair, parks and recreation, and more.

Historically, American cities and counties are known for their lack of ethics and integrity in carrying out the people's business. Courthouse gangs and city hall bosses once ruled a vast number of cities and counties by handing out jobs, contracts, and other favors to friends and political cronies. Senator George Washington Plunkitt of New York City's Tammany Hall fame once proudly proclaimed, "I seen my opportunities and took 'em!" Indeed he did, becoming a millionaire in his lifetime as a power-broker. Corrupt local officials still roam the corridors, although not as freely as in the past. Monmouth County (New Jersey) is a prime example. Eleven officials, including three mayors, were arrested in early 2005 on federal corruption or money-laundering charges as a result of an FBI sting (Smothers 2005).

Ethics management in and among local governments is even more varied than that at the state and national levels. Among America's cities and counties, some have impressive ethics management programs: To name a few, King County (Seattle, Washington), Miami-Dade (Florida), Anne Arundel (Annapolis, Maryland), and Cook County (Chicago, Illinois) have local ethics commissions armed with substantial investigatory powers. The city of Los Angeles has one of the most comprehensive programs in the United States. Jacksonville, Florida, also has a proactive program with an ethics code that touts "aspirational goals for the conduct of city employees" (City of Jacksonville, Florida n.d). Unlike many cities, St. Petersburg, Florida, has an appearance standard in its code of ethics. "City employees and officers," the code states, "must act in a completely trustworthy manner and avoid even the appearance of a conflict of interest if they are to gain and keep public confidence" (St. Petersburg, City 2004).

An *appearance standard* is a very high standard. It requires an employee to behave in a way that a reasonable person would consider ethical.
In other words, an appearance of unethical behavior is as unwelcome
as an actual occurrence of unethical behavior.

Some local governments struggle to put in place sound ethics management practices. Consider Salt Lake County, Utah. Reform measures to foster
ethical governance in Salt Lake County, Utah, were launched in 2004 in
response to a scandal in which the county's mayor at the time was forced
from office. She had been accused of a felony—misusing public funds.
Court documents alleged that the mayor had misused health department
funds to hire bookkeepers at a boys and girls club where her daughter was
the chief financial officer. The scandal set in motion a call for ethics reform.
The county council set to wrangling about specific measures and failed to
come up with a coherent proposal. Then, the deputy mayor, standing in for
the mayor, put together a set of proposals for consideration as a whole. The
Democratic mayoral candidate (then mayor-elect) offered a similar list of
proposals, with some additions. Many, but not all, of the proposals have been
adopted. They include:

1. adopting an ethics statement that all county officials and employees must read and review before taking office;
2. requiring ethics training for all county officials and employees
   every 2 years;
3. encouraging county officials to hold open records and meetings
   consistent with state statutes and county ordinances;
4. requiring the disclosure of outside interests and conflicts of interest;
5. placing strict limits on employees from accepting or soliciting
   gifts, honoraria, or requests for employment;
6. banning for 1 year county officials and employees from directly
   communicating, for compensation, with their former county agency
   for the purpose of influencing any matter pending before that county
   agency;
7. prohibiting the appointment or hiring of a relative to any county
   position except for seasonal employment;
8. prohibiting officers and employees from engaging in political
   activities, including the solicitation of political contributions, during
   the hours of employment;

9. prohibiting employees from using county resources in connection with any political activity (Salt Lake County, Utah 2011);
10. requiring lobbyists to register with the county and disclose lobbyist's clients (Anderson 2011).

Exhibit 5.2
Chapter 2.07—Salt Lake County Ethics Code

Sections

2.07.010—Ethics statement.
2.07.020—Employee training.
2.07.030—Government in the sunshine.
2.07.201—Conflicts of interest.
2.07.203—Definitions.
2.07.204—Gifts.
2.07.205—Gifts and the procurement process.
2.07.206—Honoraria.
2.07.207—Exceptions.
2.07.208—Restrictions on post-county employment.
2.07.209—Nepotism.
2.07.401—Political activities of employees.
2.07.402—Prohibitions on political use of county resources.

(Salt Lake County, Utah 2011)

These measures have put Salt Lake County on a steady ethics management path. No significant ethics issues have surfaced since 2004. The reform measures acknowledge that ethics and integrity in governance are important and require the commitment of county resources to build a strong ethical climate. While the county takes a legalistic approach to ethical governance, it recognizes that this approach is not sufficient—thus the requirement for ethics training for all officials and employees.

Salt Lake County appears to have learned from ethical failure, but has it learned enough? A proposal to create an ethics commission, while discussed several times since 2004, is yet to become a reality. Gavin Anderson (2011), deputy district attorney, notes: "I think the potential cost has been the discouraging factor."

Has Salt Lake County embraced comprehensive ethical reform? Apparently not. Will the reform measures introduced to date instill a vibrant ethical culture in Salt Lake County governance? Maybe; maybe not. Time will tell.

Agency rules that define acceptable behaviors for employees are commonplace among local governments. In Kansas City, Missouri, for example, the ethics handbook issued to all employees asserts that it is unacceptable behavior to spend several hours a week on city time downloading Internet information on a relative's medical condition (Rabin 2003, 466). In California, local governments typically place restrictions on employees receiving gifts, benefits, or using their position to "induce or coerce any person to provide, directly or indirectly, anything of value which shall accrue to the private advantage, benefit, or economic gain of the City Official or his or her immediate family" (City of San Diego, California 2002). In the California town of Los Gatos, administrative regulations are very restrictive. For example, one rule states, "no employee shall accept money or other consideration or favor from anyone other than the town for any reason" (Simmons, Roland, & Kelly-DeWitt 1998).

Smaller municipalities are less likely to devote resources to ethics and integrity in governance—and some experts contend that this is a significant deficiency. Mark Davis, executive director of the New York City Conflicts of Interest Board, asserts that, contrary to what many people think, "small municipalities are most in need of ethics boards, because in small municipalities conflicts of interest are absolutely unavoidable" (1999, 408).

Some small communities have joined arms and resources to promote ethical governance. In Northwest Indiana, for example, five communities in 2005, including Whiting, formed the Shared Ethics Advisory Commission, adopted a common ethics code, and began ethics training for municipal employees and elected officials. As president Calvin Bellamy states:

> The Shared Ethics Advisory Commission is an all-volunteer agency created by an inter-local agreement among five Lake County communities—Crown Point, Highland, Munster, Schererville and Whiting . . . We are not an adjudicatory body. Judgment on specific cases is left to each community or law-enforcement officials. Our mission is to provide training on ethical issues facing municipal employees in their day-to-day experience. We have developed a Shared Ethics Code, which sets out broad principles of ethical conduct. We then make those

broad principles more concrete and specific through commission-designed training programs.

(Bellamy 2010)

While cities and counties are recognizable local governments, there are thousands (an estimated 37,381, according to the U.S. Census Bureau 2009) of special districts that provide a wide variety of public services (airports, buses, housing, taxation, lighting, water conservation, and the like). Yet, they are mostly out of ethical sight, since many do not have elected boards or officials. Special districts are often referred to as "invisible governments." Larger special districts usually have a code of conduct (Berman & West 2012), but few have launched comprehensive ethics management initiatives.

One notable exception is the Los Angeles County Metropolitan Transportation Authority, that has an impressive program directed by a chief ethics officer and six colleagues in a separate ethics department and a budget of $800,000. The ethics staff "educates and advises employees, board members, contractors and the public about ethics rules and maintains the records concerning lobbyist reports and employee statements of economic interest disclosures" (Council of Governmental Ethics Laws 2004). Los Angeles County Metropolitan Transportation Authority (2011) has issued three ethics codes—an 11-page code for the 13-member board of directors, a six-page code for contractors, and a ten-page code for the authority's 10,000 employees.

Even though special districts are often out of the public eye, it is quite clear that they have their share of ethical problems. In fact, California became so concerned about ethical issues in special districts and other local governments in 2005 that the legislature passed Assembly Bill 1234, requiring all local agencies—officers and employees—to receive at least 2 hours of training in general ethics principles and ethics laws relevant to their public service. Moreover, every official is required to receive at least 2 hours training every 2 years thereafter (California 2015).

Nonprofits in State and Local Environments

The local and state environments in which nonprofit managers carry out their duties is challenging to characterize because of the enormous diversity in the types and sizes of nonprofits. Additional diversity is mirrored across states in rules and regulations that nonprofits must comply with. Even within a given state, different statutes may govern a nonprofit, depending on how the nonprofit is formed. In North Carolina, for example, state statutes define nonprofit organizations as either corporations or unincorporated associations. Those formed as corporations are governed by one set of North Carolina statutes while a different statute governs unincorporated associations.

Most of the 30,000 nonprofits in North Carolina are small organizations, with 20 percent with annual budgets greater than $100,000, while two-thirds have budgets of less than $25,000. Most rely on volunteers, part-time employees, or no more than a single full-time employee. Nonprofits that deal with local governments in North Carolina are subject to some laws that regulate governments themselves, but not all. Governments, for example, must comply with public records and open meetings laws, but nonprofits do not have to (Whitaker & Drennan 2007).

Nonprofits are regulated by the State Attorney General's Offices in each state, "arguably not the best agency for charitable oversight but it is what we have right now," says Alicia Shatteman of the Center for Non-Governmental Organization Leadership and Development at Northern Illinois University. Forming a nonprofit organization in Illinois can be a daunting process (Shatteman 2015). Any charity holding or soliciting funds in Illinois must first register with the Illinois Attorney General, file an Internal Revenue Service application for a tax exemption, and request a state sales tax exemption from the Illinois Department of Revenue. Further, an organization may need to complete additional paperwork with:

- the Illinois Department of Revenue to obtain a city or county license for door-to-door solicitation;
- the Illinois Department of Employment Security if the organization has employees;
- a city or town if local business registration is required;
- the chief county assessment officer to obtain a local property tax exemption (Shatteman 2015).

Filing and Investigating an Ethics Complaint

An ethics complaint filed against a public official, elected or appointed, is a serious matter for the accused official, even if it is eventually dismissed. The filing of a malicious complaint can be tempting for a citizen who wishes to "get even" with a public official or for a person who wishes to seek a political advantage. Consequently, cities and counties are careful about investigating a complaint unless there is persuasive evidence that a violation has occurred.

The handling of a complaint involves a series of steps and stages. The process conducted in Miami-Dade County is illustrative (Exhibit 5.3). First, a citizen must file a written, notarized complaint. Second, the commission staff examines the complaint to assist the commission in determining if it is "legally sufficient"—that is, relevant to the city's ethics ordinance. A complaint such as "city council member Jones interferes with the work of the city manager" would not be legally sufficient. An example of a legally sufficient complaint would be if a council member voted for the purchase of a parcel of land that

Exhibit 5.3   **Citizen Complaint Process in Miami-Dade County**

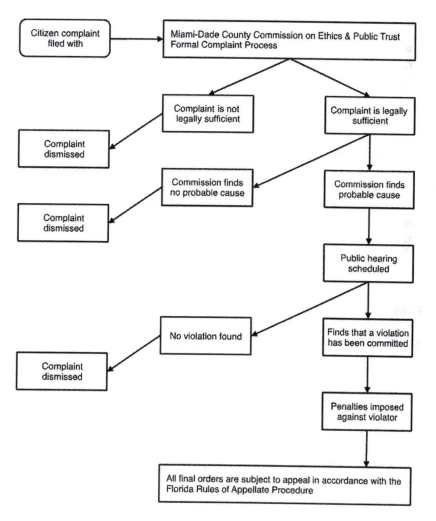

was owned by his spouse. Third, if the complaint *is* found to be legally sufficient, then the commission must rule on whether or not "probable cause" exists. That is, is there sufficient reason and evidence to believe that a violation has occurred? If the commission finds there is no probable cause, then the complaint is dismissed. However, if a finding of probable cause is rendered, then a public hearing is scheduled before the ethics commission. Evidence and arguments presented at the public hearing are the basis for the commission's ruling on either a finding of a violation or a finding of no violation.

Summing Up

This chapter highlights the diverse approaches taken by the American states and local governments to deter wrongdoing and encourage ethical behavior. What was said over 20 years ago by Elder Witt (1992, 343) about the absence of uniformity across the states in their ethics infrastructure might well be echoed today. "What has emerged," Witt said then (1992, 343), "is not a clear system of rules, but an inconsistent and confusing patchwork."

Ethics management is more than laws, rules, and regulations and the processing of ethics complaints. Obeying the law and following ethics regulations may keep state officials and employees out of legal difficulty, but abiding by the law is not sufficient to ensure ethical governance. Many states have ethics statutes, commissions with investigatory powers, and training programs, but there is little evidence that states employ the full complement of ethics management tools available to them.

The nonprofit environment is not altogether dissimilar to that of the public-sector environment recounted in this chapter. U.S. charitable organizations, like their governmental counterparts, are "subject to a wide variety of government regulations, including regulations mandated by local governments (usually relating to fundraising solicitations), state governments, and the national government" (Herman 2013b, 357). State laws set parameters on what a nonprofit can and can't do, especially in how a nonprofit conducts its business operations and engages in charitable solicitations. Nonprofits, by definition, are not in the business of generating a profit that is returned to stakeholders but they can and do generate revenues (perhaps considered profits) needed to carry out their mission.

Despite considerable regulation, nonprofits can cross the line into potential criminal behavior. In May 2015, for example, the U.S. Federal Trade Commission filed a lawsuit against a cancer nonprofit in Tennessee involving a family with ties to four charities. The charities are said to be sham charities accused of a

$187 million fraud. Family members, the Federal Trade Commission suit states, "operated as personal fiefdoms characterized by rampant nepotism, flagrant conflicts of interest, and excessive insider compensation." Most of the money was spent on telemarketers, vacations, cars, sporting events, and high-paying jobs for family and friends (McWhirter 2015). Charitywatch (2015), an independent watchdog in the charitable nonprofit environment, gave an "F" to one of the four cancer nonprofits under investigation.

Unethical behavior and worse is not limited to the governmental community. Is it?

Ethics Management Skill Building

Practicum 5.1. Follow the Law or Your Conscience?[2]

On July 24, 2011, it became legal for gay and lesbian couples in New York State to receive marriage licenses. Assume you are an elected town clerk with responsibility to issue same-sex marriage licenses but feel strongly from a religious perspective that same-sex marriages are immoral. When asked by a friend how you feel about same-sex marriage, you say "Based on my Christian faith and my belief in God and what the Bible teaches, I cannot and I don't support gay lifestyles." You also add, "The oath I took places my duty to God above my duty to faithfully execute the law." Here is the oath:

> I, ..., do swear that I will well and truly discharge the duties of the office of Town Clerk, according to the best of my skill and judgment, making the due entries and records of all orders, judgments, decrees, opinions and proceedings and carefully filing and preserving in my office all books and papers which come to my possession by virtue of my office; and that I will not knowingly or willingly commit any malfeasance of office, and will faithfully execute the duties of my office without favor, affection or partiality, so help me God.

Discussion Questions

1. Does the oath above place your duty to God above the law?
2. Do you have an obligation as a public official/civil servant to issue marriage licenses? Or, does this violate your conscience to the point that you refuse to do it? Should you plead for an exemption given your religious views?

3. Should you look for another job?
4. What should you do?

Practicum 5.2. Getting a Code Adopted

As a newly arrived senior manager in a large state agency, you are dismayed to find that the agency has never adopted a code of ethics or considered requiring employees to sign an oath stating something like:

> I do solemnly swear that I will support the Constitution of the United States and the Constitution of the state of Lincolnland, faithfully discharge the duties of my office, and abide by and adhere to the provisions of the agency's code of ethics. So help me God.

Convinced that codes and oaths contribute to ethical workplaces, you appoint a committee drawn from many different departments to draft a code and an oath for your agency. Six months later, the committee chair reports that the committee is hopelessly deadlocked over whether the code should specify appropriate behavior that could be monitored and therefore sanctioned when violations occur, or whether a statement of values and principles might suffice.

Discussion Questions

1. What advice would you offer the committee chair? Would you send him back to the committee to try once more? Would you disband the committee and start anew? Would you appear before the committee and attempt to persuade them to adopt an enforceable code and a stringent oath? A values statement? Neither?
2. What arguments would you put forward for the adoption of an enforceable code and oath? A values statement?
3. What course of action would produce the best outcome?

6

U.S. Ethics Management Environment

Where a man assumes a public trust, he should consider himself a public property.

—Thomas Jefferson, quoted in *A Winter in Washington* (1807/1824)

This chapter examines ethics management and governance at the national level in the United States.[1] We begin with a look at the views of the Founding Fathers and map the evolution of efforts to encourage ethical behavior and discourage wrongdoing. This evolutionary history is followed by an overview of U.S. ethics laws and institutions, concluding with a look at judicial ethics.

In the Beginning . . .

The Founding Fathers believed that democratic governance required leaders with impeccable moral and ethical credentials. Those who occupied office, whether appointed or elected, were expected to demonstrate the highest degree of integrity and conduct themselves in honorable ways. A democratic government—one that is open and accessible to popular will and thought—could be achieved only through the good works of morally committed men and women. According to Louis C. Gawthrop (1998), in *Public Service and Democracy: Ethical Imperatives for the 21st Century*, the 55 men who gathered in Philadelphia in 1787 to draft the Constitution for a new republic wove a garment threaded with ethical values and moral virtues. Those values "constituted an indivisible presence in all of the practical and pragmatic decisions made concerning the structure and functions of the new government" (38).

A cursory examination of the historical record—the Constitution and the Federalist Papers—to identify the framers' expectations of the qualifications one must possess to hold office suggests that, beyond age and residency requirements, members of Congress (especially the Senate) should have "stability of character" and be "truly respectable." A morally imbued constitution required nothing less than morally imbued officials to ensure that a true democracy would prosper. Still, the framers recognized a darker side of the human spirit—ambition, greed, and revenge. In *The Federalist* #6, Alexander Hamilton asserts that in creating a government of the people we must not forget that "men are ambitious, vindictive, and rapacious" (1787). James Madison shared Hamilton's view, arguing in *The Federalist* #51 that "ambition must be made to counteract ambition" (1788). Checks and balances, the separation of powers among the three branches of government, and the division of power between the national government and the states (federalism) were put forward as the structural means to "counteract ambition." And, as Madison (1788) so eloquently proclaimed, "In framing a government which is to be administered by men over men, the great difficulty lies in this: you must first enable the government to control the governed; and in the next place oblige it to control itself."

Government of, by, and for the People

The framers' clashing views of human nature and the struggle to govern ethically came to the fore in the early decades of the new republic. George Washington's secretary of war, Henry Knox, found himself deeply in debt as a result of an extravagant lifestyle and gambling obligations incurred by his wife (Gilman 1995b). In 1791, in an effort to cope with his debts, Knox engaged in land speculation in Maine that resulted in lawsuits challenging the transactions. Friends came to his legal rescue, and he later rewarded them with recommendations for public office (1995b, 63). Embezzlement was also a problem in the early republic. "A pointed example," Gilman (1995b, 64) notes, "is the embezzlement case of Dr. Tobias Watkins, a close friend of President John Quincy Adams (1824–1828) and a high-ranking officer in his administration." Dr. Watkins was later tried and imprisoned by the Jackson administration.

These transgressions, however, paled alongside the rampant patronage bestowed on political followers when Andrew Jackson (1828–1836) occupied the White House. Jacksonian Democracy, as historians dubbed it, meant that the common man could lay claim to any job in the federal government. And, perhaps most importantly, the credentials for this claim were neither the possession of moral character nor workplace competency; rather, they were rooted in political and personal connections. Thus, the spoils system—whereby those who won political office rewarded their friends and supporters—was in full swing.

Patronage politics was to dominate much of American government for the next five decades. Even during the Civil War (1861–1865), President Abraham Lincoln spent much of his time receiving and responding to federal job seekers. The war itself bred numerous accounts of corruption, ranging from exorbitant fees for the purchase of rifles to public expenditures for the purchase of meat in food rations for soldiers. "Corruption in the procurement of war supplies led to the dismissal of Secretary of War Cameron and the passage of the first set of conflict-of-interest statutes" (Gilman 1995b, 66). Widespread corruption, as Gilman (1995b, 65) notes, resulted in "America's development of a legal foundation for ethical behavior." Conflict-of-interest statutes were drafted in the postwar years under the Grant administration in an attempt to stop federal officials from "participating in negotiations that might bring financial benefits to the employee either directly or indirectly" (Roberts 1988, 12).

Still, government by incompetent, immoral, and unethical officials approached epidemic proportions by the end of the nineteenth century. Courthouses and state capitols became breeding grounds for the corrupt and ambitious. In New York City, for example, the Boss Tweed gang and a string of Tammany Hall political successors handed out jobs and dollars with impunity. Among the more famous personalities was New York state senator and ward boss George Washington Plunkitt, a son of Irish-American immigrants who entered politics to amass and lose a fortune in his lifetime (1842–1924). Plunkitt's ethics—or, more appropriately, lack of ethics—eventually became the anathema of good government reformers.

> This civil service law is the biggest fraud of the age. It is the curse of the nation. There can't be no patriotism while it lasts. How are you goin' to interest our young men in their country if you have no offices to give them when they work for their party?
> —Senator George Washington Plunkitt,
> "The Curse of Civil Service Reform" (1903)

Despite the lively condition of big city political machines and patronage government in the second half of the nineteenth century, reformers applauded when the Pendleton Act of 1883 (also known as the Civil Service Act) became law. This new law aimed to inject "merit" and "political neutrality" into the operations of the national government, presumably leading to a modern civil service imbued with an ethical impulse. Joining the reformers, then Princeton professor Woodrow Wilson (1887/1941, 217) called for "a civil service cultured and self-sufficient enough to act with sense and vigor"—a system in which "administration lies outside the proper sphere of politics" (210). The result of civil service reform, Wilson argued, is "but a moral preparation for what is to follow. It is clearing the moral atmosphere of official life by establishing the sanctity of public office as a public trust" (210).

Administration, Science, and Ethics

Wilson sought to ensure that the American system of government remain effective and moral. His plea to remove the running of government from the "hurry and strife" of politics required two additional considerations: (1) that the field of administration be viewed as a "field of business"; and (2) that efforts be undertaken to build a "science of administration" (209). These pronouncements, when taken together, provide an embryonic definition of public management and, as the industrial age roared into the twentieth century, found an intellectual home with the emergence of the scientific management movement founded by Frederick Taylor.

Taylor, an engineer who believed that America suffered enormous inefficiencies in the workings of its factories and its government, advocated "one best way" to accomplish work. He introduced tools such as time-and-motion studies to find that one best way. The application of scientific management principles in industry and government, Taylor argued, would lift America out of its wasteful and unproductive habits to the benefit of all. His call resonated with government reformers and with members of the movement to create an impartial, merit-based civil service. Inefficiency, after all, was closely identified with corruption and other misdeeds that prevailed in America's cities and states. Moreover, in creating a "neutral" cadre of public servants to carry out the work of government, the proper emphasis would be placed on work processes, not on personal or political friendships.

Scientific management is an approach to management that emphasizes the application of "scientific" knowledge to work processes. Frederick W. Taylor (1856–1915), an engineer and the father of scientific management, published *The Principles of Scientific Management* in 1911.

A science of administration and Taylorism, as the scientific management school became known, served as the model for the evolution of public management and administration. The ethic associated with this paradigm was utilitarianism (or instrumentalism—getting the job done right benefits the greatest number), and it found overt expression in the evolution of the city management profession. Staunton, Virginia, appointed the first person to hold the title of city manager in 1908. The manager was expected to be competent, politically neutral, and well versed in getting the city's streets repaired and its sewer and water lines working properly. This separation of management from politics was exactly what Wilson had in mind, and the fact that the prevailing ethic was utilitarian was not especially concerning to anyone. Indeed, utilitarianism fit very well with a work ethos. It also fit well with the evolution of the City Managers' Association, which was established in 1914, although it should be noted that the association recognized early on that it was important for its members to live by a strict code of ethics. Today, the rebranded association (International City/County Management Association) is widely regarded as a leader and model in advocating ethical behavior by its members.

Morally Mute Public Management

Efforts to turn administration into a scientific practice began to waiver with the onset of World War II, but they continued to stir the imaginations of managers and organizational theorists well into the 1960s. Science, progress, and modern management, inextricably interwoven, had become dogma by the late 1930s (Stillman 1999). The scale, planning, and execution of the war effort brought a new reality and thinking. The politics–administration dichotomy drew unfavorable attention as policy makers administered wartime programs and administrators became heavily involved in policy making. The planning, coordination, and execution of programs and policies were not driven by scientific principles but by the necessity to get the job done quickly, efficiently, and effectively. And, with the advent of nuclear weapons, and resulting concerns about their destructive potential, many observers began to question whether progress needed to be redefined.

The war years contributed to a proactive management style and led to the so-called "golden years" of federal government employment in the 1940s and 1950s. Gone was some of the theoretical baggage, especially the identity of managers as "neutrally competent" problem solvers. Neutrality, as epitomized through local, state, and federal civil service, had grown larger than the Wilsonian legacy of removing partisanship from government work. In conjunction with the ethic of utilitarianism and Weberian norms of impartiality and hierarchy, neutrality meant either public servants had no claim to values (personal, social, political), especially insofar as they might enter into the carrying out of their official duties; or at best, as a professional, one could make an argument for a preferred course of action but was expected to fall into line once a policy decision was made by organizational or political superiors. The end result of these influences was the emergence of amoral management—organizations led by men and women who may have been moral but refused to voice their beliefs.

Indeed, as managers and organizations became more morally and ethically sterile, a movement was launched to do something about it. In the late 1960s, at the height of civil unrest and diminishing confidence in the ability of the United States to become the Great Society, as espoused by President Lyndon B. Johnson, a group of young academics gathered in upstate New York at a retreat called Minnowbrook and put forth a call for a new public administration. This "new" public administration would be one in which administrators and managers accepted responsibility for promoting social justice and equity. This value-infused movement was seen by many as an antidote to the perilous plight of the morally mute manager.

What was new about the *new public administration*? Namely, that administrators could and should become proactive in promoting the welfare of the less-advantaged members of society. The old public administration required administrators to be obedient and passive purveyors of the wishes and demands of their elected superiors.

For a variety of reasons, the new public administration did not have as great an impact as some had hoped. Terry L. Cooper (2001, 12) asserts, however, that:

> when one surveys the history of administrative ethics during the last hundred years it seems clear that this movement made an important contribution to the emergence of a field of study focused on ethics in public administration . . . [especially] around a commonly shared ethical concept—social equity.

Nonetheless, the proactive posture of the new public administration made many managers and public officials question whether it was a proper role for nonelected officials to be so presumptuous in defining the public interest. After all, is that not the responsibility of legitimately elected officeholders?

Low Road, High Road, or No Road?

There's a saying with relevance to the role and place of ethics in public management during the past several decades: "If you don't know where you're going, then any road will get you there!" The tumultuous 1960s came to a close with a quest to make managers more relevant morally and ethically, but then there was Watergate—and its aftermath. The secret White House tapes not only revealed that President Richard M. Nixon had conspired with others to cover up a politically motivated break-in of the Democratic headquarters at the Watergate Hotel, but they also showed that the president's moral compass was broken. President Nixon's resignation in 1974 spawned a wave of legislative initiatives in Washington, D.C., and the states to prevent wrongdoing in government and punish those who choose to break the law. State after state enacted ethics laws and established ethics boards or commissions, with some given substantial powers to investigate alleged cases of wrongdoing by officials. At the federal level, Congress enacted the Ethics in Government Act of 1978—a law that, among other things, created the U.S. Office of Government Ethics (OGE) and the controversial independent counsel, whose broad investigatory powers were put on display in Kenneth W. Starr's 1998 investigation of President Bill Clinton's financial and personal affairs.

Efforts to legislate the ethical behavior of federal officials, including high-ranking appointed managers and often-frontline members of the government workforce, have produced dubious results. There is precious little empirical evidence that ethics laws, ordinances, or boards have given us good government. Indeed, some say that this legislation allows officials to employ the lowest common denominator in deciding right and wrong behavior. That is, by stating in law what constitutes various punishable offenses, lawmakers have given elected and appointed officeholders the opportunity to define ethics as "behaviors and practices that do not break the law," but may come close to it. Stated in the vernacular, if it's not illegal, it's OK. John Rohr, a noted ethics scholar, labeled this approach as the "low road." The low road features compliance and adherence to formal rules. "Ethical behavior," Rohr asserts in *Ethics for Bureaucrats: An Essay on Law and Values* (1989, 63), "is reduced to staying out of trouble" and results in "meticulous attention to trivial questions."

> While compliance systems can work, their failure is surprisingly high, often at great expense to employers. But the primary danger of compliance systems lies in their contortion of the decision-making process. Suddenly, instead of thinking about doing the right thing, employees focus on calculating the costs and benefits of compliance versus non-compliance—and about trying to outsmart the system.
>
> (Bazerman & Tenbrunsel 2011, 113)

But is the low road the only road? It is hard to argue that it's the "best" road. In fact, many scholars believe it is even a poor substitute for "no road." What, then, might be a more agreeable or desirable alternative? The "high" road to ethics behavior for public managers, Lewis and Gilman argue in *The Ethics Challenge in Public Service: A Problem-Solving Guide* (2012), is the path of integrity: "Relying on moral character, this route heads toward moral judgment; it counts on ethical managers individually to reflect, decide, and act" (14). Such an approach blends the acceptance of personal responsibility for one's behavior with honorable intentions and personal integrity—that is, adherence to moral and principles. But to whose morals and principles should one adhere? Herein lies the challenge of the high road.

The legislative flurry to enact ethics-based laws in the 1970s is regarded by some as an important step forward. However, insofar as this step fosters the "low road" of compliance to ethical behavior, it may actually be a tiny step at best. To be sure, scholars are not advocating a blanket repeal of ethics laws and ordinances. Rather, they are calling for an awakening, perhaps a reawakening, of what might be referred to as the "moral sense" that exists in every single human being. A tall order? To be sure. Indeed, it is one that is fraught with real-world challenges that were amply illustrated in the decade of the 1980s.

The thrashing around to find an ethical road to follow fluctuated throughout the "me" generation of the 1980s. Scandals on Wall Street, in the U.S. Department of Housing and Urban Development (HUD), and in the White House with the Iran-Contra affair (a clandestine arms deal with Iran that occurred during Ronald Reagan's presidency) sent ethical compasses spinning wildly. Why would an inside trader like the notorious Ivan Boesky risk his reputation and a prison sentence to skim off millions of dollars in illegal stock trades? Why would Samuel Pierce, the head of HUD under Reagan, sell out to the highest bidders? And, why would Reagan, a popular American president, deny involvement in an illegal and covert scheme to fund anticommunist activity in Nicaragua by selling arms to an unfriendly Iranian regime?

The answer to the first two questions is greed, with some overtones of Plunkitt ethics—"I saw my opportunity. . . " The Wall Street and HUD scandals clearly involved men and women of ambition and avarice. Some believe that these incidents were merely symptoms of the 1980's "me" mentality. Neither government officials nor private-sector managers and chief executive officers seemed immune to the question, what's in it for me?

> The Iran-Contra affair of the mid-1980s involved the secret and illegal sale of high-priced missiles to Iran by the Reagan administration to support the Contra rebels in Nicaragua—a move that had been banned by the passage of the Boland Amendment. The Contras were fighting to overthrow the Socialist-led Sandinista government in Nicaragua. Top administrators in the Reagan White House tried to funnel proceeds from the Iranian arms sales to the guerrillas bent on toppling the Sandinista regime. At the same time, U.S. officials believed that the arms deal would move Iranian leaders to use their influence to win the release of the American hostages in Lebanon.

Lying, as in the Iran-Contra affair, was equally troublesome and symptomatic of the moral malaise that seemed to grip America in the 1980s. This particular scandal was especially disturbing because the chain of command from the president through his top security advisers, and eventually U.S. Marine Lieutenant Colonel Oliver L. North, seemed to be an unbroken lie bound together by patriotism, duty, and blind loyalty. As North explained to Congress, "Lying does not come easily to me. But we all had to weigh in the balance the difference between lies and lives" (U.S. Senate 1987). That President Reagan actually lied is arguable, however, given the congressional testimony of Admiral John M. Poindexter, the president's national security adviser. Testifying before a joint Senate and House hearing in July 1987, Poindexter stated:

> I made a very deliberate decision not to ask the president [about whether arms should be sold to Iran to raise money for the Nicaraguan Contras to fight the Socialist-controlled Nicaraguan government] so that I could insulate him from the decision and provide some future deniability.

In other words, Poindexter purposely withheld information from Reagan about the money-for-arms transactions against which Congress had specifically legislated. Lying? No. Evasiveness? Yes. Poindexter provided the president with plausible deniability that, in effect, undermined the constitutional responsibility of the highest elected official in the nation.

The ethical angst of the 1980s spilled into the world of public management, as well—so much so that a number of countermeasures were initiated. One was the promulgation in 1984 of a code of ethics by the American Society for Public Administration (ASPA). ASPA was established in 1939 by the New Deal generation to promote professional values and ethical behavior in public service. Yet it took more than 40 years to build the consensus needed to adopt a code. Another countermeasure was the recognition by many schools of public affairs and administration that it was time to place ethics courses in their curricula. By the end of the 1980s, 40 schools had added an ethics course to their graduate program of study (Menzel 1997). The National Schools of Public Affairs and Administration (NASPAA) took a related initiative in 1989, when a new curriculum standard on ethics was introduced. Schools seeking accreditation, NASPAA asserted, must demonstrate that their programs have the capacity and means to "enhance the student's values, knowledge, and skills to act ethically."[2]

Scholarship on administrative ethics also expanded significantly in the 1980s, with an unprecedented number of ethics books and journal articles appearing in print.[3] These collective efforts by individuals and professional associations constituted a major push to ensure that men and women who entered public service could contribute to ethics and competency in government. Whether these results have been achieved remains an important but mostly unanswered question. In fact, the pluralistic nature of these initiatives, in combination with the rethinking of administration and management in the 1990s, may have diffused the presumed desirable outcomes.

The evolutionary history of strengthening ethics in American governance suggests how bumpy the road is and why it remains a work in progress. We turn next to the evolution of federal ethics laws.

Federal Ethics Laws

A variety of statutes govern the conduct of federal employees, with the oldest one—dating from the Civil War era—aimed at curbing abuses in government procurement. A 2015 compilation (104 pages) of federal ethics laws by the U.S. OGE lists laws dealing with conflicts of interest, procurement and contracting, gifts and travel, employment, government property and information, taxes, and political activities (US OGE 2015a). A variety of executive branch agencies, including the Executive Office of the President, the U.S. Department of Justice, the Inspectors General, the Merit Systems Protection Board, the Office of Special Counsel, the General Services Administration, the Office of Personnel Management, the Federal Elections Commission, and the General Accountability Office, have ethics responsibilities. Complex? Yes. Confusing? Yes.

> The Ethics in Government Act is . . . one of the few happy results of the Watergate scandal. History teaches us of the periodic eruption of bad government and has lessons for us. I am well aware that many find the law unduly detailed and tedious, but the Government is better for it. It would be easier by far to fill vacancies, to contract, and to run departments of government as little fiefdoms as they sometimes were earlier in our history. But it would not be easier to govern ethically.
> —Robert I. Cusick (2010),
> Director, U.S. Office of Government Ethics

The two most significant federal statutes are the Ethics in Government Act of 1978 and the Ethics Reform Act of 1989. The 1978 act followed on the heels of the Watergate crisis of the early 1970s. This legislation established the U.S. OGE within the Office of Personnel Management and "charged it with providing overall leadership and direction for the ethics program within the executive branch" (Gilman 1995a). The 1978 act also "established a comprehensive public financial disclosure system for all three branches" of the federal government (Gilman 1995a). Additionally, this legislation authorized the president to appoint an independent special prosecutor to investigate high-profile cases. Do you recall special prosecutor Ken Starr and the Clinton/Lewinsky scandal?

The Ethics Reform Act of 1989 expanded previous legislation in several areas. Post-employment restrictions were applied to members of Congress and top congressional staff. Moreover, the public financial disclosure system was strengthened by "authorizing all three branches of government to implement a system of confidential financial reporting" (Gilman 1995a). The prohibition on solicitation and acceptance of gifts was expanded to include all three branches. Other provisions dealt with limitations on outside earned income and compensation received for service as an officer or board member of an association or corporation. Further, the 1989 act placed restrictions on the compensation that a federal official might receive for teaching without prior notification and approval of the appropriate ethics office.

Other federal legislation that should be noted is the Office of Government Ethics Reauthorization Act of 1988, the Whistleblower Protection Act of 1989, and the Lobbying Disclosure Act of 1995. The Lobbying Disclosure Act (P.L. 104–65) was signed into law by President Bill Clinton on December 19, 1995, and took effect January 1, 1996. It expanded the definition of who a lobbyist is, thereby greatly "increasing the number of registered lobbyists and the amount of information they must disclose" (Tenebaum 2002). Failure to comply with the act can result in a civil fine of up to $50,000.

The Whistleblower Protection Act of 1989 established the Office of Special Counsel as an independent agency within the executive branch to receive complaints and "safeguard the merit system by protecting federal employees and applicants from prohibited personnel practices, especially reprisal for whistleblowing" (U.S. Office of Special Counsel 2010). The Office of Special Counsel is a small agency with 106 employees who are primarily personnel management specialists, investigators, and attorneys. The original version of the act was amended in 1994 with the passage of Public Law 103–424, which expanded the coverage to some government corporations and employees in the U.S. Department of Veterans Affairs.

Some critics point out that, while the U.S. whistleblowing regulatory system is a positive development, there is still much room for improvement. The current approach, according to Sheryl Groeneweg (2001), is based heavily on how much money is saved by blowing the whistle on misconduct, fraud, or abuse of authority. She asserts that the U.S. system is reactive, not proactive, and therefore puts the whistleblower's career in a precarious situation. Most importantly, "at its core, the U.S. model displays the failure to focus on the spirit of whistleblower protections" (15). Roberta Johnson (2003, 21), writing in *Whistleblowing: When It Works—and Why,* adds: "Studies of whistleblower protection suggest that the protection offered is far from perfect."

Honest Leadership and Open Government Act of 2007

On September 14, 2007, president George W. Bush signed S.1, the Honest Leadership and Open Government Act of 2007 (P.L. 110–81), into law. The act amended the Lobbying Disclosure Act of 1995 to provide, among other changes to federal law and House and Senate rules, additional and more frequent disclosures of lobbying contacts and activities.

Specifically, the act tightened revolving-door rules by prohibiting:

- retiring senators from directly lobbying members or employees of either House for a period of 2 years; retiring members of the House are banned from lobbying for 1 year;
- senior Senate staff and Senate officers from lobbying contacts with the entire Senate for 1 year, instead of just their former employing office.
- senior House staff from lobbying their former office or committee for 1 year after they leave House employment (Straus 2008).

The Honest Leadership and Open Government Act of 2007 is the most recently enacted federal legislation concerning Congress and lobbyists. It attempts to slow the revolving door that enables former members of Congress and top staff members to use their knowledge and connections to lobby their colleagues and federal agencies. The Jack Abramoff Indian lobbying scandal, along with several other high-profile cases (including one involving the former deputy secretary of the Department of the Interior, Steven Griles, who pleaded guilty in 2007 to obstruction of justice in the Senate investigation of the Abramoff scandal), triggered the legislation. The lobbying bans, which many regarded as a step in the right direction, are viewed by some legal experts as too lenient. University of Minnesota law professor and former White House chief ethics lawyer Richard W. Painter (2009, 150) notes:

> A former member usually has a lot of influence with former colleagues for well beyond two years. A better rule might bar former members of the House or Senate from lobbying back to Congress for a period equivalent to their time in office . . . up to a maximum perhaps of five or seven years.

Honest Services Fraud

Federal prosecutors have been aggressive over the past 15 years in their pursuit of government officials—federal, state, local—and corporate executives who have defrauded the public. When members of Congress rewrote mail and wire fraud laws in 1988, they included 28 words that made it illegal to "deprive another of the intangible right of honest services" (Wikipedia 2011a). In a *San Diego Union-Tribune* article, assistant U.S. attorney Shane Harrigan described the law (18 U.S.C. § 1346) as an "extremely effective tool to fight public corruption," adding, "The essence of public corruption is that public officials deprive people in the community of their honest efforts to represent them. That's theft of honest services and that's what the statute covers" (Thornton 2006). Bribery, kickbacks, and extortion are often difficult to prove. In other words, it is much easier to prove to a jury that honest services fraud has occurred. Critics contend it "is a way for prosecutors to convert almost any kind of behavior into a felony" (Thornton 2006). Moreover, it is asserted that the language is vague and interpreted inconsistently across cases.

Convicted of Honest Services Fraud

- Jack Abramoff—Washington, D.C., lobbyist
- Joseph L. Bruno—New York state senator (R)
- Wayne R. Bryant—New Jersey state senator (D)
- Randy "Duke" Cunningham—congressman (R) from San Diego, California
- Kevin Geddings—North Carolina lottery commissioner
- William J. Jefferson—congressman (D) from New Orleans, Louisiana
- Mary McCarty—Palm Beach, Florida, county commissioner
- Bob Ney—congressman (R) from Ohio
- Don Siegelman—governor (D) of Alabama

Honest services fraud was among the charges brought against Jeffrey K. Skilling, chief executive of Enron just prior to its 2001 collapse, and Conrad M. Black, a newspaper executive accused of defrauding his media company. Both were convicted and appealed their cases to the U.S. Supreme Court (for information on Skilling, see *Skilling v. United States*, 130 S. Ct. 2896 [2010]). In June 2010, the court—in a unanimous decision—called the broad interpretation of the law unconstitutionally vague (Liptak 2010). The justices did not strike down the law entirely; rather, the majority said the law must be limited to the offenses of bribes and kickbacks. The court remanded both Skilling's and Black's convictions to the lower court for reconsideration.

The Supreme Court's decision is widely viewed as narrowing, if not eviscerating, the honest services fraud law. Elizabeth R. Sheyn, law clerk in the U.S. Court of Appeals for the Sixth Circuit, writes:

The Supreme Court's recent decision in Skilling greatly narrowed the scope of the honest-services statute, which criminalizes schemes or artifices designed to deprive another of the intangible right of honest services, by limiting the statute's application to schemes to defraud involving bribes or kickbacks.

(Sheyn 2011)

The initial reaction from Congress was swift. Senate Judiciary Committee chairman Patrick Leahy (Democrat: Vermont) introduced the Honest Services Restoration Act on September 28, 2010. The aim of the bill was to restore the scope of the statute to cover improper, undisclosed self-dealing (Aguilar 2010). The Leahy bill died when the 111th Congress (2008–2010) closed.

Nonprofits and Dark Money

In Chapter 1 it was noted that the U.S. Internal Revenue Service (IRS) is an important actor in the nonprofit's environment. The IRS determines whether or not a nonprofit is exempt from federal taxation under section 501(c)(3) of the Internal Revenue Code. Qualified 501(c)(3) nonprofits also allow donors to deduct their contributions from their taxes, another important consideration. IRS rules prohibit a nonprofit from using a "substantial part" of an organization's expenditures for lobbying but can lobby for the adoption or rejection of bills under consideration by legislative bodies. Nonprofits can also express opinions about initiatives being voted upon by communities (Idealist 2015). Indeed, "charities can undertake some nonpartisan activities related to elections, including get-out-the-vote campaigns and voter registration. They can also invite candidates to speak and host candidate forums, as long as the structure of those events ensures they are nonpartisan" (Aprill 2014).

Automatic Exemption for Churches

Churches that meet the requirements of Internal Revenue Code Section 501(c)(3) are automatically considered tax-exempt and are not required to apply for and obtain recognition of tax-exempt status from the Internal Revenue Service (IRS).

Although there is no requirement to do so, many churches seek recognition of tax-exempt status from the IRS because this recognition assures church leaders, members, and contributors that the church is recognized as exempt and qualifies for related tax benefits. For example, contributors to a church that has been recognized as tax-exempt would know that their contributions generally are tax-deductible.

Source: Internal Revenue Service https://www.irs.gov/pub/irs-pdf/p1828.pdf Retrieved November 6, 2015.

Nonprofits are specifically prohibited from endorsing partisan candidates for any public office. That being said, the U.S. Supreme Court decision in 2010, called Citizens United, that allows corporations and unions free to contribute directly to political efforts, has ushered in a new era for nonprofits. Social welfare nonprofits are now vehicles for raising funds in support of a candidate's campaign. And here's the catch—donors are not identified, thus there is "dark" money slushing around. The news media has noted that the 2016 presidential aspirants are "taking advantage of a morally corrupt—and perfectly legal—campaign finance system" (Ruth 2015). Dark money, although legal, can be considered tainted money, thus unethical in the nonprofit world. As the lead editorial in the *Tampa Bay Times* states forthrightly:

> The court rulings opened the door for the creation of nonprofits that have little or no reason to exist except to promote political candidates with anonymous contributors. They are exploiting a loophole in Internal Revenue Service guidelines to get away with it.
>
> (*Tampa Bay Times* 2015)

Are stealthy donors on the loose in American politics? So it seems.

The dark-money issue extends beyond nonprofit political mischief to include suspicions of self-dealing, improper loans, and unfair business practices, asserts California attorney general Kamala Harris (Democrat) (*Wall Street Journal* 2015). In 2014, Harris ordered nonprofits to disclose the identities of donors who contributed more than $5,000 in a single year. This decision became a flashpoint in the battle over money and free speech. Lawsuits quickly followed challenging the disclosure requirement. A federal appeals court in May 2015 ruled that the requirement did not violate First Amendment rights to freedom of association. This ruling prompted an appeal to the U.S. Supreme Court (Dolan 2015), but the court declined to hear it.

Most of the dark money making its way into politics comes not from campaigns themselves but outside groups including nonprofit 501[c] groups or social welfare organizations that are spending tens of millions of dollars.

(Murse 2015)

Executive Branch Ethics

The development of a clear set of ethical standards for officers and employees of the executive branch was initiated in January 1989, when President George H.W. Bush issued Executive Order 12668. This order established the Commission on Federal Ethics Law Reform, which, in turn, produced a report titled "To Serve with Honor." The report made 27 recommendations, including one that a "1965 executive order prescribing the standards of conduct be revised and that the Office of Government Ethics be directed to consolidate all executive branch standards of conduct in a single set of regulations" (Gilman 1995a). A second executive order on the subject, Executive Order 12674 (April 12, 1989—see Exhibit 6.1), set forth 14 principles of ethical conduct for government officers and employees and directed the OGE to "promulgate a single, comprehensive, and clear set of executive branch standards of conduct that shall be objective, reasonable and enforceable" (Gilman 1995a). In August 1992, the OGE issued a final rule promulgating standards of conduct for executive branch employees, effective February 3, 1993.

Exhibit 6.1
Principles of Ethical Conduct for
Government Officers and Employees

By virtue of the authority vested in me as President by the Constitution and the laws of the United States of America, and in order to establish fair and exacting standards of ethical conduct for all executive branch employees, it is hereby ordered as follows:

(continued)

Exhibit 6.1 *(continued)*

Part I: Principles of Ethical Conduct

Section 101: Principles of Ethical Conduct

To ensure that every citizen can have complete confidence in the integrity of the Federal Government, each Federal employee shall respect and adhere to the fundamental principles of ethical service as implemented in regulations promulgated under sections 201 and 301 of this order:

(a) Public service is a public trust, requiring employees to place loyalty to the Constitution, the laws, and ethical principles above private gain.

(b) Employees shall not hold financial interests that conflict with the conscientious performance of duty.

(c) Employees shall not engage in financial transactions using non-public Government information or allow the improper use of such information to further any private interest.

(d) An employee shall not, except pursuant to such reasonable exceptions as are provided by regulation, solicit or accept any gift or other item of monetary value from any person or entity seeking official action from, doing business with, or conducting activities regulated by the employee's agency, or whose interests may be substantially affected by the performance or nonperformance of the employee's duties.

(e) Employees shall put forth honest effort in the performance of their duties.

(f) Employees shall make no unauthorized commitments or promises of any kind purporting to bind the Government.

(g) Employees shall not use public office for private gain.

(h) Employees shall act impartially and not give preferential treatment to any private organization or individual.

(i) Employees shall protect and conserve Federal property and shall not use it for other than authorized activities.

(continued)

Exhibit 6.1 *(continued)*

(j) Employees shall not engage in outside employment or activities, including seeking or negotiating for employment that conflicts with official Government duties and responsibilities.

(k) Employees shall disclose waste, fraud, abuse, and corruption to appropriate authorities.

(l) Employees shall satisfy in good faith their obligations as citizens, including all just financial obligations, especially those such as Federal, State, or local taxes that are imposed by law.

(m) Employees shall adhere to all laws and regulations that provide equal opportunity for all Americans regardless of race, color, religion, sex, national origin, age, or handicap.

(n) Employees shall endeavor to avoid any actions creating the appearance that they are violating the law or the ethical standards promulgated pursuant to this order.

(Executive Order 12674 of April 12, 1989, as modified by Executive Order 12731)

President John F. Kennedy made ethics a major policy theme during his administration. An ethics czar was appointed to work with the head of the Civil Service Commission. Executive Order 10939, issued May 5, 1961, established conflict-of-interest standards for presidential nominees and appointees, including members of the White House staff.

The U.S. Office of Government Ethics

The Office of Government Ethics Reauthorization Act of 1998 is significant because it removed the OGE from the Office of Personnel Management and established it as a separate executive agency. The OGE is responsible for promulgating and maintaining enforceable standards of ethical conduct for more than two million civilian employees and military members in over 130 Executive Branch agencies (U.S. OGE 2015b).

The director is appointed to a 5-year term by the president with the consent of the Senate. The office has no investigatory powers and does not serve the legislative or judicial branches of government. OGE'S mission is to advance a strong, uniform executive branch ethics program by interpreting and advising on ethics laws, policies, and program management; holding executive branch agencies accountable for carrying out an effective ethics program; contributing to the professional development of ethics officials; and modernizing and implementing the ethics rules and regulations (Exhibit 6.2).

Exhibit 6.2
Who Is Responsible for Investigating the
Alleged Misconduct of Federal Employees?

The inspector general of the department or agency involved and, when necessary, the Federal Bureau of Investigation of the Department of Justice. The sixty-four inspectors general (IG) in the executive branch of the U.S. government conduct the majority of investigations into government wrongdoing. In addition they also coordinate investigations with their regular financial and management audits of federal agencies and programs. The coordinating body for the inspectors general is the President's Council on Integrity and Efficiency (PCIE), of which the Office of Government Ethics is a member.

(U.S. Office of Government Ethics 2016)

Each executive agency has a designated agency ethics official(DAEO) and an alternate deputy tasked with supporting the agency's ethics program and with whom OGE primarily deals. DAEOs provide guidance on how to interpret and comply with conflict-of-interest regulations, standards-of-conduct regulations, and financial disclosure policies and procedures. Pamela A. Gibson (2009, 105) examined the moral reasoning of DAEOs and found that they engage in conventional reasoning which "mirrors and supports the legalistic practice of public administration expected at the national level." In other words, federal ethics officials in the executive branch have a law-and-order orientation toward resolving ethical issues.

Approximately 4,500 full-time and part-time ethics officials work in the executive branch to provide employees with assistance in identifying and resolving potential conflicts of interest. Their duties include collecting and reviewing employees' financial disclosure reports, providing employees with ethics training, counseling employees on ethics and standards of conduct issues, and maintaining compliant agency ethics programs (U.S. OGE 2015b).

As might be surmised, knowing how to stay out of trouble in the executive branch of the U.S. government has become a major challenge given the numerous laws, rules, and regulations regarding unacceptable practices and behaviors. Thus, a primary mission of the OGE is to help federal employees comply with those rules and regulations so that they can avoid unintentional ethical lapses.

The OGE does not have civil or criminal enforcement authority for violations of the Standards of Ethical Conduct for Employees of the Executive Branch. However, evidence of suspected violations can be turned over to the U.S. Department of Justice for possible prosecution. If an Executive Branch employee violates a criminal statute, such as those involving conflicts of interest, he may be dismissed from his job, fined, and imprisoned. The OGE 2014 annual survey of conflict-of-interest prosecutions identifies 11 new prosecutions by the U.S. attorneys' offices and the Antitrust Division of the Department of Justice. Among these prosecutions, the sentences ranged from fines of $1,000–$20,000, imprisonment up to 30 months, probation, to community service (U.S. OGE 2015c).

The ethics infrastructure in place in the executive branch of U.S. government is built on rules, regulations, enforcement, education, and training. This is both good news and bad news. Rule-driven ethics management, with its legal compliance overtones, is regarded by many ethicists as reactive and punitive—a minimalist approach. Moreover, it can cause major disruptions in an agency. Consider the National Institutes of Health initiatives offered by the Director Elias A. Zerhouni in early 2005 to force staff to divest their holdings in drug and biotechnology companies. Six thousand employees among the agency's 18,000 would have been affected had the director not backed off from the rules in August 2005. Threats of high-level defections and 1,300 mostly critical comments by employees about the proposed rules motivated the director to loosen the conflict-of-interest rules (Connolly 2005).

Rules are inescapable, but a more comprehensive and inclusive approach requires officials to lead with integrity and find avenues to motivate public-service employees and professionals "to serve with honor," as the 1989 President's Commission on Federal Ethics Law Reform report reads.

Presidents

Do the "Principles of Ethical Conduct for Government Officers and Employees" apply to presidents? Surely, one might think. But life in the White House can be more challenging than one might suppose. Consider President Lyndon B. Johnson (LBJ: 1963–1968) and the U.S. involvement in the Vietnam War. The military buildup of troops and equipment in Vietnam proceeded steadily in the 1960s, despite repeated claims by the president that the United States did not want to escalate the conflict. As Daniel Ellsberg, a member of the State Department who gained notoriety when he leaked the Pentagon papers to the *Washington Post,* recalls: "On election day 1964, I spent the day with an interagency working group to expand the war—contrary to Lyndon Johnson's assertion that the administration seeks no wider war" (Ellsberg 2004). Did President Johnson lie to the American public? So it would seem.

Fast-forward to President Bill Clinton (1992–2000). He took the ethical high ground immediately upon taking office by requiring senior members of his administration to take a "five-year" pledge that they would not represent private parties in dealing with the government after leaving office. Executive Order 12834, "Ethics Commitments by Executive Branch Personnel," President Clinton hoped, would put an end to the perception that the federal government was "hostage to special interests" (Gilman 1995b). Alas, a few years later, the president found himself in a legal and political morass of his own making when it became known that he had a sexual tryst with a young White House intern, Monica Lewinsky. The scandal grew into a political firestorm when President Clinton testified under oath that he did not have sex with Ms. Lewinsky. Many members of Congress concluded that the president lied. Consequently, the Republican-controlled House proceeded to impeach President Clinton. The Senate, however, did not convict him—that is, the U.S. Senate did not vote to remove him from office. Did President Clinton lie? So it would seem. Was lying under oath sufficient grounds for removal from office? No. Not surprisingly, the 2000 presidential campaign of George W. Bush promised to restore dignity to the office of the president.

But President Bush had his share of ethical issues as well. The list includes the invasion and occupation of Iraq, stem cell research, privacy rights, government secrecy, domestic spying by the National Security Agency without court approval, and charges that his administration sought political revenge by leaking information that revealed the name of Central Intelligence Agency (CIA) undercover agent Valerie Plume. The administration's contention that Saddam Hussein possessed weapons of mass destruction, which was the rationale for the invasion of Iraq, turned out to be untrue. Nor was a credible link found to exist between Iraq and the terrorist attacks of September 11, 2001. Many citizens have asked, "Did President Bush lie to the American public?"

The investigation into who leaked information about CIA agent Plume resulted in the indictment in 2005 of I. Lewis "Scooter" Libby, Vice President Cheney's former chief of staff, and threatened to bring down Karl Rove, President Bush's chief political adviser. Later that year, President Bush ordered mandatory ethics training for all White House staff. On June 13, 2006, it was announced that special prosecutor Patrick J. Fitzgerald would not bring charges against Rove. Scooter Libby, however, was not as fortunate. He was tried and found guilty of perjury and obstruction of justice and sentenced to 30 months in prison for stifling a CIA leak investigation. In July 2007, however, before Libby was to be imprisoned, President Bush commuted his sentence, asserting that the length of the sentence was excessive.

> A *pardon* is a forgiveness of an offense or crime and the punishment associated with it. A *commutation* is a waiver or lessening of a punishment without a forgiveness of the crime or punishment. Pardons and commutations are granted by heads of state (presidents and governors in the United States).

President Bush, critics assert, turned the ethics management clock in the federal government backward, as evidenced by appointments of individuals to high-ranking positions who used their office to advance the president's political agenda over the objections of senior managers. One example can be found in a 2005 General Accountability Office report concerning a decision made by top officials in the Food and Drug Administration (FDA). The FDA officials in question rejected an application to allow over-the-counter sales of morning-after birth control pills, ignoring contrary recommendations by both an independent advisory committee and the agency's own scientific review staff (Harris 2005). Similar intervention by top Department of Justice officials is reported to have taken place in the decision to reject senior staffers' advice on possible Voting Rights Act violations. The redistricting of congressional districts in Texas in the early 2000s, spearheaded by house majority leader Tom DeLay (Republican), clearly diluted minority-voting rights.

President Obama has also encountered strong ethical headwinds. As a candidate, he pledged to clean up the special influence of lobbyists; on his first day in office, he issued Executive Order 13490, which imposed strict rules on lobbyists entering government positions and appointees leaving government for lobbying positions. Two days later, President Obama faced a skeptical public as he sought an "exception" for William Lynn's appointment as Deputy Secretary of Defense. Mr. Lynn previously served as a lobbyist for defense industry giant Raytheon.

President Obama's Ethics Guidelines

Transparency and the rule of law will be the touchstones of this presidency . . . We need to close the revolving door that lets lobbyists come into government freely and lets them use their time in public service as a way to promote their own interests over the interests of the American people when they leave.

(Tapper 2009)

No president is above the law, but these cases point to the fine line between telling the truth and knowing when to do so is or is not in the public interest. Americans expect the president to do both.

Executive Order 13490 Pledge

Generally, appointees must commit to:

- not accept gifts or gratuities from registered lobbyists or lobbying organizations;
- recuse, for 2 years, from any particular matter involving specific parties in which a former employer or client is or represents a party, if the appointee served that employer or client during the 2 years prior to the appointment;

- if the appointee was a registered lobbyist during the prior 2 years:
  - recuse, for 2 years after appointment, from any particular matter on which he or she lobbied during the 2 years prior to appointment (or any particular matter that falls within the same specific issue area);
  - not seek or accept employment with an agency or department that he or she lobbied during the prior 2 years;
- if the appointee is subject to the senior employee post-employment restriction in 18 U.S.C. § 207(c), to abide by such restriction for 2 years after termination of the appointment;
- not to lobby any covered executive branch official (as described in the Lobbying Disclosure Act) or any noncareer SES [Senior Executive Service] appointee for as long as President Obama is in office;
- agree that any hiring or other employment decisions will be based on the candidate's qualifications, competence, and experience.

Congress

While federal ethics statutes have steadily expanded the coverage of the law over the past several decades, Congress has also found it necessary to ensure that its members and top staff are engaged in appropriate behavior. As noted earlier, the Founding Fathers designed a system of government that separated and divided power among institutions and officeholders. Horizontally, the separation of powers between U.S. Congress, the president, and the judiciary sought to prevent the concentration of power. Similarly, the division of power (federalism) between the central government and the states created multiple power centers. The Founding Fathers understood that men and women of ambition would seek the power of public office and, unless checked in some manner, might threaten the well-being of the republic. "Ambition must be made to counteract ambition," wrote James Madison (1788) in *The Federalist* #51.

House of Representatives

Over time, it has become evident that measures other than checks and balances are needed to prevent the misuse and/or abuse of public power. For example, Congress has found it necessary to constrain the unacceptable behavior of its own members. The Committee on Standards of Official Conduct, a ten-member bipartisan committee, is the ethics enforcer of the House of Representatives. Complaints brought to the committee are investigated if a majority finds probable cause to do so. In the event of a 5–5 Republican–Democrat deadlock, investigations automatically resume in 45 days. In January 2005, the Republican-controlled House, by a vote of 220 to 195, changed this provision so that, in the event of a deadlock, ethics investigations are dismissed. The politics behind this change had to do with the behavior of the House majority leader, Representative Tom DeLay (Republican: Texas), who was admonished three times in 2004 for egregious behavior. By changing this deadlock rule, Republicans claimed that the House would be able to protect the members from what could be purely partisan attacks.

Democrats strongly disagreed, arguing that the change would make the ethics committee impotent. By the end of April, after new revelations surfaced about Mr. DeLay's international travel supported by a lobbyist and the Democrats' vocal resistance, Speaker of the House J. Dennis Hastert of Illinois relented. By a vote of 406 to 20, the House approved a resolution that restored the rules that had been in place at the beginning of the year.

The House disciplinary procedures for dealing with an alleged violation of the ethics rules are shown in Exhibit 6.3. Several highly visible members of the House, both Democrats and Republicans, have been investigated and punished over the years (Exhibit 6.4). They include Newt Gingrich, Republican Speaker of the House (1994–1997), and Representative James C. Wright Jr., a Democrat from Texas who resigned in 1989 over improper lobbying on behalf of a constituent. An earlier case involved the flamboyant Democratic representative from New York, Adam Clayton Powell, Jr., who was fined $25,000 and excluded from his seat following his reelection to the 91st Congress in 1967. He appealed the House's action to the U.S. Supreme Court, which ruled that his exclusion was unconstitutional. Powerful Chicago Democratic congressman Dan Rostenkowski used his office for many years to secure political favors. In 1994, he was indicted for corruption and lost his bid for reelection. He later pleaded guilty to mail fraud and was sentenced to 17 months in federal prison. Rostenkowski served 15 months before President Bill Clinton pardoned him in 2000.

Exhibit 6.3
U.S. House of Representatives
Procedures for Handling an Ethics Complaint

Step 1: A complaint is filed in writing and submitted to the Committee on Standards of Official Conduct.

Step 2: The committee chairman and ranking minority member have 14 days to determine if the complaint meets rules that define a complaint.

Step 3: If the complaint is deemed legitimate by the chair and ranking minority member, the full committee must decide to either investigate or drop the case.

Step 4: Investigations are carried out by subcommittees that can lead to a sanction hearing to determine the level of punishment, if any. The possible sanctions include:

- expulsion;
- censure;
- reprimand;
- fine;
- limitations of rights or privileges;
- other, as determined by the committee, such as letters of reproval.

(U.S. House of Representatives 2008)

Exhibit 6.4
House Censures and Reprimands

A *censure* is a more serious punishment than a *reprimand*. Twenty-three members have been censured in House history and nine have been reprimanded. Examples include:

(continued)

Exhibit 6.4 *(continued)*

Censures

December 2, 2010	Charles Rangel of New York for violating House gift rules.
July 20, 1983	Gerry E. Studds of Massachusetts for sexual misconduct with a House page.
June 6, 1980	Charles H. Wilson of California for receipt of improper gifts, "ghost" employees, and personal use of campaign funds.
July 31, 1979	Thomas L. Blanton of Texas for unparliamentary language.

Reprimands

September 15, 2009	Joe Wilson of South Carolina for a breach of decorum when President Obama spoke to the Congress.
January 21, 1997	Newt Gingrich of Georgia for allowing a member-affiliated tax-exempt organization to be used for political purposes and providing inaccurate information to the ethics committee.
July 26, 1990	Barney Frank of Massachusetts for using political influence to fix parking tickets and to sway probation officers for a personal friend.
July 31, 1984	George V. Hansen of Idaho for false statements on financial disclosure documents.

(*New York Times* 2010b)

The House of Representatives was stunned in 2005 when a popular senior California Republican, Randy Cunningham, a decorated combat pilot in Vietnam, resigned his seat after admitting that he received more than $2 million in money and favorable considerations from a defense contractor. In November 2003, for example, the contractor MZM purchased

Mr. Cunningham's Del Mar house for $1,675,000, then put it back on the market for the same price, where it sat for nearly 9 months until it sold for $975,000—a nifty $700,000 loss, or gain, depending on your point of view. Representative Cunningham sat on the House Defense Appropriations Subcommittee. In December 2005, on the heels of Cunningham's resignation, Speaker of the House Hastert proposed that lawmakers receive ethics training.

Ethics Reform

Much criticism has been directed at Congress's seeming inability to ensure that its members behave ethically. Ethics lapses and issues in recent years have received considerable attention. For instance, there was the involvement of Ohio Republican Bob Ney in the Jack Abramoff scandal. Ney pleaded guilty to conspiracy to defraud the U.S. government and served 17 months in a federal penitentiary. And you might recall William J. Jefferson, a Democratic congressman from Louisiana, who found himself in deep trouble after the Federal Bureau of Investigation discovered $90,000 in his freezer. In all honesty, however, the clock on congressional ethics violations began ticking a long time ago. As Mark Twain (1897) once put it, "It could probably be shown by facts and figures that there is no distinctly native American criminal class except Congress."

The House of Representatives won a Democratic majority in 2006. Shortly thereafter, future House speaker Nancy Pelosi spoke out loudly and clearly about Congress's plans to bring an end "to the culture of corruption," stating, "We will drain the swamp." In March 2008, the House established the Office of Congressional Ethics (OCE), a six-person board of directors consisting of private citizens with the authority to investigate alleged wrongdoing and *advise* the House ethics committee. The OCE's authority is limited in that it cannot issue subpoenas; nor can it compel witnesses or lawmakers to testify or investigate cases. In April 2009, a *New York Times* editorial asked: "is the House swamp drained yet?" A year later, another editorial declared: "They [OCE] must be doing their job."

The Charlie Rangel Case

The case of Harlem Democrat Charlie Rangel could be considered the tipping point in the short life of the OCE. Would the OCE take on such a powerful member of Congress? After all, the 80-year-old Mr. Rangel wielded the gavel on the influential Ways and Means Committee, a much-coveted post that his seniority enabled him to claim. He was first elected to Congress in 1970.

Mr. Rangel's ethical lapses involved his use of rent-stabilized apartments in Manhattan and the misuse of his office to preserve a tax loophole worth half a billion dollars for an oil executive who pledged a donation for an educational center being built in Mr. Rangel's honor (Lipton & Kocieniewski 2010). He was also charged with failing to report or pay taxes on rental income from his beachfront Dominican villa. The House ethics committee concurred with the OCE investigation and set in motion a public trial before an adjudicatory subcommittee. The subcommittee found Representative Rangel guilty of 11 counts of ethical violations. The full committee, with the concurrence of the House by a vote of 333 to 79, censured him. Speaker Nancy Pelosi read House Resolution 1737 with Mr. Rangel standing in the well of the House before her: "Resolved, that, one, Representative Charles B. Rangel of New York be censured." Chastised but not repentant, Mr. Rangel said: "I am confident that when the history of this has been written, people will recognize that the vote for censure was a very, very, very political vote . . . I did not curse out the speaker. I did not have sex with minors. I did not steal money" (Kocieniewski 2010).

The aggressive staff director and chief counsel of the independent OCE, Leo J. Wise, announced on October 16, 2010—only a few weeks before the midterm elections—that he was stepping down to join the U.S. attorney's office in Maryland. That move allowed Wise to avoid a political fight over the future of the OCE should the Republicans recapture the House, and recapture they did. Before the election, "speculation was rampant that if the Republicans took over the House, they would kill the fledgling Office of Congressional Ethics" (Nixon 2011). After all, newly installed Speaker John Boehner had vigorously opposed the creation of the office. Would he move to kill the OCE? No; in fact, he reportedly had no plans to change the office's mandate, mission, or funding. But, as Norman J. Ornstein of the American Enterprise Institute put it: "The question is, how is the Republican leadership going to react when the OCE starts going after its people?" (Nixon 2011).

U.S. Senate

The U.S. Senate has assigned responsibility for ethics investigations to a six-member bipartisan Select Committee on Ethics. A 511-page *Senate Ethics Manual* (2003) guides the deliberations of the Select Committee and provides rules for gifts, conflicts of interest, outside earned income, financial disclosure, political activity, use of the franking privilege (free mail) and Senate facilities, employment practices, and more. The review and investigative process followed by the Senate Select Committee are similar to that followed in the House.

A four-member majority must vote in support of moving an investigation forward. The Senate Select Committee on Ethics also issues letters of admonition. For example, former senator Robert G. Torricelli (Democrat: New Jersey) was severely admonished for violating Senate rules for gifts he received. The committee of three Republicans and three Democrats wrote in a three-page letter, stating, in part: "Your actions and failure to act led to violations of Senate Rules (and related statutes) and created at least the appearance of impropriety, and you are hereby severely admonished" (U.S. Senate Select Committee on Ethics 2002). Some critics regarded this punishment as little more than a "slap on the wrist."

The 2014 Annual Report of the Select Committee states there were 45 alleged violations of Senate rules. Twenty-seven were dismissed for lack of subject-matter jurisdiction—allegations did not violate Senate rules, even if true. Seventeen were dismissed because sufficient facts were not provided to document a material violation of the Senate rules. The committee staff conducted a preliminary inquiry of the one remaining alleged violation; no action was taken by the committee (U.S. Senate Select Committee on Ethics 2015).

Sex, Politics, Ethics: A Hazardous Mix?

Unlike the House, there has been less effort made by the Senate to more closely monitor and investigate alleged ethical breaches. Does this mean that Senators and their staff are less inclined to fall from a wobbly ethical ladder? Not likely. Consider the case of Nevada Republican Senator John Ensign and his administrative assistant Douglas Hampton—and Mr. Hampton's wife. The senator had an extramarital affair with, yes, Mr. Hampton's wife, who worked on the senator's last campaign. Mr. Hampton was let go after learning of the affair. Some $96,000 in hush money, it was alleged, was paid to Mr. Hampton by Senator Ensign's parents. Moreover, the senator is reported to have helped Mr. Hampton land a lobbying job as a government affairs consultant to a Las Vegas airline company and an energy company. The Senate Ethics Committee launched an investigation into the scandal. In the meantime, Senator Ensign announced that he would not seek reelection in 2012. And, in December 2010, the Justice Department prosecutors, following a year-long investigation, dropped the charges against Ensign. But, in March 2011, Mr. Hampton was indicted by a federal grand jury in the District of Columbia for violating criminal conflict-of-interest laws, charging that he violated post-employment lobbying restrictions mandated by The Honest Leadership and Open Government Act of 2007. More specifically, he was accused of repeatedly contacting Senator Ensign's office in 2008 and early 2009 seeking assistance for the Nevada companies. Mr. Hampton claims that the senator encouraged him to contact his office.

As a nearly 2-year-long Senate ethics investigation entered its final phase, Senator Ensign resigned his seat effective May 3, 2011, one day before he was to have answered questions under oath about the charges against him. In his letter of resignation, he asserted:

> While I stand behind my firm belief that I have not violated any law, rule, or standard of conduct of the Senate . . . I will not continue to subject my family, my constituents, or the Senate to any further rounds of investigation, depositions, drawn out proceedings, or especially public hearings . . . This continued personal cost is simply too great.
>
> (Lipton 2011)

Congressional ethics is not an oxymoron. Those who serve in the U.S. Congress are placed in the proverbial fishbowl of high media visibility. Acts of wrongdoing—real or perceived—receive enormous public attention. With a majority of Americans saying that members of the House and Senate have low ethical standards, congressional representatives need to stay on the high road. Sixty-one percent of respondents in a 2014 Gallup poll ranked the ethics of members of Congress as "low" or "very low," one notch below car salespeople (Gallup 2014). The honesty and ethics ratings for members of Congress reached their highest rating of 25 percent in 2001, and since 2009, they have been at or near the bottom when compared with professions such as car salespeople, lobbyists, telemarketers, and stockbrokers (Gallup 2014).

Federal Judiciary

Judges are widely viewed as ethical public officials. Yet, it has long been recognized that judges need ethical guidance and advice as much as other public officials do. Federal judges receive lifetime appointments when approved by the U.S. Senate in its capacity to "advise and consent." The Code of Conduct for United States Judges (U.S. Courts 2011) sets forth seven canons to which all federally appointed judges must subscribe.

Canons are a body of standards, rules, or principles accepted as universally binding.

As can be seen in Exhibit 6.5, the canons are both proscriptive and prescriptive. Judges must "uphold the integrity and independence of the judiciary" while also "avoiding the appearance of impropriety in all activities" and "refraining from political activity." Judges who find themselves in ethically questionable situations can seek advisory opinions from the Committee on Codes of Conduct of the Judicial Conference. The Judicial Conference serves as the principal policy-making body concerned with the administration of the U.S. courts.

Exhibit 6.5
Code of Conduct for United States Judges

Canon 1: A judge should uphold the integrity and independence of the judiciary.

Canon 2: A judge should avoid impropriety and the appearance of impropriety in all activities.

Canon 3: A judge should perform the duties of the office impartially and diligently.

Canon 4: A judge may engage in extrajudicial activities to improve the law, the legal system, and the administration of justice.

Canon 5: A judge should refrain from political activity.

(U.S. Courts 2011)

With lifetime appointments, federal judges cannot be easily removed from the bench for ethical lapses. In *The Federalist* #78 (1788), Alexander Hamilton argued that judges should be appointed to serve "during good behavior" and insulated from the political process so that they could be a check on the legislative and executive branches. However, when a judge's behavior is egregious, he or she can be removed by a House vote of impeachment and a Senate trial to determine guilt—an action taken only eight times in Senate history. The most recent removal occurred on December 8, 2010. All 96 senators present voted to oust New Orleans-native G. Thomas Porteous, Jr., of the Federal District Court in Louisiana, for a "pattern of conduct incompatible with the trust and confidence placed in him" (Steinhauer 2010). One impeachment article states Porteous was "so utterly lacking in honesty and integrity that he is guilty of high crimes and misdemeanors and is unfit to hold the office of federal judge and should be removed from office" (Alpert 2010).

What did Judge Porteous do? He sought and accepted kickbacks and other gifts, including money, trips, and free meals at expensive restaurants from lawyers and a bail bond company with business before him. He also knowingly and intentionally made false statements, under penalty of perjury, related to his personal bankruptcy filing and violating a bankruptcy court order (Wikipedia 2011c). Mr. Porteous's behavior cost him dearly. Not only did he lose his lifetime job, he lost his $174,000 annual federal pension and was forever disqualified from holding any office of honor or profit under the United States.

An Unfinished Portrait

Ethics in American governance has a long, evolutionary history. The portrait sketched here, however, remains unfinished in light of the challenges to ethical governance. These challenges are in no small measure exacerbated by the forces of privatization, globalization, computerization, and the rapidly changing world of information technology.

The threat of the resurrection of the morally mute manager is real and must be taken seriously. The new public management movement has yet to define itself ethically or morally. Rather, it has aligned itself with a pernicious brand of moral muteness that reduces citizens to customers and public service professionals to businesspeople whose major task is to make citizen-customers satisfied with what they want and receive from government. This pathway, as Gawthrop (1998) reminds us, is certainly not a pathway to the common good. It even raises the question of whether such an approach can avoid the worse pitfalls of unethical behavior and practices in government.

Moral courage is the willpower to do the right thing with the knowledge that it will cause pain for another person or for members of one's organization.

Public managers who do not understand why the word public cannot be removed from their job descriptions or cannot grasp why ethical competence is essential to effective governance should ply their trade in less demanding occupations. "No web of statute or regulation," as President John F. Kennedy (1961) put it, "can hope to deal with the myriad possible challenges to a man's integrity or his devotion to the public interest" (Lewis 1991, 14). And, according to the then U.S. comptroller David M. Walker: "We need more leaders with three key attributes: courage, integrity, and innovation . . . We need leaders who have the integrity to lead by example and to practice what they preach" (2005).

The Evolution of Government Ethics in the United States

1792–1828: Character and Integrity in Governance

George Washington set the moral tone of the new government by insisting that public officeholders be men of integrity and high moral character. He served as an exemplar of the values he exalted and appointed men to the federal bureaucracy who were reputed to be persons of character as well as competence (Henry 1995, 240). Some appointees, however, possessed questionable character at best.

1828–1870: Age of Patronage Governance

The election of the Tennessee populist Andrew Jackson to the office of the president of the United States in 1828 ushered in patronage politics and the spoils system. Government jobs were handed out freely to friends and political supporters. Corruption reached alarming levels as time passed and political machines in New York, Philadelphia, and Chicago put down deep roots among immigrants needing help.

Postmaster General Amos Kendall developed the first code of public ethics for the U.S. government in 1829.

1870–1900: Antipatronage Movement

In 1883, U.S. Congress passed the Civil Service Act (also known as the Pendleton Act), which called for a federal civil service system based on competence and merit in appointments and advancement. Federal administrators were to conduct themselves in a politically neutral manner. The law followed the assassination of President James A. Garfield in 1881 by a disappointed office seeker.

In 1887, then Princeton professor Woodrow Wilson penned the famous essay "The Study of Administration" (1887/1941), which calls for the separation of politics and administration. Civil servants were expected to carry out their duties in an efficient and ethical fashion.

1900–1930: Zeal for Government Integrity

Demands to end corruption and advance good government resulted in a zealous approach to reform the entire political system, not just the bureaucracy. Progressive reformers advocated removing partisanship from office holding, especially at the municipal level; staggering election cycles so that local elections were not held in the same year as state or federal elections; eliminating ward-based districts and replacing them with at-large districts; establishing independent commissions and authorities; and ending patronage appointments.

Theodore Roosevelt waged a vigorous campaign to end patronage appointments as a U.S. civil service commissioner (1889–1895). He led efforts to investigate fraud and political abuse in government and expose corrupt government officials. As president, he championed the expansion of competitive civil service, which was increased from 110,000 to 235,000, approximately 63.9 percent of the whole executive civil service. And for the first time, the merit system surpassed the spoils system in numbers of jobs in the executive service (U.S. Office of Personnel Management n.d.).

The early twentieth century also witnessed the adoption of new local-government models such as the council-manager plan, which recognized the growing need for professional public management. New professional associations sprang up with the founding of the International City Managers Association (ICMA) in 1914. Thirty-two local governments in the United States and Canada became charter members as the ICMA became the front line in the battle for good government. A decade later (1924), the ICMA adopted the first public service code of ethics for local government administrators.

In 1914, the Society for the Promotion of Training for the Public Service was created. It was "a forerunner of the American Society for Public Administration, which was established in 1939" (Henry 1995, 23).

University of Chicago professor Leonard D. White published the first edition of his textbook *Introduction to the Study of Public Administration* in 1926, creating a benchmark for public administration as a professional field of study and practice.

Scientific management, as described by its inventor Frederick Winslow Taylor (1919), demanded greater planning, specialization, standardization, and "one best way" to accomplish the work of the organization. As a moral code, Taylor claimed that scientific management "aids the worker in general intellectual and moral development" (Fry 1989, 63). But the reality is quite different. The worker is trained to follow orders and be obedient. Attention to moral self and ethical behavior gives way to moral muteness and amoralism.

1930–1960: Administration as Science

Decades of strife, war, and recovery ushered in new views, attitudes, and realities of government and governance. Government was widely viewed as a positive instrument for social and economic advancement. Can-do administrators armed with the science of administration occupied senior posts in government and became social engineers. Many brought to their work a philosophical view of ethics that was both pragmatic and utilitarian.

States began to focus on ethics issues in this period. In 1954, New York became the first state to adopt an ethics law after a series of scandals involving the bribery of public officials by organized crime.

1960s: Rise and Demise of Can-Do Government

The 1960s witnessed the can-do government of the Great Society launched under President LBJ. By decade's end, the steady erosion of public trust and confidence in government had taken its toll, and government was no longer seen as an instrument to advance social justice and improve the average American's quality of life. Social upheaval, spawned by disillusionment with the Vietnam War and the inability of the federal government to resolve difficult social problems, pushed administrators into a defensive and ethically challenging corner. By decade's end, growing concern with the irrelevance of public administrators motivated a call for a "new" public administration. Administrators were challenged to reconnect themselves ethically and morally and commit themselves to placing social equity at the forefront of the public interest. Most failed to respond.

The first government-wide executive order on standards of conduct affecting all executive branch employees was promulgated on May 8, 1965 (Executive Order 11222).

1970s: Ethical Meltdown

In 1972, Republican operatives attempted to break into Democratic National Headquarters at the Watergate Hotel in Washington, D.C. The unsuccessful burglary attempt spawned a cover-up that shocked the nation and forced President Richard M. Nixon to resign from office in 1974. A year earlier, Vice President Spiro T. Agnew had been charged with accepting bribes and falsifying income tax returns. He entered a plea of "no contest" to the income tax falsification charges and was forced to resign. Agnew was fined $10,000 and placed on probation for 3 years.

The U.S. Congress enacted the Ethics in Government Act in 1978 to prevent future Watergates. Many states followed the lead of Congress and enacted ethics statutes before the decade's end.

1980s: Into the Ethical Wilderness

Despite the flurry of legislation to discourage unethical behavior at all levels of government, problems continued in both the private and public sectors throughout the 1980s. Wall Street scandals involving insider trading brought attention to the ugly underbelly of the "me" generation and eroded public trust in America's financial institutions. Scandals rocked the federal government and reached the highest office of the land with the Iran-Contra affair— an illegal arms deal orchestrated in the name of anticommunism—during the Reagan administration.

ASPA unveiled its first public service code of ethics in 1984 with a decided emphasis on the public interest. Laws were enacted to regulate and investigate charges of unethical practices at the state and local levels and included provisions dealing with gifts, outside employment, and post-employment rules.

Congress passed the Ethics Reform Act of 1989, placing greater restrictions on federal employees in the solicitation and acceptance of gifts, outside earned income from professional services, and financial reporting.

President George H.W. Bush issued Executive Order 12674 in 1989, outlining "Principles of Ethical Conduct for Government Officers and Employees." For the first time, as many as 250,000 federal employees received annual training on the laws and regulations (Gilman 2005, 73).

The legal-punishment trend toward outlawing corruption and cracking down on unethical behavior intensified, but not everyone viewed this as a positive development. Frank Anechiarico and James B. Jacobs describe the decade as dominated by a "panoptic vision," one in which public employees were regarded as similar to "probationers in the criminal justice system" (1994, 468).

1990s: Benign Neglect and Reawakening

Governmental ethics and reform moved to the sidelines in the early 1990s as the first Gulf War occupied the attention of both the public and President George H.W. Bush. Democratic nominee Bill Clinton was elected president in 1992, and the "reinvention" of the federal government got under way in 1993 with much sound and fury. Vice President Al Gore, in charge of the reinvention process, issued a report in October outlining a government that would work better and cost less. The Gore report called for reforming the federal bureaucracy, not political institutions, and failed to mention the need for ethical governance. Benevolent neglect of government ethics prevailed during this time.

In 1998, the Bill Clinton–Monica Lewinsky scandal ensnarled all within its reach, especially President Clinton. The White House was lambasted by critics for moral indignities that eventually placed the president on the path to impeachment. The country recoiled at the tawdry details publicized during the Senate impeachment trial in 1999 as questions were raised about the president's behavior, including his lying under oath. Clinton was eventually cleared of the charges.

2000s: Restoring Ethical Governance?

George W. Bush was elected president of the United States in 2000 with his campaign promise to restore "integrity in the White House." He put the country on the road toward a moral America. The White House pushed for restrictions on stem cell research and abortion. After 9/11, a wartime president emerged with an agenda that challenged the moral fiber of the nation. By 2005, accusations of White House deception, misinformation, secrecy, domestic spying, torture, and leaking classified information abounded.

In October 2005, President Bush ordered ethics training for all executive office personnel.

2016 and Beyond

Ethical governance in America remains a work in progress. At the national level, President Barack Obama moved swiftly after taking office on January 20, 2009, launching a call in his inaugural address for a "new era of responsibility" by issuing Executive Order 13490, "Ethics Commitments by Executive Branch Personnel." Noncareer political appointees are expected to sign a pledge that they will not accept gifts from lobbyists or act on matters involving a former employee or former client. Furthermore, the pledge requires a signature that "I agree that any hiring or other employment decisions I make will be based on the candidate's qualifications, competence, and experience" (Executive Order 13490 2009). State and local governments are on the move as well, although a patchwork of laws, regulations, and reform initiatives remains an apt description.

Summing Up

Ethics management in the U.S. national environment remains a work in progress, with no end in sight. While much has been accomplished since the ethical meltdown called Watergate, there is no clear road ahead given the size and complexity of the undertaking. Still, one must remain optimistic in spite of the mind-numbing surprises that reach the media all too often. Sexting (sending sexually explicit texts), a creation of the high-tech age, surprised the American public in June 2011 when Anthony Weiner, a Democratic congressman from New York, admitted to placing revealing pictures of himself on Facebook and tweeting young women.

All the rules and regulations on the books and those yet to be invented are unlikely to prevent errant public officials from straying from the ethical path. In the end, the responsibility for ethical behavior remains with the individual, regardless of his or her official rank. The key for instilling those values that enable one to pursue the ethical course remains something of a mystery.

In this era of postmodernism, it is unclear what type of ethic might infuse American government. The economic collapse of 2008–2009 set in motion what is now known as the Great Recession, which—in combination with globalization—has resulted in much ethical soul searching within and outside government.

Equally troublesome is the shocking legacy of the case of moral and administrative failure at Abu Ghraib, Iraq, where torture became the norm for treating prisoners captured during the Iraq War. A report written by Major General Antonio M. Taguba, the senior commander in Iraq, found that between October and December of 2003 there were numerous instances of "sadistic, blatant, and wanton criminal abuses" at Abu Ghraib (Hersh 2004). Soldiers who abused prisoners also suffered from lack of leadership oversight, and leaders who were indifferent to the needs and concerns of their subordinates (Reinke 2006, 141). Further administrative complications added confusion to the situation as the relationship between the 800th

Military Police Brigade commander, Brigadier General Karpinski, and the commander of the 205th Military Intelligence Brigade, Colonel Pappas, was unclear. While the military police were placed under the command of the military intelligence unit, this put the ranking officer (Karpinski) under the authority of a lower-ranked officer (Pappas). These failures and others "resulted in an untrained, undisciplined, and undermanned unit" (Reinke 2006, 143). While the soldiers who abused prisoners were not without fault, the Justice Department's narrow definition of torture justified the use of coercive interrogation policies and contributed to the conditions that "led to the torture and abuse of Iraqi prisoners in Abu Ghraib prison" (Reinke 2006, 144).

Other analysts (Pfiffner 2005) who have examined U.S. prisoner torture practices at Guantanamo and Abu Ghraib point to several key legal memoranda that set the conditions for torture: (1) the suspension of the Geneva Conventions on the treatment of prisoners of war; and (2) the 50-page, single-spaced document written in 2002 by Assistant Attorney General Bybee dealing with the question of what would constitute torture under U.S. law. While there is no public evidence that President Bush or Secretary Rumsfeld ordered or condoned the torture of prisoners, civilian and military leaders took seriously the legal memorandum justifying "actionable intelligence" that "set the tone that allowed abuse to occur" (Pfiffner 2005, 323).

Is it any wonder that the American public has become increasingly dubious of those who govern? Is it any surprise to learn that we are experiencing significant levels of public distrust and outright cynicism of government and large institutions in America?

Ethics Management Skill Building

Practicum 6.1. Ethics Challenges in Disasters

On August 29, 2005, Hurricane Katrina made landfall near New Orleans, Louisiana. A day or two later, the levees protecting the city (New Orleans actually sits below sea level) were breeched; water spewed into the streets and residences, flooding nearly all of the city, with some water levels reaching 18–20 feet. As conditions worsened, law and order broke down. Looters sacked stores and gangs roamed the streets. The New Orleans police force of 1,500 was overwhelmed by the lawlessness. Scores of police officers were cut off by the storm and floodwaters, and as many as 500 others either walked off their posts in the days after the storm or otherwise couldn't be accounted for. Many officers experienced high levels of stress and distress—the rising floodwaters endangered their lives, as well as the lives of their loved ones, and some became targets of angry residents and mob violence, in some cases dodging sniper bullets as they rescued victims. The city's police superintendent put it this way: "I had officers in boats who were being shot at as they were pulling people out of the water." Two officers committed suicide (Treaster & Desantis 2005).

Discussion Questions

1. Assume you are the New Orleans chief of police. What explanations do you have for the failure of some police officers to carry out their duties? Was this an ethical failure of the individuals? The New Orleans Police Department? Something else?
2. How would you deal with the stress experienced by New Orleans Police Departmentofficers? Raise their pay? Hire counselors? Send them to Las Vegas for a 5-day vacation? Give them time off to visit relatives? None of the above?
3. What would you do to discourage desertions by police officers in the event of a disaster? Would you launch a major ethics training program? Emphasize a code of ethics? Hire a consultant to assess the organization's culture? Nothing, as this is a matter of duty?

Practicum 6.2. Polish This Draft!

Annual performance appraisals typically result in anxious moments for all, especially the person receiving the appraisal. Others can be drawn into the anxiety circle as well, with ethical or not-so-ethical overtones. Let's say you are an employee who works in a large federal agency as a staff member for a senior manager. You are routinely expected to provide "input" for the manager's annual evaluation. Suppose your input goes directly to his secretary and thus to him: Is anyone going to say anything but glowing things about what happened under his watch? Probably not.

Now consider an even more uncomfortable situation. Suppose you, as the best writer on the staff, are given the task of polishing the draft of the senior manager's performance evaluation—an evaluation put together using the "input" that everyone had provided. Trying not to violate your own ethical standards, you simply edit it, correcting grammar and rewording so it will read more smoothly. You return it to his secretary, who shares it with her boss. Then, the boss sends it back to you and pronounces, "It's not good enough. Make me look like a god."

Discussion Questions

1. Would you voice your ethical concerns to the boss?
2. Would you report your boss to his boss?
3. Would you request a transfer to another agency?
4. Would you simply turn your head and make your boss "look like a god?"

Notes

1. The discussion in this chapter draws in part from Menzel (2001a).

2. NASPAA has adopted a new approach to accreditation that emphasizes "values," including ethical values.

3. See Burke (1986), Cooper (1982, 1984, 1987), Denhardt (1988, 1989), Gawthrop (1984), and Rohr (1989).

7

The International Ethics Management Environment

All men are good at birth. Same are their natures
Different are their habits.

—Wang Yinglin (1223–1296), renowned Confucian
scholar in the Song Dynasty (*New Land* 2015)

This chapter explores international actors and initiatives that endorse strong ethics management, and then takes a close look at ethics management in Europe and Asia, with specific attention focused on developments in four countries—the United Kingdom, the Netherlands, China, and Japan.

Good Governance

Interest in conceptualizing and building "good" societies with a strong ethics infrastructure has become a worldwide endeavor. This movement was undoubtedly prompted in part by the breakup of the Soviet bloc in the late 1980s and 1990s. The democratization movement, as it is sometimes labeled, found fertile ground in emerging countries around the globe in the decades that followed. Thus early efforts to describe and account for integrity reform and desired change found expression in the metaphor of the "Greek temple," whose pillars (institutions, laws, values) needed to function effectively to ensure a satisfactory quality of life for the citizenry (Pope 2000). The Greek temple metaphor spawned interest in National Integrity country studies sponsored by Transparency International (TI). Since 2001, more than 70 National Integrity System country studies have been conducted (Lewis, Shacklock, Conners, & Sampford, 2013, 244).

Nongovernmental Organization (NGO)

The United Nations defines an NGO as a not-for-profit group, principally independent from government, which is organized on a local, national, or international level to address issues in support of the public good. NGOs are also referred to as "civil society organizations." As Steve Ott explains,

In the United States we use "nonprofit" to mean a domestic organization and "NGO" to mean either international nonprofit or a domestic nonprofit in another country. In the rest of the world, everyone (essentially) uses "NGO" to mean all of the above, i.e., no distinction between domestic, foreign and/or international.

(Ott 2015)

Jeremy Pope, the founder of TI and an activist European lawyer, notes that when TI was launched in the early 1990s, the guiding philosophy was to fight corruption by building a country's "national integrity system." More than a decade later, he concluded that, no matter how hard people work trying to strengthen public institutions and implement international standards, little seems to change. The bottom line is that "it does not really matter how strong one's institutions are if the wrong people are inside them" (Pope 2005). An individual's ethics, however acquired and influenced, cannot be ignored. Thus, education and training programs are essential to building an ethical infrastructure.

Moreover, Pope points out that the differences between ethics "best practices" in Western Europe and the United States are apparent. He suggests that the American approach can be seen in a famous cartoon in which a company's ethics advisor is shown addressing his board of directors: "My role," the advisor says, "is to draw a line between what is acceptable, and what is not. And then get the company as close to that line as possible." Drawing the line and then getting as close to it as possible is a risky, low-road proposition. The Western European approach to ethics management is not, as Pope puts it, "simply a case of 'lawful conduct'."

Given the dark consequences wrought by corruption in developing and developed countries, it is not surprising that reform efforts place considerable emphasis on first, building institutions and laws that combat corruption and second, putting in place an ethics infrastructure to promote ethical behavior.

Internationally, corruption has received much more attention than ethics. This is largely because the costs and consequences associated with corruption are more visible than they are with unethical behavior, although both can be difficult to measure in a way that yields confident results. A recent report by Global Financial Integrity finds that "illicit trade in 'goods, guns, people, and natural resources' is a $650 billion enterprise, which most negatively impacts the developing world" (Global Financial Integrity 2011).

Unethical and corrupt acts are sometimes viewed as two sides of a common coin—wrongdoing. Corruption can be viewed as unethical behavior at its worst, although this might be an oversimplification. And, when placed in an international context, one might ask, are both ethics and corruption culture-bound? Does the prevailing culture define what is acceptable or unacceptable behavior? Maybe. Consider the story in Exhibit 7.1.

Exhibit 7.1
A Different View of Corruption

Gathered in the guest room of a Berber friend's house in the Atlas Mountains of Morocco after Friday prayers, Hussein turned from the assembled village to me and asked me: "Is there corruption in America?"

"Yes," I answered.

"Give us an example," he gently inquired.

So, as the room quieted, I gave an example of a kickback arrangement. "Ah, no," said Hussein, as the others' heads shook in unison, "that is just buying and selling." So I mentioned the Watergate scandal. "No, no," Hussein replied to common assent, "that is just politics." So I gave an example of nepotism. "No, no, *no*," all voices cried out, "that is just family solidarity." So, as I struggled to think of an example that would maintain the honor of my country for being every bit as corrupt as anyone else's, Hussein turned to the others and said, with genuine admiration: "You see why America is so strong—the Americans have no corruption!"

(Rosen 2010)

This story, although humorous, presents a view of corruption that differs from that espoused in the Euro-American context. "Corruption is the failure to share any largess you have received with those with whom you have formed ties of dependence," muses Lawrence Rosen (2010). Is corruption culture-bound? Is ethics culture-bound? You will have to decide for yourself, as there is no universal agreement. However, as one well-known corruption scholar, Susan Rose-Ackerman (1999, 2), suggests:

> Obviously, subtle differences in culture and basic values exist across the world. But there is one human motivator that is both universal and central to explaining the divergent experiences of different countries. That motivator is self-interest, including an interest in the well-being of one's family and peer group. Critics call it greed . . . Endemic corruption suggests a pervasive failure to tap self-interest for productive purposes.

International bodies, including the United Nations (UN), TI, Global Integrity (GI), the Utstein Group (United Kingdom, the Netherlands, Norway, Sweden, Canada, and Germany), and the Organisation for Economic Co-operation and Development (OECD), have launched a number of anticorruption initiatives. The UN, for example, promulgated an International Code of Conduct for Public Officials in 1996 (Exhibit 7.2). Additionally, the UN International Centre for Crime Prevention has developed "Anti-Corruption Tool Kits" to:

> help UN Member States and the public to understand the insidious nature of corruption, the potential damaging effect it can have on the welfare of entire nations and suggest measures used successfully by other countries in their efforts to uncover and deter corruption and build integrity.
>
> (Amundsen 2006)

Exhibit 7.2
UN General Principles of the
International Code for Public Officials

1. A public office, as defined by national law, is a position of trust, implying a duty to act in the public interest. Therefore, the ultimate loyalty of public officials shall be to the public interests of their country as expressed through the democratic institutions of government.

(continued)

Exhibit 7.2 *(continued)*

2. Public officials shall ensure that they perform their duties and functions efficiently, effectively, and with integrity, in accordance with laws or administrative policies. They shall at all times seek to ensure that public resources for which they are responsible are administered in the most effective and efficient manner.

3. Public officials shall be attentive, fair, and impartial in the performance of their functions and, in particular, in their relations with the public. They shall at no time afford any undue preferential treatment to any group or individual or improperly discriminate against any group or individual, or otherwise abuse the power and authority vested in them.

(United Nations Economic and Social Council 1996)

These meritorious efforts by international bodies are sometimes challenged from within when an international agency's ethical compass is adrift. Consider the case of the International Monetary Fund (IMF), with 187 member countries. In May 2011, the agency's managing director, Dominique Strauss-Kahn, was arrested and charged with sexually assaulting a hotel housekeeper in New York City. Given this allegation of egregious behavior, the media began to take a close look at the ethical culture of the IMF; what turned up was surprising. Several years previously, the IMF tightened up its internal systems for catching misconduct among its 2,400 staff members. This included establishing a telephone hotline for complaints like harassment and appointing and empowering an ethics adviser to pursue allegations of unethical behavior. But—and it is a big "but"—the IMF's ethics policy applied only to staff, not to the managing director! The director and the IMF's 24 executive board members are above the policy and beyond the reach of the ethics adviser. Rather, the board is responsible for policing its own directors via a five-person ethics committee whose work is confidential. Moreover, the only way the board can discipline its executive members is to write a warning letter to them or to their home countries. "There are a lot of controls in place when it comes to the staff, but not for the leadership," said Katrina Campbell, a compliance and ethics expert at Global Compliance (Bowley 2011).

International Nonprofit Actors

TI is a nongovernmental organization devoted to combating corruption and fostering integrity through information and education. TI publishes a Bribes Payers Index, a Global Corruption Report, and a Corruption Perceptions Index (CPI) that track corruption in 175 countries. According to the 2015 CPI, Denmark, Finland, Sweden, New Zealand, and the Netherlands are the five most corruption-free countries in the world, in that order. The five most corrupt countries, according to the CPI, are Somalia, North Korea, Afghanistan, Sudan, and South Sudan. The United States is tied with Austria at number 16, one slot ahead of Ireland, Hong Kong, and Japan, and one spot behind Belgium, ranked number 15.

> Ultimately, ethics in the public service must be understood as an integral element of the role of public administrations in the achievement of good governance.
>
> (United Nations 2001)

TI also publishes guides and books that promote integrity in governance. A National Integrity System source book, available in over 20 languages, offers "a holistic approach to transparency and accountability and embraces a range of accountability 'pillars'—democratic, judicial, media and civil society" (Pope 2000).

GI is a newcomer to the international nonprofit watchdogs. The organization views

> corruption as a universal challenge, not a problem specific to low-income countries. It is not just about national governments, but about local government and communities as well as key sectors within economies. Corruption is not a "development" issue; it is a political and economic one.
>
> (Global Integrity n.d.)

GI evolved from a team working at the Center for Public Integrity in Washington, D.C., and it became an independent nonprofit organization in

2005. A year later, GI released the first full-length *Global Integrity Report* (2006), which provided in-depth anticorruption assessments for 43 countries on five continents. GI uses online collaboration tools via a network of more than 1,200 in-country journalists, academics, and social scientists to assemble and report data that allow stakeholders to "implement evidence-based reforms" (Global Integrity n.d.). GI's comprehensive web site (www.globalintegrity.org/) contains a blog, a set of country corruption notebooks written by journalists, and easy downloads of past *Global Integrity Reports.*

The Utstein Group, with headquarters in London, is another international actor. The ministers of international development from Germany, the Netherlands, Norway, and the United Kingdom established it when they gathered at the Utstein Abbey in Norway in 1999. The group has created an online resource center (www.cgdev.org/section/publica tions?f%5B0%5D=field_document_type%3A2023) that lists studies, reports, and anticorruption projects currently under way throughout the world.

OECD

The OECD, with 30 member countries and a history dating to the early 1960s, has long been at the forefront of promoting good governance. The OECD was instrumental in putting forward the 1997 Anti-Bribery Convention that is "the first global instrument to fight corruption in cross-border business deals" (OECD 2004). Thirty-six countries, including six non-OECD members, have enacted antibribery laws based on the OECD Convention. Estonia is the most recent party to the convention.

In 1998, the OECD also adopted a 12-principle recommendation to improve ethical conduct in the public service (Exhibit 7.3). These principles, according to the preamble to the OECD recommendation, are intended to be a point of reference for member countries "when combining the elements of an effective ethics management system in line with their own political, administrative and cultural circumstances." The extent to which these principles have been drawn on by member countries and other countries to develop an effective ethics management system is difficult to say. Nonetheless, the 12 principles are noteworthy, and the intention is certainly meritorious.

Exhibit 7.3
OECD Published Principles for
Managing Ethics in the Public Service

1. Ethical standards for public service should be clear. Public servants need to know the basic principles and standards they are expected to apply to their work and where the boundaries of acceptable behaviour lie.
2. Ethical standards should be reflected in the legal framework. The legal framework is the basis for communicating the minimum obligatory standards and principles of behaviour for every public servant.
3. Ethical guidance should be available to public servants. Guidance and internal consultation mechanisms should be made available to help public servants apply basic ethical standards in the workplace.
4. Public servants should know their rights and obligations when exposing wrongdoing. Public servants also need to know what protection will be available to them in cases of exposing wrongdoing.
5. Political commitment to ethics should reinforce the ethical conduct of public servants. Political leaders are responsible for maintaining a high standard of propriety in the discharge of their official duties.
6. The decision-making process should be transparent and open to scrutiny. The public has a right to know how public institutions apply the power and resources entrusted to them.
7. There should be clear guidelines for interaction between the public and private sectors. Clear rules defining ethical standards should guide the behaviour of public servants in dealing with the private sector, for example regarding public procurement, outsourcing, or public employment conditions.
8. Managers should demonstrate and promote ethical conduct. An organizational environment where high standards of conduct

(continued)

Exhibit 7.3 *(continued)*

are encouraged by providing appropriate incentives for ethical behaviour . . . has a direct impact on the daily practice of public service values and ethical standards.

9. Management policies, procedures, and practices should promote ethical conduct. Government policy should not only delineate the minimal standards below which a government official's actions will not be tolerated but also clearly articulate a set of public service values that employees should aspire to.

10. Public service conditions and management of human resources should promote ethical conduct. Public service employment conditions, such as career prospects, personal development, adequate remuneration, and human resource management policies, should create an environment conducive to ethical behaviour.

11. Adequate accountability mechanisms should be in place within the public service. Accountability should focus both on compliance with rules and ethical principles and on achievement of results.

12. Appropriate procedures and sanctions should exist to deal with misconduct. Mechanisms for the detection and independent investigation of wrongdoing such as corruption are a necessary part of an ethics infrastructure.

(Organisation for Economic Co-operation and Development 1998)

The principles are consistent with the OECD's recommendation that countries build their ethics infrastructure "to regulate against undesirable behaviour and to provide incentives to good conduct" (OECD 1997). A well-built ethics infrastructure would include politicians who are advocates and exemplars of ethical governance; an effective legal framework; accountability mechanisms; workable codes of conduct, education, and training, and an active civic society. Admirable? Without question. Doable? Not easily.

As a working model, OECD classified nine countries along two dimensions—an integrity–compliance dimension and a public administration–managerialism dimension (Exhibit 7.4). The United States is characterized as having an ethics infrastructure that is a mix of compliance-based ethics and managerialism; that is, the emphasis is on "getting the job done" while at the same time complying with ethics rules and regulations.

Exhibit 7.4 The Integrity–Compliance and Public Administration–Managerialism Dimensions

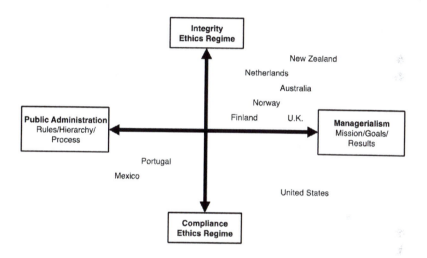

Ethics Laws and Codes Internationally

Ethics laws and codes of conduct are widely used tools in the international ethics manager's toolbox. For example, Australia's Northern Territory placed a code of conduct in the 1993 Public Sector Employment and Management Act. Neighboring New Zealand passed a nationwide code of conduct in 1998 that emphasizes obligations generally expected of civil servants in their professional lives. Each agency has been encouraged to develop specific codes of conduct consistent with the standards set out in the national code. The U.K. Committee on Standards in Public Life, known as the Nolan Committee, promulgated the "Seven Principles of Public Life" that have been incorporated into codes of conduct by various agencies (Exhibit 7.5).

Exhibit 7.5
U.K. Committee on Standards in Public Life:
Principles of Public Life

1. *Selflessness*: Holders of public office should take decisions solely in terms of the public interest. They should not do so in order to gain financial or other material benefits for themselves, their family, or their friends.
2. *Integrity*: Holders of public office should not place themselves under any financial or other obligation to outside individuals or organizations that might influence them in the performance of their official duties.
3. *Objectivity*: In carrying out public business, including making public appointments, awarding contracts, or recommending individuals for rewards and benefits, holders of public office should make choices on merit.
4. *Accountability*: Holders of public office are accountable for their decisions and actions to the public and must submit themselves to whatever scrutiny is appropriate to their office.
5. *Openness*: Holders of public office should be as open as possible about all the decisions and actions that they take. They should give reasons for their decisions and restrict information only when the wider public interest clearly demands.
6. *Honesty*: Holders of public office have a duty to declare any private interests relating to their public duties and to take steps to resolve any conflicts arising in a way that protects the public interest.
7. *Leadership*: Holders of public office should promote and support these principles by leadership and example.

These principles apply to all aspects of public life.

(U.K. Committee on Standards in Public Life 2001)

In Brazil, the Public Ethics Commission (in Portuguese, the Comissão de Ética Pública) was established in 1999 to promote ethical behavior in the federal executive branch. The commission is also responsible for the implementation of the Federal Code of Conduct for the Senior Government Officers in the executive branch, and it oversees and coordinates decentralized ethics initiatives in order to ensure the adequacy of the Brazilian administration's ethical standards. Another aspect of the agency's duties is to ensure that the relevant rules and procedures are known and understood, which includes publicity and training for officials and guidelines and help in dealing with ethical dilemmas (Transparency International 2012).

Despite these steps by Brazil to shore up its ethical infrastructure, corruption scandals have reaped discord and discontent among the citizenry. Executives at the partially state-owned oil company Petrobras have been charged with a complicated kickback-and-bribery scheme involving legislators. Petrobras officials are charged with taking a cut of the cash from inflated contracts, funneling the rest to lawmakers. Three former congressmen were arrested and have been accused of money laundering and involvement with a currency dealer (Jelmayer 2015).

South Korea adopted a code of conduct for maintaining the integrity of public officials in 2003. This code specifies the standards of conduct to be observed by both state and local public officials and covers conflicts of interest, the use of one's office for private purposes, and the obligation of officials to exercise neutrality and impartiality in their agencies.

The Philippines, with a workforce of 1.4 million men and women in the civil service, enacted a Code of Conduct and Ethical Standards for Public Officials and Employees in 1989. The standards include upholding the public interest over and above personal interest; discharging duties with the highest degree of excellence, professionalism, intelligence, and skill; acting with justness and sincerity; not discriminating against anyone, especially the poor and the underprivileged; and leading modest lives appropriate to their positions and income. Officials are expected to avoid extravagant or ostentatious displays of wealth in any form. The code also emphasizes positive incentives for exemplary behavior, stating that incentives and rewards to government officials and employees may take the form of bonuses, citations, directorships in government-owned or controlled corporations, local and foreign scholarship grants, and paid vacations. Public officials so honored are automatically promoted to the next higher position, with the commensurate salary suitable to their qualifications (Republic of the Philippines 1989).

One ethics management tool under development by the Philippines Civil Service Commission is an Ethics-Based Personality Test. The commission believes that prescreening candidates for employment with this test will result in the "recruitment of the right people in all aspects and dimension"

(Valmores 2005). The test will "determine the behavioral tendencies and personality profile of a job applicant [to] address the longstanding problem of hiring otherwise qualified people who are deficient on the moral and ethical requirements of public service." Ariel Ronquillo (2007) notes that the Ethics-Based Personality Test "aims to objectively evaluate the behavioral competencies and ethical values of persons wanting to enter the government service as well as existing government personnel as a critical approach to further promote ethics, transparency, and accountability."

In Africa a notable good government and ethics initiative is the "Charter for the Public Service in Africa." The charter puts forth a highly meritorious set of principles to strengthen public service throughout Africa. Included in the charter is a code of conduct for public service employees that emphasizes professionalism and ethics. Public service employees are expected to carry out their duties with "integrity and moral rectitude," avoid conflicts of interest, declare assets upon taking and leaving office, be politically neutral, and respect the confidentiality of official information to which they are privy. The African Union meeting in Addis Ababa, Ethiopia, in 2011 adopted the African Charter on the Values and Principles of Public Service and Administration and called on all member states to take the necessary measures, as soon as possible, to sign and ratify the charter (African Union 2011).

Ethics Codes in Europe

Perhaps the most active regions of the world today in the development and implementation of codes of ethics are Central and Eastern Europe, where many countries are in transition from authoritarian to democratic regimes. A study by J. Palidauskaite (2006), a scholar from Lithuania, tracked the approaches taken in ten countries—Albania, Bulgaria, the Czech Republic, Estonia, Latvia, Lithuania, Macedonia, Poland, Romania, and the Slovak Republic. She reports that two trends are discernable—some countries focus on the behavior of public servants through laws and codes, while other countries rely on statutory regulation only. The implementation of ethics codes and/or laws follows one of two paths. The first path is the use of an impartial council or board much like that found in the United States and the United Kingdom. The second path is left up to the individuals themselves "to interpret and apply the code of ethics" (45). The latter approach is consistent with the professional norm of self-enforcement, which is central to the codes adopted by many professional societies in the United States.

The European Union (EU) has also been quite active in the development of official ethics, declare Moilanen and Salminen (2006). A two-step process is followed. First, core values are identified and then promoted. As the discussion on public service ethics advances, the state becomes ready to move to the second step—the development of a code of ethics with specific standards. Their study finds that half of the EU countries use general (i.e. applies to all civil servants working in the central state administration) value statements and the other half use general codes of ethics.

Ethics codes and statutes are not, of course, sufficient tools to ensure ethical governance. Mike Nelson (1999) notes,

> The problem with Codes of Conduct is that it is easy to stick them on the wall, but hard to make them stick in practice . . . Without an effective development and implementation strategy which is integrated and engages with the heart and bowels issues of concern to the organization, the net result seems consistently the same: That the Code of Conduct remains a mere piece of paper, displayed or appealed to when convenient, but ignored the rest of the time.

In assessing the role of codes in EU countries, Bossaert and Demmke (2005, 7) conclude:

> Despite their popularity, codes of ethics make little sense unless they are accepted by the personnel, and maintained, cultivated and implemented with vigor . . . Codes are useless if staff are not reminded of them on a regular basis and given continuous training on ethics. Codes are only effective if they are impressed upon the hearts and minds of employees.

Alas, even with a vigorous implementation strategy, a code may still not deter unethical behavior.

Whistleblowing Laws

Whistleblowing laws and practices vary enormously throughout the world. The United States has numerous laws that encourage and protect individuals who blow the whistle on those who engage in corruption, waste, fraud, and abuse of power. And, there is a high incident of whistleblowing. Like those of the United States, Israel's laws provide extensive protection for whistleblowers, although there is a low incident of whistleblowing there. India, the largest democracy in the world, has no statutes that encourage or protect whistleblowers. "In fact, whistleblowing is technically illegal, according to civil service rules, and might even be personally dangerous" (Johnson 2005, 1057). Still, there is a growing grassroots movement in India to expose government wrongdoing.

Until the collapse of the Soviet Union in 1991, whistleblowing in Russia was encouraged as a form of spying that enabled the government to sustain itself and control its citizens. This historic and unique Russian history, Roberta Johnson contends, is changing; there is evidence that a new breed of whistleblowers is emerging who are motivated to serve the public interest (2005, 1056). Johnson's case study of the United States, Israel, Russia, and India has led her to conclude that there is no direct correlation between the law and the incidence of whistleblowing. Rather, she contends that the "cultural context, more than any other factor, helps explain why in some countries whistleblowers play an important role in opposing corruption and in other countries they do not" (1051).

To further assess ethics management internationally, in the next section a closer view of ethics management in Europe is presented. After which, a more in-depth look at national integrity systems in China, Japan, The Netherlands, and the United Kingdom is detailed.

Europe

Lawful conduct has a distinctive place in Europe. Seventeen of the 28 EU countries prohibit accepting gifts and invitations, with eight of those countries prohibiting gifts above a certain amount—Austria, Cyprus, Italy, Latvia, Lithuania, Slovenia, and Sweden, and United Kingdom. All but five EU countries—Belgium, the Czech Republic, Denmark, Germany, and Luxembourg—require public officials to disclose financial interests (Bossaert and Demmke 2005, 105). Seventeen EU countries provide for punitive measures for those who violate ethics rules.

The EU has stepped up its efforts to promote public service ethics. A 2004 survey (Bossaert and Demmke 2005) of member states resulted in a voluntary, nonlegally binding European Code of Ethics, also known as the Ethics Framework. Six general core values were identified, and in a follow-up study (Moilanen 2007) those six were divided into eight values for analytical purposes:

1. rule of law;
2. impartiality/objectivity;
3. transparency;

4.   accountability;
5.   professionalism;
6.   duty of care;
7.   reliability (confidence, trust);
8.   courtesy.

The survey of EU states found that these "values were well reflected in the official documents with only minor exceptions" (Moilanen 2007, 4). The Ethics Framework, the study concludes, has had a positive impact on the EU, especially in helping member states draft their own code of conduct.

Ethics management among Western European countries, asserts Aive Pevkur (2007), spans a continuum of value-based, rule-based, and law-based approaches. According to Pevkur, Finland and Denmark take a value-based approach, Portugal and Great Britain pursue a rule-based approach, and Germany and France follow a law-based approach to ethics management (Exhibit 7.6). She notes that, while there is a movement away from the law or rule-based system and toward a value-based system, it remains uncertain whether it is "possible to go directly to an integrity-based system or whether a rule-based system is a necessary transitory phase" (Pevkur 2007, 20).

Exhibit 7.6   **Basis of Ethics Management in Countries**

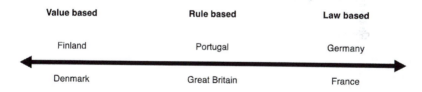

Value based	Rule based	Law based
Finland	Portugal	Germany
Denmark	Great Britain	France

Source: Pevkur (2007)

Russia, a non-EU country, is struggling with rampant corruption (estimated at $318 billion in 2009, one-third of gross domestic product) in many sectors. "Surveys show that the vast majority of Russians encounter corruption at almost every turn in their daily lives, from dealing with traffic policemen to securing a place in a good school or getting a vital personal document renewed" (Weir 2009). Bribes paid by businesses are mostly directed at low-level local officials to secure licenses and fix the bidding for contracts. Higher-level officials, however, are not immune, as some businesspeople claim that they pay monthly bribes to federal ministries.

Russian native and scholar Jasmine Martirossian (2004, 105) describes the situation in this way:

> Russia, today, has been likened to America's "wild west." Criminal elements seem to be unchecked, and it appears that people believe that efforts to expose wrongdoing are fruitless because corrupt public institutions and agencies will fail to act upon complaints, or, if they are acted upon, that the apparatus of corrupt practices will spring into action, bribes will change hands, favors will be exchanged, and no punishments will be meted out.

We turn next to an examination of ethics management in the United Kingdom and the Netherlands.

United Kingdom

The United Kingdom, composed of Great Britain and Northern Ireland, is a unitary government, although local governments exercise a great deal of autonomy. Nonetheless, the Seven Principles of Public Life put forth by the Nolan Committee in 1995 provided a starting point for more aggressive efforts to deal with ethical challenges in government. This landmark event found expression in the 2000 Local Government Act that set forth three principal components for ethics management in the United Kingdom:

1. a requirement that every local authority adopt a code of conduct that all councilors must sign up to;
2. a requirement that authorities set up a standards committee to oversee ethical issues and provide advice and guidance on the code of conduct and its implementation;
3. the establishment of an independent body (the Standards Board) with responsibility for investigating alleged breaches of a Council's code of conduct and promoting and maintaining high standards of conduct (Committee on Standards in Public Life 2004).

The Standards Board became operational in March 2001 and has regulatory responsibility for 386 local authorities, 8,000 parish councils, 31 fire and civil defense authorities, and 44 police authorities. It also covers the Greater London Authority and other regional assemblies. More than 4,000 complaints have been received by the Standards Board, with less than half investigated. Lecturer Michael Hunt describes this number of complaints as very high (Hunt 2005). A significant number of complaints deal with a failure to register a personal or financial interest. Other complaints allege that councilors bring disrepute on their community and do not treat others with respect. Eighty-two councilors have been disqualified from holding office, and 15 members were suspended following a hearing by the adjudication panel, an independent judicial tribunal that hears and adjudicates serious matters concerning the conduct of elected officials (Committee on Standards in Public Life 2004, 13–14).

Another agency, the Audit Commission, is involved in ethics management, although its primary mission is to monitor local government spending. The commission describes itself as an "independent body responsible for ensuring that public money is spent economically, efficiently and effectively, to achieve high-quality local and national service for the public" (Audit Commission 2003, ii). Its approach is not to define ethical governance but to include it as part of an overall definition of governance in the public sector—that is, the commission is expected to audit the ethical standards and practices of local governments. The audits can result in a Public Interest Report that focuses on any governance issue, including failure to maintain high ethical standards.

Of central importance to the Audit Commission is determining whether poor ethical governance adversely affects performance—a very difficult task. Indeed, the commission's more traditional focus has been on performance compliance and risk assessment. However, it has developed a toolkit, *Changing Organisational Cultures*, that tests "the operation of ethical standards." This includes an assessment of officers' understanding of the local authority's code of conduct.

In 2004, the Audit Commission conducted ethical audit reviews of 38 local authorities and concluded, "it is questionable as to whether or not the problems identified by these audits will lead to service failure or poor quality services" (Fawcett & Wardman 2005, 10). At the same time, more than 1,700 middle and senior managers completed the *Changing Organisational Cultures* exercise and were quite positive about their local government's commitment to combating fraud and corruption.

These meritorious efforts were strengthened even more in 2006, when the head of the civil service, Sir Gus O'Donnell, published the new Civil Service Code. Among other things, the code calls for greater transparency, responsiveness, and professionalism in government. "Creating a culture of excellence," Sir Gus asserts (2006), is an achievable goal. "My vision is for a civil service that exudes pride, pace, passion and professionalism" undergirded by the core values of honesty, objectivity, integrity, and impartiality.

As mentioned, the Audit Commission's ethics management work was secondary to its fiscal auditing responsibilities. Consequently, legislation in 2010 set in motion steps to decentralize and outsource the commission's auditing work. Thus in 2015 the commission was shut down and part of its work privatized. Other functions were absorbed—the Public Sector Audit Appointments, the National Audit Office, and the Financial Reporting Council. A new local audit framework was also put into place. The results of these structural changes are expected to save local public bodies £250 million (U.K. Department for Communities and Local Government 2012). The agency's ethics management responsibilities have apparently come to an end.

Altogether, the approach taken to ethics management in the United Kingdom is not as heavily compliance-driven as that in the United States, but it may be moving in that direction, despite Sir Gus O'Donnell's vision for a revitalized civil service. Pope points out that, should a litigation culture take hold in the United Kingdom and Western Europe like that in the United States, "the ethics scene here may well shift to that of the United States"—adversarial and "gotcha" oriented (Pope 2005, 6).

The Nonprofit Sector

The evolution of the nonprofit sector in the United Kingdom into a vibrant third-sector actor has similar features to the experience in the United States. Historically, charitable nonprofits responded to the needs of people in the absence of government intervention. That history, however, began to change in the post World War II environment as the government increasingly assumed social welfare activities. As in the United States, nonprofit organizations began to partner with government, thus entering the governance process in a more defined manner. This development became most prominent in the 1980s, "which brought a rise in government partnership, a new resource environment, and a return to a greater role for nonprofits" (Bies 2010).

Growing engagement in the governance process also raised issues about consistency in nonprofit reporting and accountability. Consequently, the Charities Act of 1993 accorded the independent regulatory U.K. Charities Commission, an agency that combines the functions similar to that of the Internal Revenue Service and state attorneys general in the United States, greater power and resources to regulate nonprofits.

This additional authority and resources, while certainly welcomed, has been used in recent years to cope with serious misconduct but it has not removed the taint of scandal that has plagued the nonprofit sector. "Last year [2014]," reports Commission Chairman William Shawcross, "we used our regulatory powers 2,060 times compared to 188 times the year before; in 2011–12, we opened 12 investigations, last year 103" (Sussex 2015). Still, charitable non-profits such as Kids Company, a prominent charity founded in London in 1996 to help inner-city children escape drug addiction and sexual abuse, closed its doors because millions of pounds granted from the government were spent on frivolous services, such as a hypnotist "who used weird methods to treat young drug addicts" (*Daily Mail Online* 2015). Unethical fundraising by a telephone fundraising company, GoGen, also shuttered its doors in 2015. An investigation by the *London Daily Mail* reported that "Britain's biggest charities ruthlessly" hounded the vulnerable and elderly for cash (*Daily Mail Online* 2016).

Unethical behavior and scandal know no national boundaries. Do they?

The Netherlands

The Netherlands, a decentralized unitary state with a population of 16.5 million, has begun to shift its ethics and integrity policy from a strong focus on complying with rules and regulations to one that emphasizes personal integrity and moral judgment (Hoekstra, Belling, & Van Der Heide 2005). This has been described by senior policy advisers in the Ministry of the Interior and Kingdom Relations as going "beyond compliance": The government recognizes the need for rules and regulations but also recognizes that these are not sufficient to ensure ethical governance. Thus, the emerging strategy is one that combines "structure and rules on the one hand and . . . culture and awareness on the other" (7). This shift in emphasis began slowly in the 1990s but has moved rapidly since 2003. That year, an investigation into the building industry found that many attempts had been made to bribe civil servants. Responding to this situation, lawmakers in the Netherlands amended the Civil Servants Act in 2005. The act obligates government bodies to adopt a code of conduct for civil servants and requires all new civil servants to take an oath of office.

The central government's commitment is reflected as well in the establishment in 2005 of a Bureau for Ethics and Integrity Stimulation in the Dutch Ministry of Interior and Kingdom Relations. The bureau provides guidance to managers on the development and implementation of ethics management programs, supports various studies, and analyzes trends and international developments in the ethics management field.

Another significant development occurred in March 2006, when the Netherlands required all government organizations to develop an integrity policy, which includes a mandatory code of conduct. To facilitate the adoption of this policy, the government published a Model Integrity Code as a guide and reference. Most important among its stipulations is that the "Model Code can be adopted only if the changes reflect stricter regulations than required" (Moilanen & Salminen 2006). In other words, an agency cannot simply copy the Model Code as its own and go about its business as usual.

The Netherlands Tax and Customs Administration is suggestive of a Dutch agency's attempt to go beyond the establishment of a code of ethics. In 2000, the Tax Administration embarked on an ambitious project to infuse its 30,000 employees with values inherent in the nature of the agency's work. As the director general states, "Due to the nature of their work, employees of the Tax Administration can easily find themselves in uncertain or even precarious situations . . . where guidelines and rules alone are not sufficient" (Van Blijswijk, van Breukelen, Franklin, Raadschelders, & Slump 2004, 725). Tax employees must deal with the public fairly and apply the rules in a consistent manner, which is not always easy to do on a case-by-case basis. Thus, rules are not enough. Other necessary steps include: (1) training new and current employees on how to handle dilemmas; (2) appointing integrity counselors who will "serve as the first line of inquiry to employees' questions with regard to integrity"; (3) creating reflection groups from among integrity counselors to "discuss real-life cases and what actions have been taken"; and (4) offering intranet group discussion opportunities for employees (723). The integrity project strikes a balance between codifying ethics and meeting the day-to-day challenges of acting with integrity.

The Nonprofit Sector

The Netherlands is often described as a welfare state, one in which the social compact rests on a societal commitment to the welfare of the people. Indeed, "in the Dutch case," as Brandsen and van de Donk (2009, 151) assert, "the third sector has been one of the foundation stones of the welfare state" (156). Nonprofit organizations are heavily involved in the delivery of human services such as health care, education, and housing and are subject to the influence of government inspections. In short, these service-providing nonprofits are tightly interwoven in Dutch governance. As Brandsen and van de Donk (2009, 145) put it, "the third sector networks have regular interactions with the government, yet they are not legally or financially recognized as a 'third sector' in a general sense."

On the other hand, philanthropic nonprofits are lightly regulated. Does lightly regulated mean that nonprofit misbehavior is largely invisible? No, there are other means to monitor nonprofit behavior. Among fundraising foundations, for example, a code of conduct has been drawn up and the Central Office for Fundraising, itself a nonprofit foundation, offers accreditation procedures that enable an organization to collect money for charitable purposes (Brandsen & van de Donk 2009, 147). "Its work is independent from that of the Ministry of Finance, which judges if associations and foundations are eligible for fiscal privileges" (Brandsen & van de Donk 2009, 147).

In sum, the nonprofit ethics management environment in the Netherlands can best be described as a hybrid system that mixes government oversight and voluntary self-policing.

Asia

Asian values—with an emphasis on personalism, paternalism, and particularism—are often asserted to be different than Western values, which emphasize impersonalism, merit, and rationalism. Thus, the giving of gifts in return for favors, for example, is commonplace in much of Asia. Indeed, bribing public officials for favorable considerations is not uncommon. Consider the small South Pacific island country of Vanuatu, located about three-quarters of the way from Hawaii to Australia. With a tiny population of 205,754, one might expect high ethical standards to prevail. Apparently this is not so, according to Marie-Noelle Ferrieux-Patterson (2003), the president of TI, Vanuatu. She asserts that there is no recognizable moral or ethical code to define right and wrong in the public sphere. Conflicts of interest are especially rampant in Vanuatu because people are linked by strong tribal allegiances and "take actions or decisions to pay back past favors or to store up future favors or rewards, such as jobs or contracts."

The biggest democracy in the world, India, has been wracked by corruption and governmental inaction for decades. A 2005 study involving more than 14,000 Indians across 20 states found that "corruption in public services affecting the day to day needs of citizens is far more serious than is commonly realized" (Transparency International 2005). The worst cases involved the police, judiciary, and land administration. Indeed, the history of corruption in India has been so persistent and severe that, in April 2011, a long-time anticorruption activist, Anna Hazare (aged 74), began a hunger strike to persuade the government to draft new legislation for a *Lokpal* (ombudsman). In August, the police in New Delhi arrested Hazare and detained more than 1,200 protesters who had joined with him in an upsurge of popular outrage. Hazare's arrest fueled even more unrest and brought about peaceful demonstrations throughout India (*New York Times* 2011). The protest movement has prompted the Indian Parliament to agree to "create an independent ombudsman with the staff and powers to investigate and prosecute corruption at every level of Indian governance," asserts Tom Friedman (2011) on a recent visit to India. And, he adds, "A furious debate is now raging here over how to ensure that such an ombudsman doesn't turn into an Indian 'Big Brother,' but some new ombudsman position appears likely to be created."

The situation in all Asian countries is certainly not as dire as suggested by the Indian or Vanuatu experience. There is a strong movement to embrace the rule of law throughout the Pacific, Asia, and Southeast Asia. Many countries are putting into place legal and institutional barriers to combat corruption and promote ethical governance. Let's look at what's happening in China and Japan.

China

Public service ethics in China in the twenty-first century is embedded in a Confucian legacy, one that emphasizes "a system of ethics that focuses on virtues that officials and governments should possess" (Dong, Yang, & Wang 2010). The former Chinese president Jiang Zemin put it this way in 2001: "We should combine the rule of law with the rule of virtue in order to build a lofty . . . ethical foundation for maintaining a good public order and practice" (Jiang 2001). Law and virtue in combination would indeed be a powerful antidote to corruption and unethical behavior. China, with a population of 1.3 billion and more than 6 million persons in the civil service, has long strived to break the grip of corruption. Since 1981, five major anticorruption campaigns have taken place, but the struggle continues. The 2015 CPI published by TI places China 83 among 167 countries—tied with four other countries. In 1995, the first year that TI published the index, China placed next to last among the 41 countries surveyed.

Building organizations of integrity among China's 29 ministries of the central government, 32 provincial governments, 1,735 counties, and 48,000 townships is a substantial challenge. Nonetheless, it is one that officials are committed to meeting. China is a single-party-dominated government. The Communist Party, as represented by the Central Disciplinary Committee, and the government Ministry of Supervision share responsibility for disciplining civil servants who engage in illegal and unethical acts.

The approach taken by China, according to Robert W. Smith (2004), is strikingly similar to that of the United States, although more formalistic; there are fewer opportunities for informal, negotiated settlements of cases in China than in the United States.

Smith (2004) also asserts that China has many anticorruption and ethics entities, perhaps more than any other country (311). Audit bureaus, centers for reporting corruption, offices of general inspection of financial and fiscal discipline, nonofficial corruption monitors, and nonofficial bureaus of anti-graft and bribery have been established at various levels of government. These bodies possess strong investigatory and sanctioning powers and invoke harsh penalties, even death penalties, on offenders. In 1999, 4,322 public servants were found guilty of ethics violations, 58 senior officials among them. In corruption cases, the death penalty "has been exercised with great frequency during the past few decades" (Smith 2004, 314). Fast forward to 2015—more than 138,000 officials were subject to disciplinary action (*China Daily* 2015).

Are China's leaders winning or losing the battle with corruption? The emerging consensus is that China's leaders are well aware of the gravity of the situation, but are up against the powerful forces of state capitalism, opportunity in a high-growth economy, human ambition. and the pursuit of personal wealth in China is in full speed and, along with it, the ugly face of greed has become all too evident.

This is not a pretty picture. President Xi Jinping launched a vigorous anti-corruption campaign shortly after becoming the Communist Party Chairman in 2012 and president in 2013. As he cautioned, the failure to reign in corruption could cause the "collapse of the Party and the downfall of the state." Speaking before the disciplinary arm of the Chinese Communist Party, he said: "Power should be restricted by a cage of regulations." That is, sound disciplinary, prevention, and guarantee mechanisms are needed "to ensure that people do not dare to, are not able to and cannot easily commit corruption" (cited in *China Daily USA* 2013). Both "flies" (low-level functionaries) and "tigers" (high-level officials) should be caged (caught). He further advocated restraint in official excesses. Senior officials agreed, according to the PRC's official news agency Xinhua that there should be "no welcome banner, no red carpet, no floral arrangement or grand receptions for officials' visits" (The Two-Way 2012).

In 2005, after 6 years and 13 drafts, the Chinese national legislature approved a code of conduct law that outlines the rights and obligations of civil servants. China's civil servant law stipulates that civil servants must (Dong et al. 2010, 106):

- abide by the constitution and laws;
- work responsibly and effectively;
- serve the public interest wholeheartedly with oversight from people;
- be devoted to their duties;
- obey their superiors;
- scrupulously follow work ethics;
- work with senses of courtesy, integrity, and honesty.

The law, however, stopped short of requiring top civil servants to disclose their personal financial obligations, which critics assert is a significant omission. "There should be no doubt that the public's right to know should weigh more heavily than officials' right to privacy," noted the author of an article that appeared in the *China Daily* (2005). As this criticism suggests, mainland China's approach to ethics management is limited in scope.

Whistleblowing is encouraged in some Chinese provinces. For example, the Guangdong provincial government began rewarding whistleblowers in 1995 to root out corruption in its ranks. Financial rewards were paid out to 55 whistleblowers totaling 140,000 yuan—at that point in time approximately $18,000 U.S. dollars (Gong 2000). Whistleblowing in China can be done by telephone, letter, or personal visits. Whistleblowing "centers" also exist in many localities; they provide toll-free hotlines for reporting wrongdoing. The effectiveness of whistleblowing in China is difficult to estimate. Ting Gong, who has studied whistleblowing in the Chinese culture, claims that many potential whistleblowers remain silent because corrupt officials "are often protected by an organizational network involving lower and higher ranking officials and sometimes even people in anti-corruption agencies. They collaborate with each other to cover up their corrupt activities" (2000, 1915).

The civil servant law stresses administrative ethics but there are no codes of ethics directed specifically at public administrators (Dong et al. 2010, 106). Ethics management in China remains a reach—with the possible exception of Hong Kong.

Hong Kong

Hong Kong, a crown colony of Great Britain until 1997, is a Special Administrative Region in China with a population of 7 million. Scholars describe the prevailing brand of administrative ethics in Hong Kong as "a curious mix of modern Weberian notions on the one hand and traditional Confucian values on the other" (Lui & Scott 2001, 650). Hong Kong civil servants are expected to be competent administrators who subscribe to the values of neutrality and loyalty to the hierarchy—Weberian notions. Confucian values enter in as well, stressing virtue and rule by scholar-officials; that is, good government depends on the kindness and wisdom of those who rule. This is a form of "rule by man," whereas the Weberian notions emphasize the "rule of law." The result, according to Lui and Scott, is that the Hong Kong bureaucracy "operates as a corporate moral entity" (657). As the authors note,

> The individual official remains a faceless, anonymous bureaucrat, a cog in a machine who has no moral identity outside his place in the collectivity. An "ethical" civil servant is one who abides by the norms of the organization and the orders of his superiors (657).

Hong Kong civil servants do not espouse values "beyond what the bureaucracy has inculcated in them" (653). Although rules and regulations abound, "they are largely designed to facilitate efficient organizational operations rather than to prescribe norms of moral behavior" (653). While Hong Kong has an ombudsman and an anticorruption body, the Independent Commission Against Corruption, they have not been capable of drawing much attention to the significance of administrative ethics (653). Professionally oriented codes of conduct also exist but are not well publicized and remain nearly unenforceable (Lui 1988).

Ethics management in China, as well as in Hong Kong, is at a nascent stage in its development, with much distance to go before a claim to ethical governance can be asserted. At the same time, there is promise of a more professional civil service; the management of civil servants is increasingly merit-oriented, with an emphasis on performance, character, ability, self-discipline, and achievement as the basis for promotion and reward (Zhu 2000). Nonetheless, administrative behavior is dependent on self-control, because there are few significant controls outside the institution of government (Zhu 2000, 1961).

The Nonprofit Sector

The nonprofit sector in post-Mao China is an amalgam of government and nongovernment organizations along with an estimated 8–10 million unregistered social organizations. Approximately 460,000 nonprofit organizations are registered with the Ministry of Civil Affairs. The unregistered social organizations focus mainly on recreation and entertainment and do not have any offices or paid staff. The registered nonprofit organizations vary in the extent to which they are autonomous and voluntary. Indeed, the national associations are mostly government-organized nongovernmental organization. Included in the registered nonprofit organizations are those registered as a for-profit business but operating on nonprofit principles. The reason for this apparent anomaly is that the formal registration process is slow and cumbersome. "There are no formal statistics on how many registered businesses are NPOs [nonprofit organizations] 'in disguise,' but estimates suggest there are probably some hundreds of thousands in all of China" (Guo, Xu, Smith, & Zhang 2012).

Public-interest nonprofit organizations, for example, those advocating environmental causes, are subject to heavy government scrutiny and regulation. China's one-party state discourages advocacy work that could lead to possible civic disruptions that, in turn, challenge the Communist regime. Other government-imposed constraints include strict donor rules that discourage public fundraising. Despite these difficulties, there is a growing realization among government leaders that the nonprofit sector can make a positive contribution to China's civil society and the deliverance of vital public services. As Guo and his colleagues (2012) write: "much progress has been made since the totalitarian period under Mao, but much future change is still needed to achieve a valid civil society."

Japan

Japan has 4.4 million public employees, of which one-quarter work for the national government and the remaining three-quarters work for local governments in prefectures, cities, towns, and villages. Schoolteachers are considered public employees and constitute one-fifth of the public-employee workforce.

Ethics management in Japan is a work in progress. In 1999, the Japanese Diet (the National Assembly) enacted the National Public Service Ethics Law. This law set in motion a limited, but nonetheless important, approach to advancing ethics and integrity in the governance of Japan. Among other things, the law set forth three general ethical principles, established an ethics board in the national administration, created ethics supervisors, called for the promulgation of a National Public Service Officials Ethics Code (Exhibit 7.7), and provided for the introduction of ethics management in local government.

Exhibit 7.7
General Ethical Principles in Japan's
National Public Service Ethics Law

1. Employees shall not give unfair, discriminative treatment to the public . . . and shall always engage in their duties with fairness, recognizing that they are servants of the whole nation and not of any group thereof.
2. Employees shall always distinguish between public and private affairs and shall not use their duties or positions for private gain for themselves or the organization they belong to.
3. Employees shall not take any actions that create public suspicion or distrust against the fairness of public service while performing their duties, such as receiving a gift from entities influenced by their duties.

Source: 72.14.209.104/search?q=cache:J6djWtg-XnQJ:unpan1.un.org/intradoc/groups/public/documents/APCITY/UNPAN019109.pdf+japan%27s+national+public+service+law&hl=en&gl=us&ct=clnk&cd=1&client=firefox-a (accessed June 26, 2006).

The ethics board was placed in the National Personnel Authority (NPA), an independent agency whose mission is to ensure fairness in personnel management and develop personnel management policies. The board comprises a president and four members. The Cabinet appoints all members of the board. A 15-person staff supports the work of the board (Kudo & Maesschalck 2005). The board's central ethics management responsibilities include:

- preparing and revising standards for disciplinary action against employees who violate ethics principles or rules;
- planning and coordinating ethics-training programs within and across ministries and agencies;
- investigating alleged violations of the ethics law and taking disciplinary actions against violations or requesting ministers to do so for violations in their ministry.

The law also called for the appointment of an ethics supervisory officer in each ministry or agency. The ethics supervisory officers are expected to provide guidance and advice to coworkers on ethics issues and to establish management systems that foster ethical behavior consistent with directions provided by the National Public Service Ethics Board.

The ethics code incorporated the three earlier-mentioned ethical principles and added two more standards for ethical behavior:

- Employees shall, in performance of their duties, aim at increasing public interests and exert their utmost efforts.
- Employees shall always behave recognizing that their actions may influence the trust in the public service, even outside of their official hours.

Following the inclusion of these two principles, the code then becomes "very specific and in fact focuses on only one issue of ethics management: Whether or not public servants can accept favours (presents, hospitality, benefits, etc.) from individuals or entities" that could be affected by the actions of government officials during the course of their work (Kudo & Maesschalck 2005, 13–14).

The NPA is responsible for the development of two types of training programs: General training for improvement of administrative duties and professional training that focuses on specific skills and techniques (NPA n.d.b). Ethics sensitivity training is available to junior and mid-level managers, although senior-level administrators are exempted (NPA n.d.a). Training for ethics managers is organized by the ethics board and is typically a "detailed explanation of the Ethics Law and Ethics Code and the discussion of specific cases, including actual case of violations against the Law or the Code" (Kudo & Maesschalck 2005, 15). The board has also published and distributed an ethics handbook that explains ethics regulations.

In summary, ethics management in Japan is narrowly focused on compliance with the ethics law and code, as evidenced by the fact that, among other things, it is directed at curbing expensive wining and dining of senior bureaucrats by those who seek favors from them. The approach taken in Japan parallels closely the legalistic approach taken by many American states, with an emphasis on prescribing and proscribing acceptable behavior.

Nonprofit Sector

The nonprofit sector in Japan is quite different than that in the United States and the United Kingdom. It is much smaller and operates under more governmental restrictions. Of the 90,000 nonprofit organizations, only a very small number (223) have a special tax status—a number that compares unfavorably with the 1.8 million in America and 160,000 in Britain (*Economist* 2011). Government-certified nonprofit organizations are only 10 percent tax-deductible, thus providing little incentive for contributors to donate. Moreover, Japan lacks a tradition of private philanthropy and government officials tend to regard nonprofit organizations as "meddlesome amateurs" (*Economist* 2011). Change is under way, however, stimulated partly by the earthquake and tsunami that lashed northern Japan in March 2011. The cumbersome process for certifying nonprofit organizations for a special tax status that deters many from seeking certification is shifting from the national tax agency to municipal authorities. Thus, some 70 percent of the nonprofit organizations will move into the special tax status that allows tax deductibility of contributions to increase to 50 percent.

Moving Forward

Are nations around the globe embracing ethics management strategies? Yes, but primarily from the perspective of combating corruption through laws, rules, and regulations. The limitations of this approach are straightforward: It reduces ethical behavior to a minimalist conception (don't break the law or regulations) and encourages a narrow, legalistic approach to defining acceptable behavior.

However, there is reason to be optimistic about a change in direction. Kenneth Kernaghan (2003), a Canadian ethics scholar, points to changes in Australia, New Zealand, the United Kingdom, and Canada. He suggests that these countries are moving toward a value-driven approach to strengthening the ethical culture of their governments. He points to the 1999 Vision and Values Statement intended to complement the U.K. Civil Service Code as evidence. In Canada, he notes that the Office of Values and Ethics, which was established in 1999, published a Values and Ethics Code for the Public Service in 2003. In New Zealand, the State Services Commission put the accent on core values in public service with the publication of *Walking the Talk: Making Values Real* (2001). This guide encourages public servants to uphold core values such as trust and integrity in their decisions and actions. Australia, Kernaghan asserts, "is the most notable for its recognition of the central importance of leadership to effective integration of the right values into public service" (2003, 718).

Summing Up

Ethics management worldwide is important. Indeed, the UN has been at the forefront of the global push to embrace ethics and integrity in governance. At a 1997 conference on Public Service in Transition held in Greece, more than 20 countries from Eastern and Central Europe and representatives from international organizations such as the European Commission gathered to discuss what could be done to facilitate "capacity building in the broad areas of governance, public administration and finance" (United Nations 1999, 15). Ranked near the top of the list was the critical importance of probity and integrity. The raising of ethical standards and performance in government requires more than a plan to combat corruption. "Public service ethics encompass a broad and widening range of principles and values . . . objectivity, impartiality, fairness, sensitivity, compassion, responsiveness, accountability, and selfless devotion to duty" (2). More than anything else, the conference participants concluded, "the transition to a free and open society calls for rededication to democratic values, the respect of human rights, and belief in the service of citizens and of the common good" (2).

There is little question that corruption impedes the possibility of a universal public service ethic and, therefore, international agreement on the adoption of effective ethics management strategies. There is another important reason why a universal public service ethic has yet to emerge. It is the belief that cultural and religious norms and traditions strongly influence the ethics of a society. Consequently, what is an acceptable ethical practice or behavior in one society may not be acceptable in another. This culturally deterministic definition of ethics suggests that right and wrong behavior is relative, not universal. Put differently, ethical norms and behaviors are embedded in and defined by a country's culture. But does this mean that there are no values that transcend the cultural diversity of societies? Not necessarily, Gilman and Lewis contend. "There are fundamental values—treated at a high level of abstraction—that are closely associated with democracy, market economy, and professional bureaucracy" (Gilman & Lewis 1996, 518). These fundamental values include respect for human dignity, freedom from oppression, fairness, and truth and honesty in civic life.

Ethics Management Skill Building

Practicum 7.1. The Greater Good

As a contract manager for the U.S. Department of Defense with an office located in Saudi Arabia, your job is to ensure that contracts are managed properly so that the procurement of goods and equipment reaches American military forces in a cost-effective and timely manner. Several months ago, the U.S. Air Force ordered more than $250,000 worth of equipment that is now sitting at the customs agency on the other side of the country. The Saudi customs agency has held up delivery for some unknown reason, perhaps a technicality. The politics of the situation is such that the United States does not want to rock the boat by challenging Saudi officials.

As the contracting officer, you feel obligated to get the equipment released as quickly as possible. To accomplish this you know it is necessary to secure a release document notarized by a high-ranking U.S. official. The document is time-sensitive. To your dismay, you discover that the finance officer dropped the ball and will delay securing the signature by 1 day. To make matters worse, the release document will become null and void if not secured immediately.

Frantic, you make every effort to reach the official whose signature is needed but discover that he is not available. What should you do under these circumstances?

Although you have no authority to do so, you decide to call the legal officer on the western end of the country and request that he redo the whole document. Furthermore, you encourage him to do whatever needs to done, including changing the date. He asks a lot of questions, so you instruct him on how to cut, paste, and copy and reapply the official seal—in essence, you explain how to falsify the document.

You rationalize that you had no choice. The process of getting the equipment out of customs would take several months. Lining up and coordinating all of these agencies would be very time-consuming, and you are not going to let legal requirements blow the deal——"I am not about to blow it on a stupid piece of legally required document."

Furthermore, you muse, there are only two of us who will ever know the document is falsified—myself and the attorney. Your success in securing the release of the equipment motivates the Department of Defense to give you an award. Further reflecting on what you did, you say to yourself—"I did not pay for those goods, U.S. taxpayers did. And if it were my money, I'd have done the same. If I had not been able to secure the release of the equipment, it was going to go into the country's local market. They were not going to return it to the vendor."

Musing further,

> Every situation violates some person's ethics, so, whose do we choose? And at what point do we as administrators determine that our ethics are above that of another employee's? There are some things we say we'll never do—knowingly falsifying documents for one.

But, I'm thinking ... you know, there may be a situation in which doing that particular thing would be more ethical than not doing it.

Discussion Questions

1. Do you think it is ever ethical to falsify a document?
2. Did falsifying the document to secure the release of U.S. Air Force equipment justify the act?
3. Are there career risks for falsifying a document?

Practicum 7.2. Religious Expression in the Workplace

You are the chief of the State Division of Vehicular Licensing with 1,250 employees located at six district offices. The director of District 2 approaches you about a thorny problem—what to do about providing employees who are Muslims with a suitable time of the day to worship. The problem began on October 30, when the state shifted from Central Daylight Saving Time to Central Standard Time. As it turns out, the "fallback" of the clock pulled the Muslim sunset prayer back into the work hours.

A group of Muslim workers requested that the district office allow them to conduct their sunset prayer at 5 p.m. The district office closes at 6 p.m. The group said that they would be willing to work from 6 p.m. to 7 p.m. to make up for the time lost.

The director is unsure what other districts have done and does not know if state law requires public agencies to accommodate employees' religious beliefs. It is, of course, clear to all that public agencies cannot promote religious beliefs and practices, but this is not quite the same thing.

As the division chief, you inform the director that other district offices have not faced this issue before. Moreover, state law is reasonably clear—employers (public and private) must accommodate employees' religious beliefs as long as the requests are reasonable and do not create a hardship for the agency.

Discussion Questions

1. Is the request by the workers reasonable?
2. Would shifting the sunset prayer hour to 5 p.m. create a hardship for the District Office of Vehicular Licensing? (Remember that the primary work of the District Office is to issue licenses to the public on a first-come, first-served basis.)

3. Would agreeing to the request be viewed as favoritism toward one group of employees? If so, would this create morale problems?
4. What recommendation would you, as division chief, make to the district director?

8

Ethical Governance in the Twenty-first Century

Most of the things worth doing in the world had been declared impossible before they were done.

—Justice Louis Brandeis (2011)

What emerging issues and challenges should we focus on to ensure that ethical governance moves forward, not backward, in the twenty-first century? There are many. Among them are privatization, the Information Age, the global pursuit of economic well-being and democratic governance, and ethics education. The future, it so often seems, is here with the historic boundary between public and private sectors a vast blur. Equally blurred is the timeline between the past, present, and future. The time warp of cyberspace and instantaneous worldwide communication has all but collapsed our calendars. In this concluding chapter, we take a close look at the challenges that must be overcome to foster ethical governance.[1]

> *Ethical governance* is an awareness and commitment to high ethical standards by those who govern and all who enter the governance arena, including institutions and processes that are fair and just.

The Privatization Challenge

The privatization of public services and facilities is in full force worldwide. Governments of all sizes and descriptions are redefining their roles and responsibilities in providing and delivering public services. Cities, counties, states, and the U.S. government are entering into new relationships with private-sector organizations—profit and nonprofit—to "create a government that works better and costs less," to borrow the title of the Report of the National Performance Review (1993). In some instances, the result has been load shedding—disengaging entirely as a governmental service provider. In other instances, government contracting with a private profit-making firm or a non-profit organization to deliver public services has been the preferred modus operandi.[2]

When David Osborne and Ted Gaebler issued their clarion call in *Reinventing Government: How the Entrepreneurial Spirit Is Transforming the Public Sector* (1992), the response was nearly instantaneous and widespread. The reinventors endorsed privatization and called for public managers to be entrepreneurial in leading their agencies. Precious little was uttered about what privatization or entrepreneurialism might mean for ethical management. Indeed, there is no mention of ethics in their book. Perhaps Osborne and Gaebler believed there is little to be concerned about, since they are not calling for managers to engage in illegal activities—merely to manage differently within the law.

Laura Abbott (2006), who worked for 26 years as a uniformed officer of the U.S. Public Health Service in the Department of Health and Human Services, describes her experience with contractors in this way:

> It has been frustrating because even if the legal means are available to force contractors to meet their deliverables, at least in my department, the will to enforce them is seriously impaired or perhaps intentionally ignored. As government has turned to greater and greater use of contractors, supposedly for support functions, the chain of accountability and sense of common purpose has been much diminished.

H. George Frederickson (1997, 194) pulls no punches in asserting that the privatization movement will eventually collapse or, at a minimum, retreat on the heels of greed and corruption amid renewed "calls for administrative competence in government." Contracting in particular, Frederickson (193) reminds us, has "always made a tempting environment for kickbacks and fraud. Doesn't anyone remember why Spiro Agnew resigned as vice president?" Frederickson's indictment is unflinching. "As more privately inclined people are appointed to governmental positions and as more governmental services are based on the enterprise model," the more likely it is that we will experience corruption and unethical behavior (180).

Meeting the Privatization Challenge

Cuyahoga County (Cleveland, Ohio) Executive Ed FitzGerald challenged 175 construction industry contractors that to win county business they would need to "engage in the highest ethical standards; nothing less will be tolerated." He also told contractors that to work for Cuyahoga County, they must join the Northeast Ohio Business Ethics Coalition, sign a membership pledge to abide by the new county ethics ordinance, and promote a high ethical standard throughout their businesses (J. Miller 2011).

Linda deLeon takes a more optimistic view of ethics, privatization, and public management entrepreneurship. She argues that "public entrepreneurship can be, and at its best is, ethical" (1996, 496). She acknowledges, however, that the values commonly associated with successful private-sector entrepreneurs—egotism, selfishness, waywardness, domination, and opportunism—if not adequately constrained or checked may result in norms antithetical to the public interest. Self-serving, profit-seeking, calculating public entrepreneurial managers may be able, if successful, to spot opportunities and marshal resources to produce innovation, but the trade-off may be a diminished ethical environment. Nonetheless, deLeon believes that ethical entrepreneurship is possible and should be encouraged in public organizations.

But what evidence do we have that privatization or reinvention or entrepreneurialism threatens ethical management in government or, at worst, evokes corrupt and unethical behavior? Some evidence is supplied by Cohen and Eimicke (1999), who have investigated three cases of public entrepreneurship—the Orange County, California, financial bankruptcy case resulting from a $1.6 billion loss; a risky hotel partnership project in Visalia, California; and the successful privatization of Indianapolis's wastewater-treatment plants.

The Orange County, California, case is an example of entrepreneurship gone amok ethically, crossing over into the realm of the illegal. Robert Citron, the county treasurer, invested locally pooled funds in fiscal instruments known as derivatives that produced spectacular financial gains until interest rates began to rise. When this happened, the financial bottom fell out and eventually forced the treasurer out of office and Orange County into bankruptcy in 1994. Two years later, Mr. Citron was sentenced to 1 year in jail and fined $100,000.

The Visalia case is more problematic as an ethics failure or success story. What is clear is that the city took risks with taxpayer dollars. Its partnership with the Radisson hotel chain to build and operate a hotel on city-owned property floundered, which ultimately forced the city into buying the hotel and assuming its debts.

In Indianapolis, the city often cited as the epicenter of municipal privatization, the former mayor Stephen Goldsmith set about privatizing more than 40 city services in the early 1990s. Among those services were the wastewater-treatment plants. Although the city's plants were considered efficient, the city administration decided to contract out the services. The result was that a firm based in France with 51 percent ownership by the local Indianapolis Water Company won the contract and was able to achieve significant financial savings. Based upon their examination of the experiences of these three cases, authors Cohen and Eimicke conclude that public entrepreneurship can be ethical, but that a large measure of care, caution, and competence should be exercised.

As a case in point, Richard K. Ghere (1996) describes the arguable, if not unethical, results of a partnership forged between a metropolitan county in a midwestern state and a local chamber of commerce. The county sought to promote tourism, attract convention business, and develop a regional economic development strategy that would lure international business. A 3 percent hotel/motel bed tax was earmarked for this purpose, and the local chamber of commerce was contracted to provide these services. Suffice it to say that chamber officials were delighted with this arrangement and were energetic partners—perhaps too energetic. As time passed, a number of "irregularities" began to accrue. These included noncompetitive awards made to vendors who had family connections with chamber officials, falsification of expense reports and convention business activities, golf and dinner outings for county commissioners paid for by the chamber, and questionable international travel provided by the chamber for county officials. Ghere's analysis does not detail the extent to which the chamber's practices may have permeated county government as a whole, but it is clear that the relationship or partnership at the top did little to foster an ethical climate. Indeed, this case points out how the privatization of a public function amounted to the diminishment, if not privatization, of ethical behavior ordinarily expected of public officials. The contract, of course, was the vehicle for this transformation.

Other stories of privatization challenges to ethical governance can be found in Florida. The next sections illustrate three of these stories.

Use and Abuse of Insider Information

Another contractual ethical issue is the use and abuse of insider information. Consider the state of Florida, which, under the Republican governor Jeb Bush (1998–2006), moved full force into the privatization of Florida government. Insider information was apparently used by a private firm in securing a $126 million state technology contract. An investigation by the Florida Department of Law Enforcement concluded that the company had access to insider information that helped it easily win the contract over 19 competitors. Here's what happened: A company employee who was hired as a consultant also served as the de facto chief of staff for the State Technology Office, the granting agency. An editorial in the *St. Petersburg Times* (2005) described the situation as "a curious work environment, one in which government employees and those hired under contract were virtually indistinguishable." The Florida Department of Law Enforcement and the state attorney, despite having misgivings about this "curious work environment," decided they lacked sufficient evidence to criminally prosecute the company.

One unexpected outcome, however, was the finding that Florida's ethics laws do not apply to private-sector employees when they have acted in a state agency executive capacity. This "finding" prompted a 2010 statewide grand jury to call for an expansion of the definition of "public servant" to include individuals who work for any entity "authorized by law or contract to perform a governmental function or provide a governmental service" (State of Florida 2010, 17). The 2011 Florida legislature did not act on this recommendation.

Private Contracting for Prison Management

In 2008, 37 American states, Florida among them, awarded contracts to private profit-making firms to operate prisons. The state had contracted with private firms back in 1993 to manage its prison system. Florida law created the eight-member Correctional Privatization Commission (CPC) to oversee the contractors who managed five prisons at a cost of $106.4 million a year. A decade later, however, dissatisfaction with the lack of management oversight by the commission had reached the point where the Florida legislature said "enough." In 2005, the Florida legislature terminated the CPC and transferred all of its powers and duties to the Florida Department of Management Services. What happened?

A review by the Florida Office of the Inspector General (2005) of the financial transactions of the CPC uncovered sordid details about this particular form of private–public cooperation. It seems as if the two for-profit prison companies overbilled the state by $12.7 million during this period (2001–2004). The commission paid the two contractors—Corrections Corporations of America and the GEO Group—for guards that did not exist at the prisons. The overbilled funds were then remitted back to the CPC's Grants and Donations Trust Fund to enable the CPC to pay staff salaries. As it turns out, the legislature eliminated the commission's budget in 2001, but not the commission itself. Thus, the commission found a creative, entrepreneurial way to keep its ten-member staff employed. Is it any wonder that the CPC failed at overseeing the contractors?

Privatizing Home Building Reviews and Inspections

The privatization of home building plan reviews and inspections to ensure that codes are met illustrates another side to public–private cooperation in Florida. Between 2000 and 2002, many communities were experiencing a significant building boom. Consequently, the building departments of local governments were not able to process permits and conduct inspections in a manner deemed timely by the building industry. Some building departments took up to 6 weeks or more to turn around a building permit. Thus, the Florida legislature came to the rescue. In 2002, the legislature enacted the Private Provider Law (FS 553.791), enabling a building owner to use a private provider to satisfy building code compliance plans and carry out inspections for the structural, mechanical, electrical, and plumbing components of a building. The law required the builder to notify the local government of the owner's intent to use a private provider. The local building official then issued the requested permit or provided written notice to the permit applicant identifying the specific plan features that did not comply with the code within 30 business days. If the local building official did not provide a written notice of the plan's deficiencies within the 30-day period, the permit application would be deemed a matter of law and the permit would be issued by the local building official on the next business day.

The Private Provider Law has resulted in a new industry, with several engineering firms hiring plan reviewers and inspectors who, by law, must be state-certified and licensed. The president of Capri Engineering, Gary H. Elzweig, whose firm has ten offices throughout Florida, asserts that:

> The private provider law came along at the right time. It's an amazing win-win situation. The private sector takes on the responsibility of processing compliance paperwork in a timely manner while freeing up municipal resources that can be better used for more important services such as hurricane rehabilitation.

(Schweers 2005)

Others are not so sure, describing the situation as the classic "fox in the hen house." One county building official put it this way: "They are a for-profit business. Our duty is to serve the public—they're not doing this as a public service. We are here to protect the public in that sense" (Schweers 2005). The verdict is still out regarding how successful the cooperation will be between the corps of private providers and local government building departments. Time will tell.

These Florida experiences illustrate the challenging nature that the privatization movement poses for public officials who want to embrace sound ethical management practices. Frederickson (1997, 171) notes, "It is no small irony that government is moving in the direction of privatization at the same time that there is a rising concern for governmental ethics."

Nonprofits and Privatization

The astounding growth of nonprofits in the United States as privatized alternative service providers has also been accompanied by the lack of transparency in many instances. As discussed in Chapter 6, nonprofits are not bound by the same disclosure requirements that constrain government agencies. The charter school experiences suggest that all too often the lack of disclosure is a serious problem compounded by inadequate state oversight of charter schools. In Texas, for example, with nine people assigned by the Texas Education Agency to oversee more than 500 charter school campuses, charter schools would seem to have much discretion in carrying out their work. Consider the case of the Cosmos Foundation, a nonprofit charter school operator founded by a group of Turkish businessmen and professors. The foundation, operating under the name of Harmony Schools, oversees 33 Texas schools (k–12) that receive more than $100 million a year in taxpayer funds. The "Turkish schools," as they are often called, claim they "do not play favorites in awarding contracts but Turkish-owned companies have in fact been the low bidders" (Saul 2011). Then there is the issue of whether the schools use taxpayer dollars to benefit a moderate brand of Islam called the Gülen movement, named after a charismatic Turkey scholar and preacher, Fethullah Gülen. The transnational movement is active in education in more than 180 countries. Do Harmony Schools officials teach religion or promote Gülen teachings and Turkish culture? They claim to not do so but who really knows?

As Robert Wechsler (2015) plainly puts it, "One lesson that should become clear is that when government services are privatized and there is little oversight or transparency, unethical behavior is inevitable."

Information (R)Age Challenges

The privatization "rage" is occurring at a time that coincides with another "rage"—the information "rage." Americans and citizens worldwide are acquiring PCs, tablets such as the iPad, e-readers like the Nook and Kindle, and MP3 players. The language of the Internet, the World Wide Web, browsers, video sharing, search engines, e-mail, listservs, blogs, chat rooms, and more has become commonplace vocabulary. Today's workplace, whether in the central office, field office, or home office, is an increasingly high-tech, information-driven workplace.[3]

Governments throughout the United States have climbed on to the Information Highway en masse. The technical aspects of accessing the Internet pale alongside the attempt to understand and abate the undesirable, and sometimes unethical, consequences that this technology can have on group life in public agencies. A study of the negative effects of e-mail on social life in the corporate workplace found that some effects, such as making the workplace less personal, were a product of two factors—the technology itself (for example, the depersonalization of social relations due to the absence of face-to-face interaction) and intentional choices by users or employees "to avoid unwanted social interactions" (Markus 1994, 119). In other words, technology is not singularly responsible for "negative" social effects in the workplace. Employees can and do make intentional choices in deciding with whom they wish to communicate. Managers committed to promoting a strong ethical climate are likely to find this situation especially difficult, particularly in light of our rudimentary knowledge of such behavior.

Another ethical challenge facing managers is implementing and monitoring Internet usage practices. These include surfing the web on agency time for personal pleasure, downloading or viewing obscene material, advertising or soliciting for personal gain, making political statements, posting or downloading inflammatory racial or sexual material, waging or selling chances, and using pseudo names when transmitting electronic messages. What can be done to discourage these practices? One approach is to adopt Internet Acceptable Use policies. But what if these policies do not work and abuse still occurs? Ethics management leaders may then have to take further steps. This has happened in the City of Tampa, Florida, where four city parking division employees were fired after sending e-mails with discriminatory references to sex, race, and ethnicity. Human resources (HR) director Sarah Lang said that "their e-mails were specifically directed at specific employees in a pattern of e-mails that lent themselves to sexual harassment" (Varian 2005). A follow-up investigation of employees' work habits found that other city workers—44, in fact—had sent e-mails that violated the city's business-only e-mail policy. Disciplinary letters were sent to these individuals with a copy placed in their personnel file. To promote the city's zero-tolerance Internet-abuse policy, the HR director sent letters to all personnel reminding them that it is against the rules to send personal e-mails from city-owned computers. Additionally, when employees now sign on to their computers, they are greeted with an on-screen message requiring them to acknowledge the city rule banning the personal use of e-mail.

There is awareness that the Internet can be a vital gateway to innovative, responsive government. Thus, there is an incentive to provide employees access to, and encourage experimentation with, the vast storehouse of data and information on the World Wide Web.

Many cities and counties have set up community blogs to share information and engage the citizenry. Citrus County, Florida (2011), for example, has a blog primarily to disseminate news and information. Blogs promote transparency and, if managed responsibly, can aid in building trust in government (Hillsborough County, Florida 2011). City managers are also blogging on their own initiative. (See listing of city manager blogs at http://mastersinpubli cadministration.com/the-50-best-city-manager-blogs-sites-and-more.)

Blog Disclaimer

By commenting in this forum, you give Hillsborough County the right to reproduce, distribute, publish, display, edit, modify, and create derivative works from, and otherwise use, your submission for any purpose in any form and on any media. Comments to this blog are moderated. To ensure your comments are posted, they should be made in a spirit of cooperation and mutual respect and in a manner to help resolve the issue presented, no matter which side of the issue you are on. Comments that include the following will not be posted:

- Advertisements or solicitations
- Repeated instances of the same post (spam)
- Malicious links
- Material that infringes on the rights of any third party, including intellectual property, privacy or publicity rights
- Personal attacks against others, including Commissioners or staff members

- Sensitive materials including, but not limited to: illegal activities, gambling, sexually explicit materials, weapons, drugs, violence, inappropriate language, racial, discriminatory comments, defamatory statements, partisan political positions, and religious positions

Source: http://www.hillsboroughcounty.org/index.aspx?NID=2955 (retrieved November 17, 2015)

Other ethical, perhaps legal, issues go beyond citizen and employee access and use of the Internet and have to do with the posture of government itself. Online governments and their leaders must position themselves to promote democratic practices such as citizen access to public information while at the same time ensuring that sensitive information is protected. It is one thing to post data about crime rates or AIDS statistics and another to allow access to names or addresses of victims. Likewise, the question might be asked: Is a public service being provided when the county property appraiser's office creates a searchable database containing property values and locations? Or is this merely making it easier for criminals to employ the same technology to target would-be victims?

Many local governments facing lean budget years might be encouraged to adopt entrepreneurial practices such as selling advertising space on their home page or endorsing a commercial product as the official product of their government. Are these practices ethical? Legal? The commercialization of the Internet is well under way. But how far should we go in commercializing government?

Finally, there is the matter of electronic communication between and among public officials and citizens. Few (small *d*) democrats would object to e-mail replacing fax messages between citizens and officials, but it may be an entirely different matter when the communication path is between officeholders. Will the Information Age, especially in its electronic form, effectively dismantle government in the sunshine? Or, will officials exercise due care, diligence, and caution before jumping on the keyboard and sending an important message to colleagues or top managers?

The Winds of Globalization[4]

A popular saying in the 1970s was that "small is beautiful," a reaction to big government, big corporations, and big policy failures in America.

Four decades later, it can truly be said that small is beautiful globally. With the advent of high-powered technology, instant communication transmissions, endless choice through direct satellite TV programming, and shrinking travel distances and time, the world has never been so small. Elected and appointed officials in places as far-flung as Beijing, Lima, Moscow, Cairo, Johannesburg, London, and Brisbane are instantly aware of the latest political and economic developments in Washington, D.C., New York, Chicago, Sacramento, and Tallahassee.

The winds of globalization blew with powerful market-driven force during much of the 1990s. First thought to be only an *economic* force, as countries such as China, Russia, and Vietnam embraced market-based reforms, globalization began to expand its reach as a *social* and *political* agent of change with increasing democratization and engagement in increasingly transparent policy making. The rule of law became more than a mantra; it became a means through which political leaders envisioned the possibility of seismic shifts in improving their country's well-being and, in some instances, lifting their people out of poverty.

Globalization writ large began to touch Americans as well. Appointed and elected officials found themselves scrambling to connect their communities with exciting opportunities abroad. Sister-city programs sprang up, along with international trade delegations from cities, counties, and states traveling far and wide to explore the new world order, as it was sometimes labeled. In the second decade of the twenty-first century, there is scarcely a large city or county that does not have an international affairs office.

Managers soon learned that it was important for them and their organizations to "think globally." This perspective is reinforced by professional associations such as the International City/County Management Association (ICMA) and the American Society for Public Administration (ASPA). Both associations have launched initiatives that emphasize international affairs. Thus, managers are increasingly confronted by the norms and ways of different cultures. This has been especially challenging in situations where the cultures vary regarding what is and is not ethical. Giving and receiving gifts among public officeholders in Asian cultures, for example, is both commonplace and perfectly acceptable. Similar practices in the United States are viewed with suspicion, and many cities and counties have zero-gift policies.

These differences continue to be debated, with one argument calling for a global ethic—a framework for defining right and wrong that knows no social, economic, or political borders. Easier said than done? No question about it. Still, the search for a global ethic is meritorious.

Public Administration Ethics Education Challenges

Education for professional public administrators in the United States and some countries abroad is carried out primarily through nearly 300 member-institutions of higher education that provide graduate or undergraduate study in public affairs and administration. As of September 1, 2015, 192 graduate programs at 178 schools (including one each in China, Egypt, and the Republic of Korea) were accredited by the Network of Schools of Public Policy, Affairs, and Administration (NASPAA).[5] The Masters of Public Affairs/policy/administration (MPA) degree is increasingly viewed by the practitioner community as the degree of preference. The inclusion of professional ethics in the course of study adds considerable value to the MPA.

The teaching of ethics is a multifaceted and often controversial enterprise. It is multifaceted because the field of public administration ranges broadly within and across organizations, nations, and cultures. It is controversial because there is disagreement in the field of ethics on what to teach and how to teach it. Indeed, some persons believe that ethics cannot be taught in a traditional class or course context. Rather, the best that can be hoped for is to teach *about* ethics. Still, there is a widespread view among practicing administrators and educators that an ethical public service is essential to a well-functioning democracy. Accordingly, teaching ethics to men and women who occupy positions of public trust should and must be pursued regardless of the uncertain outcomes.

There are three approaches to teaching ethics: Sensitivity and awareness, moral reasoning, and leadership and exemplar modeling.

Sensitivity and Awareness Teaching

A sensitivity and awareness approach to the teaching of ethics has moved along two primary paths. The first path is legalistic and is often reflected in the advice and instruction provided by state ethics commissions to state and local public employees and elected officials. This approach puts the accent on the "do's and don'ts" of state ethics laws. These laws, as noted in Chapter 5, emphasize conflicts of interest, financial disclosure, whistleblowing protection, and confidentiality of information. Using a "how to stay out of trouble" approach brings both good news and bad news. The bad news is that this approach often reduces acceptable behavior to the lowest level of "if it's not illegal, it's OK!"—which, as John Rohr reminds us in *Ethics for Bureaucrats: An Essay on Law and Values* (1978), is the "low road" to public service ethics. The good news is it sets down benchmark behaviors that all members of an organization can understand, even if they do not always follow suit.

The second path is semi-legalistic, with a focus on professional codes of ethics or agency rules of acceptable behavior. At the professional association level, for example, nearly every public service group has a code of ethics that its members are expected to support. Two associations are illustrative in this regard—the ASPA and the ICMA.

ASPA is an 8,000-member organization consisting primarily of educators, students, and public employees drawn from local, state, and federal agencies and members of nonprofit associations. The ASPA code, first adopted in 1984, identifies five key principles: (1) serve the public interest; (2) respect the Constitution and the law; (3) demonstrate personal integrity; (4) promote ethical organizations; and (5) strive for professional excellence (ASPA 2006). Members who violate the code can be expelled from ASPA. The code was revised in 2013 to include the above principles along with three additional principles: Promote democratic participation, strengthen social equity, and fully inform and advise elected and appointed officials and governing board members and staff members (ASPA 2013). Practices and guidelines to promote the code were also adopted. Enforcement guidelines are under consideration.

The ICMA is a 7,500-member organization consisting primarily of practicing public managers in cities and counties in the United States and abroad (for example, Ireland and Australia). The ICMA code dates to 1924 and provides specific guidance on acceptable and unacceptable behaviors for local-government managers. For example, it is deemed unethical for a city manager to leave her management post with less than 2 years of service, unless there are extenuating circumstances such as severe personal (medical/mental/financial) problems. It is also viewed as unethical for a city manager to endorse a commercial product that a vendor might sell to a local government (ICMA 1998). The ICMA actively enforces the code with a half-dozen or more members sanctioned nearly every year for violations (see, for example, ICMA 2010).

The teaching of ethics based on codes or administrative rules of behavior stresses the contents of the codes or the rules themselves, which unfortunately, can become ends in themselves. The teaching of codes and rules is often conducted by personnel within a governmental agency, management consultants, and college and university instructors, especially those in graduate-degree-granting programs that prepare men and women for public service careers.

Moral Reasoning

A second approach to teaching ethics in public administration is moral reasoning. The effort here presumes that one can learn to reason through a difficult moral or ethical dilemma. Learning how to act ethically in public service is just that—a learning process, which when a real-world ethical dilemma arises can be applied with desirable outcomes. The reasoning process puts the accent on decision making through ethical reflection based on the interplay of moral rules, ethical principles, self-appraisal, and justification. At the heart of this exercise is what Cooper (2006a) calls exercising one's moral imagination to sort through right or wrong decision outcomes.

Another proponent of teaching ethical decision making is Carol W. Lewis who, in *The Ethics Challenge in Public Service: A Problem-Solving Guide* (1991) and a later edition with Stuart C. Gilman (2012), presents the reader with a problem-solving guide. Her guide engages the learner with real and hypothetical decision-making scenarios, self-assessment tools, and questions that stimulate ethical reflection. She contends that neither the "low" road of compliance nor the "high" road of integrity is a realistic guide for navigating the often stormy political and bureaucratic environments of public service. Rather, it is necessary to develop a two-pronged, systematic strategy that incorporates the path of compliance with formal standards and the path of individual integrity. She labels this approach as the "fusion route" to meeting the ethics challenge in public service (Lewis 1991).

How do we learn to engage in moral reasoning? We learn how to reason and make ethical decisions by practicing; learners can engage themselves with decision dilemmas and work through them. A teacher of ethics can use scenarios and small-group processes to help learners practice ethical decision making and acquire skill in doing so. Menzel (2010) offers many scenarios that, with hands-on practice, can help an individual become an ethically competent leader and builder of organizations of integrity.

This methodology has much in common with virtue ethics espoused by Aristotle in the age of antiquity. Aristotle believed that one could acquire a virtue only by engaging in virtuous acts. But, he was wise to add, one does not acquire a virtue by engaging in foolhardy acts. Jumping into a lion's cage to acquire the virtue of courage is not what he had in mind! Moreover, it is the pursuit of virtue—a lifelong effort—that defines the virtuous person.

Leadership and Exemplar Modeling

A third way to teach ethics centers on leadership and exemplars in public service. This approach has had a time-honored tradition in the U.S. military academies at West Point and Annapolis's Stockdale Center for Ethical Leadership and is increasingly reflected in the curricula of graduate schools that award the MPA degree. A handful of schools (for example, the Lyndon B. Johnson School of Public Affairs at the University of Texas) have established a Center for Ethical Leadership that is designed to attract men and women with a strong desire for leadership responsibilities (see the Center's web site at www.utexas.edu/lbj/research/leadership).

Leading with Integrity

To paraphrase Martin Luther King, Jr., "The ultimate measure of a leader is not where they stand in moments of comfort and convenience, but where they stand at times of challenge and controversy." For me, that requires defining a vision and goals others can embrace. Achieving that vision with integrity of leadership requires optimism, strong ethical behavior, personal accountability, decisive decision making when needed, and empathetic patience.

>   —Martin P. Black,
>   AICP, ICMA-CM, former city manager, Venice, Florida
>   and General Manager and Chair of the West Villages
>   Improvement District (Black 2011)

The study of leadership, of course, is wide-reaching, encompassing commercial, political, and educational sectors. Interestingly, the study and teaching of administrative leadership have been problematic, as Larry Terry notes in *Leadership of Public Bureaucracies* (1995). Several factors have contributed to this situation—the complexity of modern public organizations, including the growing interdependency of private- and public-sector organizations; the antibureaucratic ethos that permeates American politics; and the challenge of distinguishing administrative leadership from political leadership. New administrative leadership paths, however, are being forged by scholars such as Monty Van Wart, who offers "the competencies that organizational leaders at all levels need" (2005, xiii). More recently, Van Wart (2011) draws our attention to the rise of the postmodern perspective in leadership studies, citing topics such as discourse theory, complexity and relational theory, integral leadership studies, and network and collaboration theory.

Effectiveness of Ethics Education[6]

What can be said about the effectiveness of ethics education in graduate public affairs and administration programs? Are professional schools and programs preparing public and nonprofit administrators to be effective ethics managers? Are they making a difference? These are difficult questions to answer. There is no question that ethics educators believe they are making a difference (Menzel 1997). Survey data collected from 78 of the member schools of the Network of Schools of Public Affairs and Administration offering an ethics course showed that seven out of ten believe students find the subject matter valuable. A smaller percentage (67 percent) said they believe that students who receive ethics instruction become more ethically sensitive. Finally, one out of every two respondents asserts that, perhaps most importantly, students use the ethical knowledge gained in their program of study to resolve ethical dilemmas.

These findings are encouraging for those who believe that ethics education is important and does make a difference in the lives of practitioners. But impressions, of course, can be wrong. Moreover, since many educators may bring to their task a professional advocacy (which is presumably neither a brand of moral indoctrination nor ethical zealotry), a self-fulfilling prophecy may be at work; ethics educators may want to believe that they are making a difference and are therefore inclined to report such on a survey. A more definitive measure of ethics education outcomes is necessary.

Concern about the effectiveness of public management education prompted NASPAA to revisit its accreditation standards in 2006. Three years later, in 2009, new competency-driven standards were approved. NASPAA-accredited programs are now expected to assess student competencies and deliver educational experiences that ensure responsible and effective performance in public management.

Nonprofit Ethics Education Challenges

The challenges facing nonprofit ethics education are not altogether different from those confronting public management education. Yet, there is one difference that is noteworthy. Ethics education, especially at the university graduate level, suffers from an identity problem that also bedevils the nonprofit field. That is, should nonprofit education (ethics) be merely an extension of public administration? Business administration? Or should it be a stand-alone enterprise? A recent survey by Brudney and Martinez (2010) of teaching administrative ethics in nonprofit management found that ethics pedagogy is highly fragmented, a finding that mirrors the field at large. In other words, there is little consensus about what should be taught or how it should be taught. Insofar as nonprofit management is treated as a subfield of administrative management, ethics education and standards are defined by the host field. The Brudney and Martinez survey of 80 responding academic programs that offer masters degrees, certificates, or concentrations in non-profit management found that, while all respondents indicated their courses were devoted to nonprofit ethics, the syllabi generally did not distinguish between administrative ethics generally and nonprofit ethics specifically.

These findings, along with others concerning the identity issue, beg the question: Is ethics education languishing in nonprofit studies? Moreover, what might the state of ethics management education be? This latter question takes on even more significance given the Brudney and Martinez survey results that "the paramount objective of ethics coursework was to emphasize the centrality of personal responsibility and instill in students a sense of the duties they will face when working in a nonprofit organization" (192). This approach to nonprofit ethics education, however laudable, is short-sighted.

The "New" Ethics[7]

The proliferation of ethics courses is an important development in what Derek Bok (1990) calls teaching the "new" ethics. The applied ethics course, he contends, "does not seek to convey a set of moral truths but tries to encourage students to think carefully about complex moral issues" (73). He adds,

> The principal aim of the course is not to impart right answers but to make students more perceptive in detecting ethical problems when they arise, better acquainted with the best moral thought that has accumulated through the ages, and more equipped to reason about the ethical issues they will face in their own personal and professional lives (73).

The "new" ethics should also include a focus on teaching future public administrators how to be effective ethics managers. There is little evidence that professional education in public administration even touches on this subject, although one is hopeful that the shift in NASPAA standards, noted above, will make a difference. The irony, of course, is that the leaders of public organizations are engaged in ethics management day in and day out. The present approach is learning by the "seat of your pants." Educators and NASPAA have much to do in cultivating men and women to be ethics managers and leaders who know how to build organizations of integrity. There is no "one best way" to teach or acquire ethics, nor is there one best way to educate ethics managers. NASPAA's (2008) call for programs to "enhance the student's values, knowledge, and skills to act ethically and effectively . . . in the management of public and, as appropriate, third sector organizations" cannot be contested. At the same time, there is evidence that other factors such as the ethical environment of the educational program are at work and must be taken into account in order to obtain a more complete understanding of ethics education.

More than two decades ago, the Hastings Center released a report calling for the higher educational community to act with greater vigor and conviction in placing ethics and values in campus curricula. Educators should not lose sight of their message. The report asserted that we cannot afford, wittingly or unwittingly, to be a partner in producing "a new generation of leaders who are ethically illiterate at best or dangerously adrift and morally misguided at worse" (Jennings, Nelson, & Parens 1994, 2).

A New Generation of Leaders

The teaching of ethics in public administration has a promising future, but much more effort is needed, especially in educating men and women to be effective in leading and building organizations of integrity. The findings reported by Paul C. Light in *The New Public Service* (1999) are revealing and disturbing. Light's study focused on the graduates of the nation's leading public policy and administration programs (including those at Syracuse, Kansas, University of Southern California, University of Michigan, and Harvard). He reports that these graduates, regardless of their current sector of employment (government, nonprofit, private), placed "maintaining ethical standards" at the top of the list of skills considered very important for success in their current job. At the same time, when asked if their school was helpful in teaching skills that would enable them to maintain ethical standards, most rated their education as insufficient. In fact, Light reports that this gap between how helpful a school is in teaching ethics and how important ethics is to one's job success was the largest of all skills listed. (The list included such important skills as "budgeting and public finance," "doing policy analysis," "managing motivation and change," and "managing conflict.")

NASPAA, through its Commission on Peer Review and Accreditation, incorporated language in its previous accreditation standards (4.21) that graduates should be able "to act ethically." Standard 4.21 encouraged schools to put into place ethics courses or otherwise demonstrate that they are teaching ethics across the curriculum (NASPAA 2008). The 2009 restructured standards no longer identify "to act ethically" as a standard. Rather, NASPAA calls for programs seeking accreditation review to meet four preconditions, one of which is a commitment to public service values. NASPAA's "good" intentions to broaden the framework for considering public service values do raise questions about the emphasis placed on ethics education in preparing men and women to lead with integrity.

Public Service Values . . . include pursuing the public interest with accountability and transparency; serving professionally with competence, efficiency, and objectivity; acting ethically so as to uphold the public trust; and demonstrating respect, equity, and fairness in dealings with citizens and fellow public servants.

(NASPAA 2009)

Four years before it restructured its standards, however, NASPAA took a step toward encouraging schools to emphasize ethics with its adoption in 2005 of a Member Code of Good Practice. The code admonishes all programs holding membership in NASPAA—not just those accredited—to integrate "ethics into the curriculum and all aspects of program operation, and expects students and faculty to exhibit the highest ethical standards in their teaching, research, and service" (NASPAA 2005). Perhaps the next significant step that NASPAA should take is to require all accredited programs to place an ethics course in the core curriculum. Dennis F. Thompson (1992, 255) remarked, "From the truth that ethics is mainly instrumental, it does not follow, as many critics seem to think, that ethics is always less important than other issues." In other words, acquiring the ability to "to act ethically" should not be relegated to the educational rear.

NASPAA might also encourage MPA programs to adopt an ethics code for students. A student code might be useful in introducing students to professional ethics. Curious about whether any NASPAA school has such a code, your author placed the following question on the NASPAA listserv—does your school have a student code of ethics? Of course universities have conduct rules and codes but they are seldom discipline-specific. Thus, the answer was a resounding and deafening silence. Should a student code of ethics such as the one in Exhibit 8.1 be adopted by MPA programs? Perhaps NASPAA should draft a model student code that academic programs could draw on to fashion their own code.

Exhibit 8.1
Masters of Public Affairs (MPA) Student Code of Ethics

1. I will abide by procedures, rules, and regulations as described in the MPA Student Handbook and the college catalog.
2. I will respect the guidelines prescribed by each professor in the preparation of academic assignments and other course requirements.
3. I will be objective, understanding, and honest in academic performance and relationships.
4. I will strive toward academic excellence, improvement of professional skills, and expansion of professional knowledge.
5. I will neither engage in, assist in, nor condone cheating, plagiarism, or other such activities.
6. I will respect and protect the rights, privileges, and beliefs of others.
7. I will become familiar with and adhere to the standards of ethical conduct established by each of the professional societies to which I am admitted as a member.
8. I will not tolerate unethical conduct on the part of others who claim membership in a professional society of which I am a member and will take appropriate action to disclose a violation of ethical standards.

Sources: This code was adapted and developed by the author from the following sources: Florida Gulf Coast University 2009; University of Wisconsin–Madison 1992.

Teaching ethics is a diverse, dynamic, and challenging enterprise. There is considerable evidence that a greater emphasis will be placed on ethics in the decades ahead in the United States and abroad. A chapter in the *Handbook of Administrative Ethics* (Cooper 2001) tracks the emergence of administrative ethics as a field of study in the United States and leaves little doubt that more attention will be devoted to teaching ethics in public administration programs and schools in the years ahead. Added emphasis, as noted earlier, will be placed on defining and measuring one's ethical competence, a challenging task to be certain. Cooper and Menzel (2013) offer guidance for doing so in their book *Achieving Ethical Competence for Public Service Leadership.*.

Promoting ethical behavior in public service is not limited to MPA programs. Many universities have established ethics centers and institutes to carry out a myriad of programs and activities. The Markkula Center for Applied Ethics (n.d.) at Santa Clara University in California is one of the most active. The center's ethics programs are quite comprehensive, ranging from business ethics to global ethics, government ethics, technology ethics, and more. Among the innovative government ethics programs is the "Ethics and Leadership Camp for Public Officials." This 2-day camp, which was launched for the first time in June 2006, attracted more than two dozen local city council members and ethics officers from California, Texas, and Arizona (Brown 2006). One novelty intended to heighten the campers' sensitivity to ethics and accountability was a "moral compass" that was slung around their necks. Exercises and group discussions were directed at enabling the campers to:

- find ways to strengthen their city's ethics program;
- identify the ten most common ethical pitfalls of cities;
- learn the best practices for city ethics programs;
- fulfill California's AB1234 ethics training requirement.

Nonprofit Ethics Advocates

In addition to university-based ethics centers, there are a number of nonprofit organizations that promote ethics and integrity in the public service. The more prominent ones are the Ethics Resource Center (www.ethics.org/), the Council on Governmental Ethics Laws (www.cogel.org/), City Ethics (www.cityethics.org/), the International Institute for Public Ethics (www.iipe.org/), and the Government Accountability Project (www.whistleblower.org/).

Public service professional associations such as the ASPA (www.aspanet.org/), ICMA (www.icma.org/), and the Government Finance Officers Association (www.gfoa.org/) place a great deal of emphasis on ethical behavior. All have professional codes of ethics. ASPA and ICMA also offer resource materials and training activities for their members. ASPA's section on Ethics and Integrity in Governance is especially focused on promoting a more inclusive concept and practice of ethics and integrity in the governance process. The section's web site (www.aspaonline.org/ethicscommunity/) offers visitors access to decision scenarios, slide presentations, and an ethics compendium.

Internationally, there is considerable movement to promote ethical behavior, especially among emerging democracies that are struggling for economic and political independence. Nations like Russia and China are trying to loosen the grip of corruption and embrace the rule of law. The United Nations (UN) has stepped up its efforts to lend a hand as well. A report titled *Public Service in Transition: Enhancing Its Role, Professionalism and Ethical Values and Standards* (United Nations 1999) by the Division of Public Economics and Public Administration emphasizes "the critical importance of probity and integrity" of governments worldwide to conduct the public's business. The UN has developed an impressive web site, the UN Public Administration Network (n.d.), that provides valuable advisory and training resources. The UN has also led by example, with the establishment on January 1, 2006, of the Ethics Office. The new office has set up an ethics hotline and is counseling the UN's 29,000 personnel worldwide on financial disclosure and conflicts of interest. "Other tasks will eventually include awareness training on ethics issues" (United Nations 2006).

Staying the Ethical Course

Public and nonprofit managers are increasingly drawn into the ethical haze of privatization and the time warp of the Information Age. Privatization and entrepreneurialism are here to stay (at least for a while) and cannot be ignored. Nor can we turn our heads and ignore the realities of the Information Age and the necessity to rethink what motivates the behaviors and practices of workers in local and global workplaces. We must recognize that, while individuals are moral agents and therefore responsible for their actions, they function in a more, not less, complex and dynamic social and organizational environment.

What, then, are the implications for managers who wish to navigate these troubling waters? Most compelling is the need to think and act in terms of organizational ethics. Managers should ask themselves day in and day out: "What can and should I do to foster an ethical environment in my organization?" Leading by example is, of course, a starting point, but it is not sufficient. Another factor is recruiting honest employees. Easier said than done? Certainly.

How can managers foster a strong ethical environment in their organization? Many suggestions have been provided in this book. But to truly succeed, managers must strive to instill an ethical consciousness in their organization and in their relationships with members of other organizations, both private and public. Among other things, steps should be taken to develop and implement a code or values statement, provide ethics training, establish an ombudsman, or add an ethics element to annual performance reviews. These efforts, separately and collectively, support the view of "ethics as organization development" (Zajac & Comfort 1997).

Within Challenges to Ethical Governance

Five challenges must be overcome to bring about ethical governance. First, organizational leaders must *acknowledge* that ethics and integrity in governance are important. This challenge may appear rather obvious, almost a given. But in the local-government environment, many public managers may presume that, since cities and counties are often subject to state ethics laws, there is no need to be especially attuned to ethics and integrity. State ethics laws typically cover nepotism, conflicts of interest, and financial disclosure. In short, most states have enacted ethics laws that are minimal in their coverage and consequences. Thus, if cities and counties do not set ethical standards higher than the state requires, they are already on the low road to ethics and integrity. Cities and counties need to move beyond the standards established by state laws in order to be responsive to citizen expectations and meet the demands of modern professional management.

Effective Ethics Reform

Even well-meaning elected officials will lack the political will to self-police without a significant level of public pressure. Politicians will pay attention to their constituents. Therefore, the most effective ethics programs emerge from, and thrive within, a process in partnership with the people.

In many cases a local ethics initiative begins with a series of events that create a grassroots movement to attack the current spate of corruption in the system. After the current problems are addressed, there is a danger that outrage will dissipate and public attention will go elsewhere.

> Ethics reform is a long-term project that requires continued attention. In turn, sustained public involvement requires an effective outreach effort as well as the responsiveness of the ethics entity. Without outreach and public input, and an equally robust response, an ethics commission is no more than a glorified code enforcement board.
> —Alan Johnson (2011b)

The second challenge is to *recognize* that ethics and integrity are not limited to a single organization or a single category of employees. American counties and states, with few exceptions, are loosely coupled collections of organizations with many different kinds of employees, administrators, and elected officials. This Hydra-headed reality means that a piecemeal approach to ethical governance is not likely to succeed. It is not sufficient to put forward a code of ethics or training or orientation program that covers only one of a county's many units (such as the administrative staff, the clerk's office, the sheriff's office, the auditor's office, the assessor's office, or the property appraiser's office). Employees, appointed professional administrators, and elected officials must be included in a comprehensive approach to ethics. This approach also ensures equal treatment of all those who work in county government, regardless of position and power.

The third challenge is to *commit* sufficient resources to building and sustaining organizational integrity. Neither governmental agencies nor nonprofit organizations are in the business of producing ethical governance. Rather, they are producers of valuable public and charitable services ranging from those mandated by higher authorities—taxation, property assessment, roads, and vital statistics—to those services demanded by citizens—for example, parks and recreation, marinas, golf courses, solid-waste collection and disposal, and air and water quality management. These goods and services consume the vast majority of available revenues. Moreover, these service needs and demands compete with one another for vital resources, and there is typically never sufficient funding to meet all of the services needed or desired. In other words, managers can and often do feel that spending scarce tax or donated dollars on ethics and integrity is a low-priority matter when funds for vital services are in real or imagined short supply. This view, of course, ignores the distressing reality that corruption is a major cause of a waste of resources.

The fourth challenge is to *avoid* a narrow rules-and-regulations approach to ethics management. Remember the old saying, "There ought to be a law!" Problems, this old bromide suggests, can be best dealt with by passing a law to correct errant behavior. Laws, ordinances, codes, and new or stricter personnel policies are too often viewed as quick fixes or solutions to problems that occur. Jurisdictions that move along this path and do nothing more are engaging in "feel-good ethics." A comprehensive management strategy that fosters ethical governance demands more than a new ordinance or a revised personnel manual. What is required is an integration of standards into all aspects of management and policy, as well as unquestionable leadership commitment to the new culture of invigorated ethics standards.

Leading with Integrity

Every organization needs an honest and credible leader that establishes ethical standards and then reinforces them.
—Pam Iorio, President and CEO,
Big Brothers Big Sisters of America (2011, 38)

The fifth challenge is to *learn* from ethics failures. Public governance is a people-driven enterprise. Yes, technology, machinery, and more are the tools needed to carry out the work of governance, but human beings still make the important decisions day in and day out, and these decisions have a direct effect on the lives of residents. Human beings have ethical lapses—sometimes egregious and other times minor or modest. These failures are part and parcel of modern organizational life. Managers truly committed to building and sustaining ethical governance must be able to learn from failures and scandal and commit to corrective actions. Public officials must have an open mind and learn from ethics failures. Scandal might trigger ethics reform, but if reform measures simply become standard operating procedures, little can be achieved in effecting genuine change. Organizations that do not learn do not grow and do not become agents for building integrity in governance.

What more should public and nonprofit leaders do to meet the challenge of ethical governance? Above all, they must commit themselves to a comprehensive strategy, and they must stay the course. An ethics summit or other forum could be arranged as a first step in recognizing that ethics and integrity are important. Additionally, a code of ethics and/or a statement of principles should be adopted that applies to all employees. The development of a code and/or statement of principles should strike a balance between ethical aspirations and the practical reality of day-to-day work.

Management should emphasize training and employee development programs. Employees in all types of organizations are vulnerable to ethical lapses. A continuous, ongoing training program—one that is stitched into the daily work environment—tends to amplify the message that ethics matters. Managers must provide organizational members with clear guidelines for proper behavior, an unambiguous explanation of the ramifications of an ethical lapse, and practical tips on how to make ethics behavior an ordinary work habit.

An ethics audit could be equally valuable, perhaps invaluable as a benchmark for tracking changes in the organizational culture. An audit, whether based on a survey of employees or an assessment of occupational vulnerability, should be conducted periodically.

Organizational leaders must advocate and embrace transparency. Sunshine laws that require open meetings to let the public view the decision making of elected officials and whistleblowing ordinances can contribute to transparency, but are often insufficient. Top officials must encourage subordinates to carry out their work with full disclosure, citizen access, and a tolerance for competing claims.

The Road Ahead

There are several conclusions that can be drawn about the challenges facing ethical governance in the twenty-first century. First, ethics issues and efforts to deal with them are not limited to the American experience. These matters are ubiquitous. Moreover, it is clear that efforts to manage ethics cannot be reduced to a "one size fits all" boilerplate. Creative solutions are needed that allow for cultural differences but at the same time do not treat ethics as something that depends on the situation.

Second, building organizations of integrity is not a one-shot affair. Rather, it is an ongoing process in much the spirit that it is the journey, not the destination, that matters. Still, the destination is very important, even if it's never reached. What is that destination?—workplaces where individuals treat each other with respect, take pride in their work, care about one another, promote accountability, and place the public interest over individual and organizational self-interest. This is the idea and ideal of an organization of integrity.

A third conclusion is that a compliance approach to building an organization of integrity is not sufficient. Indeed, in its most pernicious form it can lead to the lowest common denominator that if it's legal, it's ethical. This low-road approach will never sustain an ethical workplace. Rather, the workplace becomes one in which rule evasion and dodging go hand in hand with a "gotcha" mentality. The high road of aspirational ethics must be taken. Members of the organization must always ask themselves, "What is the right thing to do?" Rules and regulations may help answer this question, but they will never be sufficient. Each person must strive to ensure that his or her ethical compass is working correctly. A faulty ethical compass is the surest way to get lost in the quagmire of today's complex organizations.

A final conclusion is that there is no checklist for building organizations of integrity. Public and nonprofit managers must engage in exemplary leadership, promote ethics training, support codes, conduct ethics audits, and find ways to promote an ethical climate through the use of HR management processes such as hiring, annual evaluations, and promotion. These tactics can be powerful when combined in a systematic, comprehensive manner—similar, perhaps, to that of an orchestra conductor who must be able to produce harmonious music from diverse musicians and instruments. No single tactic is the best one to transform the sour notes of unethical behavior into the reassuring culture of an organization of integrity.

The ethical challenges facing public and nonprofit managers are real and ever more complex, and they must be met. A failure to do so will erode public trust, confidence, and faith in our more than 200-year-old experiment called the United States of America. Are you ready to meet the challenges of ethics management?

Ethics Management Skill Building

Practicum 8.1. Nonprofit Contracting

As a recent retiree from the U.S. Air Force, you decide to take a position with a nonprofit agency that manages the city's federally funded low-income housing program. On four separate occasions over the next few months, you are told by the city's program administrator to use money from one federal grant to pay for a project that wasn't covered by the grant. One month later you are asked to approve the expenditure of $87,150 on a private residence that would sell for $70,000.

Increasingly uncomfortable with the situation, you object, asserting that federal guidelines prohibit the city from spending that much money on low-income housing. The city administrator complains to your boss that you are not attentive, productive, or responsive to city staff. Your boss decides to remove you from the project. Frustrated, but convinced that you did the right thing, you write to the mayor detailing your concerns about the misuse of federal funds. The mayor never responds.

A few months later the city's internal auditing staff reports that the city administrator has issued questionable loans, kept poor records, and awarded noncompetitive bids. Housing and Urban Development (HUD) officials warn the mayor that the administrator may have misused $1.4 million in federal funds. The administrator claims that the feds are applying ridiculous rules. The mayor backs him. The administrator appears before city council and asserts that "we do not intend to follow HUD's direction at this point." All but one member of city council praises the administrator.

Fast-forward 2 years—a federal indictment charges that the city housing administrator used government jobs to reap thousands of dollars in gratuities. HUD requires the city to return $1,402,650 to the U.S. Treasury.

Discussion Questions

1. Did your boss do the right thing in removing you from the project?
2. Did you do the right thing in going around your boss by writing directly to the mayor?
3. What policy would you draft to prevent a city administrator from misusing federal grants for low-income housing? Would your policy apply to the director of the nonprofit agency?

Practicum 8.2. Entrepreneurialism at the Office

Jan and Bill are ambitious, energetic urban planners employed by the U.S. Department of Transportation (DOT) in Atlanta's regional headquarters. Their work on several comprehensive plans brings them much praise, including several positive stories published in the *New York Times*. One day, Jan says to Bill,

> Why don't we try to make some money as planning consultants? We can advertise ourselves on the web with our own site. The costs would be minimal, and as long as we don't contract with clients doing business with our agency, there shouldn't be any ethical or legal issues to contend with.

Bill gives Jan's suggestion a few days of thought, and a week later they have a web site in place. On the site, Jan and Bill are presented as Jones & Greene Associates, Urban Planners. Services that their firm can provide include, among other things, market analysis, community planning, business site selection, and geographic information systems.

Assume you are Jan and Bill's boss at the DOT and you happen to come upon their web site. While it does not identify the U.S. DOT as Bill and Jan's employer, the site does state that they have significant government experience as urban planners. Moreover, the page contains their firm's e-mail address and Bill's home office telephone number.

Two weeks later, while at work, you happen to overhear Bill talking by telephone with an apparent client about his consulting services.

Discussion Questions

1. What would you do? Would you call Bill and Jan aside and tell them that they cannot do private business while at the office?
2. Would you consult with your agency's designated ethics officer?
3. Would you report them to the U.S. Office of Government Ethics?
4. Would you ignore the situation?

Notes

1. A comprehensive overview of the research literature on ethics and integrity in public administration is highlighted by Menzel (2015b).

2. See Henry (2011) for a critical review of contracting by the U.S. government.

3. See Bretschneider and Mergel (2011) for a comprehensive treatment of technology and public management information systems.

4. There is a growing body of literature regarding the plight of public administration in a "postglobal" world. See Schultz (2011) for an overview.

5. To reflect its growing international membership and disciplinary breadth, NASPAA changed its name to the Network of Schools of Public Policy, Affairs, and Administration effective March 1, 2013.

6. See Raffel, Maser, and Calarusse (2011) for an in-depth discussion of NASPAA competencies in education for leadership in public service.

7. This discussion draws on Bowman and Menzel (2004).

Appendix 1
Online Ethics Resources

http://blog.ethicalgovnow.org This web site provides 24/7 coverage of ethics news and issues in the United States and abroad.

http://ethicsmgt.com/ethicsmgt.com/Presentations.html This web site offers papers and presentations by the author.

http://www.ethics.org/about/mission-statement The Ethics Resource Center provides leading ethics and compliance research and best practices, networking opportunities, and certification to its membership, which represents more than 450 organizations across all industries, each dedicated to promoting the highest levels of integrity in organizations worldwide.

http://ethics.iit.edu/teaching/online-resources The Center for the Study of Ethics in the Professions was established in 1976 to promote research and teaching on practical moral problems in the professions.

http://www.scu.edu/ethics/ Markkula Center for Applied Ethics addresses the practical ethical dilemmas professionals and individuals face in their daily lives and conducts practical research to produce articles, cases, best-practice reports, podcasts, and videos.

http://www.fl-counties.com/factor-home/knowledge-center/ethics-resources This web site provides numerous educational opportunities and a wealth of information on ethics, sunshine laws, and public records for Florida County Association members.

http://icma.org/en/icma/home International City/County Management Association offers courses, guidelines, and advice on ethics issues.

http://ethics.harvard.edu Edmond J. Safra Center for Ethics, Harvard University, seeks to advance teaching and research on ethical issues in public life. Widespread ethical lapses of leaders in government, business, and other professions prompt demands for more and better moral education.

http://www.publicintegrity.org The Center for Public Integrity is a nonpartisan, nonprofit investigative news organization that serves democracy by revealing abuses of power, corruption and betrayal of public trust by powerful public and private institutions, using the tools of investigative journalism.

References

Abbott, L. 2006. Personal e-mail communication, July 8.

Adam, A.M., and D. Rachman-Moore. 2004. "The Methods Used to Implement an Ethical Code of Conduct and Employee Attitudes." *Journal of Business Ethics* 54:225–244.

African Union. Assembly of the Union. 2011. "Decisions, Declarations and Resolution." January 30–31. http://www.au.int/en/sites/default/files/ASSEMBLY_EN_30_31_JANUARY_2011_AUC_ASSEMBLY_AFRICA.pdf (retrieved October 9, 2015).

Aguilar, M. 2010. "Post-Skilling, Movement Afoot on Honest Services Fraud." *Compliance Week,* October 4. www.complianceweek.com/post-skilling-movement-afoot-on-honest-services-fraud/article/187439/ (retrieved April 17, 2011).

Alpert, B. 2010. "Judge Thomas Porteous Not Trustworthy, Task Force Declares." Nola.com, January 22. www.nola.com/crime/index.ssf/2010/01/judge_thomas_porteous_not_trus.html (retrieved March 31, 2011).

American Society for Public Administration (ASPA). 2006. "ASPA's Code of Ethics." http://www.aspanet.org/scriptcontent/index_codeofethics.cfm.

———. 2013. "Code of Ethics." http://www.aspanet.org/public/ASPA/Code%20of%20Ethics/ASPA/Resources/Code_of_Ethics/Code_of_Ethics1.aspx?hkey=7d5473b7-b98a-48a4-b409-3efb4ceaa006 (retrieved March 5, 2016).

Amundsen, I. "Political Corruption." U4 Anti-Corruption Resource Centre 2006. http://www.u4.no/publications/political-corruption/ (retrieved March 15, 2016).

Anderson, G. 2011. Personal e-mail communication, May 19.

Anechiarico, F., and J.B. Jacobs. 1994. "Visions of Corruption Control and the Evolution of American Public Administration." *Public Administration Review* 54:465–473.

———. 1996. *The Pursuit of Absolute Integrity: How Corruption Control Makes Government Ineffective.* Chicago, IL: University of Chicago Press.

Aprill, E.P. 2014. "Nonprofits and Political Activity: Lessons from England and Canada." Social Science Research Network, March 25. http://papers.ssrn.com/sol3/papers.cfm?abstract_id=2414665 (retrieved October 9, 2015).

Association of Fundraising Professionals (AFP). 2015a. https://afp.az1.qualtrics.com/jfe/form/SV_cSAeP4HYwsVleOo (retrieved July 31, 2015).

———. 2015b. "AFP Enforcement Procedures." http://www.afpnet.org/files/ContentDocuments/EthicsEnforcementProcedures.pdf (retrieved October 7, 2015).

Audit Commission. 2003. "Corporate Governance." Report, October. www.audit-commission.gov.uk/SiteCollectionDocuments/AuditCommissionReports/NationalStudies/CorporateGovernance.pdf (retrieved January 3, 2006).

Austin Statesman. 2012. "Give Ethics Commission Teeth it Needs to Force Officials' Compliance." April 11. http://www.statesman.com/news/news/opinion/give-ethics-commmission-teeth-it-needs-to-force-of/nRmtM/ (retrieved October 8, 2015).

Ayres, W.C. 2005. Personal e-mail communication.

Bailey, S.K. 1964. "Ethics and the Public Service." *Public Administration Review* 24:234–243.

Ballentine, S. 2015. "Missouri House Speaker Calls for Mandatory Sexual-Harassment Training for all Members, Staff." *U.S. News & World Report* October 23.

Barnard, C. 1938. *The Functions of the Executive.* Cambridge, MA: Harvard University Press.

Barton, P., and L. Shames. 2003. *Not Fade Away.* New York: HarperCollins.

Bass, B.M., and P. Steidimeier. 1999. "Ethics, Character, and Authentic Transformational Leadership Behavior." *Leadership Quarterly* 10: 181–208.

Bazerman, M.H., and A.E. Tenbrunsel. 2011. *Blind Spots: Why We Fail to Do What's Right and What to Do About It.* Princeton, NJ: Princeton University Press.

Beerel, A. 2014. "Why Ethics Training Doesn't Work." http://www.nhbr.com/core/pagetools.php?pageid=56987&url=%2FJanuary-10-2014%2FWhy-ethics-training-doesnt-work%2Findex.php&mode=print (retrieved October 7, 2015).

Bellah, R.N., R. Madsen, S.M. Tipton, W.M. Sullivan, and A. Swidler. 1991. *The Good Society.* New York: Random House.

Bellamy, C. 2010. "Letter to the Editor." *Chicago Tribune* September 17. http://articles.chicagotribune.com/2010-09-17/news/ct-vp-0917voicelettersbriefs-20100917_1_chicago-mayor-richard-daley-fresh-face-china-shop/2 (retrieved May 2, 2011).

———. 2015. Personal e-mail communication, March 23.

Bellomo, T. 2005. "The Making of an Ethical Executive." *New York Times* February 14.

Bennis, W.G. 1993. *An Invented Life: Reflections on Leadership and Change.* Reading, MA: Addison-Wesley.

Berman, E.M. 1996. "Restoring the Bridges of Trust: Attitudes of Community Leaders Toward Local Government." *Public Integrity Annual* 31–49.

Berman, E.M., and J.P. West. 1997. "Managing Ethics to Improve Performance and Build Trust." *Public Integrity Annual* 23–31.

———. 2003. "Solutions to the Problem of Managerial Mediocrity." *Public Performance and Management Review* 27 (December):30–52.

———. 2012. "Public Values in Special Districts: A Survey of Managerial Commitment." *Public Administration Review* 72 (Jan/Feb): 43–54.

Berman, E., J. P. West, and A. Cava. 1994. "Ethics Management in Municipal Governments and Large Firms: Exploring Similarities and Differences." *Administration & Society* 26 (August):185–203.

Better Government Association. 2013. "The BGA-ALPER Integrity Index." http://www.bettergov.org/assets/1/Page/2013%20BGA-Alper%20Services%20Integrity%20Index.pdf (retrieved October 8, 2015).

Bies, A.L. 2010. "Evolution of Nonprofit Self-Regulation in Europe." *Nonprofit and Voluntary Sector Quarterly* 39(6):1057–1086.

Black, M.P. 2011. Personal e-mail communication, March 21. Marty Black is the former city manager of Venice, Florida.

Blustein, J. 1991. *Care and Commitment: Taking the Personal Point of View.* New York: Oxford University Press.

Boeing Company. 2015. "Boeing Code of Conduct." http://www.boeing.com/resources/boeingdotcom/principles/ethics_and_compliance/pdf/english.pdf (retrieved October 7, 2015).

Bok, D. 1990. *Universities and the Future of America.* Durham, NC: Duke University Press.

Bonczek, S.J. 1998. "Creating an Ethical Work Environment: Enhancing Ethics Awareness in Local Government." In *The Ethics Edge*, ed. E.M. Berman, J.P. West, and S.J. Bonczek. Washington, DC: International City/County Management Association, pp. 72–79.

Bossaert, D. and C. Demmke. 2005. *Main Challenges in the Field of Ethics and Integrity in the EU Member States.* Maastricht, The Netherlands: European Institute of Public Administration.

Boucher, T., and S. Hudspeth. 2008. "Ethics and the Nonprofit." Commonfund Insitute. https://www.commonfund.org/InvestorResources/Publications/White%20Papers/Ethics%20and%20the%20Nonprofit.pdf (retrieved October 5, 2015).

Bowley, G. 2011. "At I.M.F., a Strict Ethics Code Doesn't Apply to Top Officials." *New York Times*, May 30:B1.

Bowman, J.S. 1977. "Ethics in the Federal Service: A Post-Watergate View." *Midwest Review of Public Administration* 11 (March):3–20.

———. 1981. "Ethical Issues for the Public Manager." In *A Handbook of Organization Management,* ed. W.B. Eddy. New York: Marcel Dekker, pp. 69–102.

———. 1990. "Ethics in Government: A National Survey of Public Administrators." *Public Administration Review* 50 (May/June):345–353.

Bowman, J.S., and D. Menzel. 2004. "Ethics Practices and Experiences in Graduate Public Administration Education." Paper presented at the 65th Annual Conference of the American Society for Public Administration. Portland, Oregon, March 27–30.

Bowman, J.S., and R.L. Williams. 1997. "Ethics in Government: From a Winter of Despair to a Spring of Hope." *Public Administration Review* 57:517–526.

Bowman, J.S., J.P., West, E.M., Berman, and M. Van Wart. 2004. *The Professional Edge: Competencies in Public Service.* Armonk, NY: M.E. Sharpe.

Brady, W.D. 2011. *Procurement Management Review.* Sarasota County, Procurement Department, Final Report, June 7. National Institute of Governmental Purchasing.

www.scgov.net/CFPO/ProcurementPurchasing/documents/NIGPFinalReport.
pdf (retrieved February 22, 2016).

Brandeis, L. 2011. http://www.goodreads.com/author/quotes/1287729.Louis_Dembitz_
Brandeis (retrieved November 16, 2015).

Brandsen, T., and W. van de Donk, W. 2009. "The Third Sector and the Policy
Process in the Netherlands: A Study in Invisible Ink." In *Handbook on Third
Sector Policy in Europe: Multi Level Processes and Organised Civil Society*, ed.
J. Kendall. Cheltenham, United Kingdom: Edward Elgar, pp. 140–158.

Bretschneider, S.I., and I. Mergel. 2011. "Technology and Public Management
Information Systems: Where We Have Been and Where We Are Going." In
The State of Public Administration: Issues, Challenges, and Opportunities, ed.
D. Menzel and H. White. Armonk, NY: M.E. Sharpe, pp. 187–203.

Brewer, G.A., and S. Coleman Selden, 1998. "Whistleblowers in the Federal
Civil Service: New Evidence of the Public Service Ethic." *Journal of Public
Administration Research and Theory* 8 (July):413–439.

Brown, M.E., and Treviño, L.K. 2006. "Ethical Leadership: A Review and Future
Directions." *Leadership Quarterly* 17: 595–616.

Brown, P.L. 2006. "At Ethics Camp, Not-So-Tall Tales from the Dark Side." *New York
Times*, June 23 http://www.nytimes.com/2006/06/23/us/23ethics.html (retrieved
May 2, 2016).

Brown, S. 2005. "Managing Municipal Ethics." www.gmanet.com/event_detail/
default.asp?eventid=6445&menuid=GeorgiaCitiesNewspaperID (retrieved December
29, 2005).

Bruce, W. 1994. "Ethical People Are Productive People." *Public Productivity and
Management Review* 17 (Spring):23–30.

Brudney, J.L. and M.J. Martinez. 2010. "Teaching Administrative Ethics in
Nonprofit Management: Recommendations to Improve Degrees, Certificates, and
Concentration Programs." *Journal of Public Affairs Education* 16(2):181–206.

Brumback, G.B. 1998. "Institutionalizing Ethics in Government." In *The Ethics Edge*,
ed. E.M. Berman, J.P. West, and S.J. Bonczek. Washington, DC: International
City/County Management Association, pp. 61–71.

Buettner, R. 2014. "Rapfogel Is Sentenced for Stealing From His Charity." *New
York Times*, July 23. http://www.nytimes.com/2015/01/07/us/bob-mcdonnell-ex-
governor-virginia-sentencing-corruption.html (retrieved August 3, 2015).

Burke, F., and A. Black. 1990. "Improving Organizational Productivity: Add Ethics."
Public Productivity and Management Review 14 (Winter):121–133.

Burke, J.P. 1986. *Bureaucratic Responsibility*. Baltimore, MD: Johns Hopkins Press.

California. 2015. Fair Political Practices Commission. *AB 1234 Ethics Training for Local
Officials*. http://www.fppc.ca.gov/index.php?id=477 (retrieved October 8, 2015).

Carnevale, D.G. 1995. *Trustworthy Government: Leadership and Management Strategies for Building Trust and High Performance*. San Francisco, CA: Jossey-Bass.

Carter, S.L. 1997. *Integrity*. New York: Harper Perennial.

Center for Public Integrity. 2015. "Enforcement Gap Reveals Difference Between State Laws and Practices." http://www.stateintegrity.org/enforcement_gap_ reveals_state_laws_practices (retrieved October 8, 2015).

Charitywatch. 2015. "Long Running Family Charity Scheme Exposed." July 27. https://www.charitywatch.org/charitywatch-articles/long-running-family-charity-scheme-exposed/160 (retrieved October 8, 2015).

China Daily. 2005. "Top Civil Servants Must Disclose Finances." April 29. www2.chinadaily.com.cn/english/doc/2005-04/29/content_438416.htm (retrieved January 3, 2006).

——. 2015. "CPC Achieves Self-Improvement with Xi's Leadership." http://www.chinadaily.com.cn/china/2016-01/10/content_23014956_2.htm (retrieved March 15, 2016).

China Daily USA. 2013. "Xi's Anti-Corruption Move Arouses Expectations." January 24. http://usa.chinadaily.com.cn/china/2013-01/24/content_16167683.htm (retrieved March 15, 2016).

Citrus County, Florida. 2011. Board of County Commissioners—Blog. http://bocc.citrus.fl.us/blog/ (retrieved February 22, 2016).

City of Jacksonville, Florida. n.d. "Ethics Office." www.coj.net/Departments/Ethics-Office.aspx.

City of San Diego, California. 2002. "Chapter 2, Article 7, Division 35: City of San Diego Ethics Ordinance." Municipal Code, April 29. http://docs.sandiego.gov/municode/MuniCodeChapter02/Ch02Art07Division35.pdf (retrieved August 8, 2011).

City of Sweet Home, Oregon. 2011. Web site. www.sweet-home.or.us/ (retrieved March 6, 2011).

Clendinen, D. 1983. "Tampa Amused but Angry at Arrests." New York Times, February 12. http://www.nytimes.com/1983/02/12/us/tampa-amused-but-angry-at-arrests.html (retrieved July 13, 2015).

CNN Library. 2015. "Penn State Scandal Fast Facts." http://www.cnn.com/2013/10/28/us/penn-state-scandal-fast-facts/ (retrieved October 5, 2015).

Cohen, S., and W. Eimicke. 1999. "Is Public Entrepreneurship Ethical?" Public Integrity 1 (Winter):54–74.

Committee on Standards in Public Life. 2004. Getting the Balance Right—Implementing Standards of Conduct in Public Life. Tenth Report. Presented to Parliament by the Prime Minister by Command of Her Majesty. http://www.official-documents.gov.uk/document/cm64/6407/6407.pdf (retrieved February 22, 2016).

Confucius. n.d. BrainyQuote.com. BrainyQuote.com Web site: http://www.brainyquote.com/quotes/quotes/c/confucius131984.html (retrieved July 2, 2015).

Connolly, C. 2005. "Director of NIH Agrees to Loosen Ethics Rules." Washington Post, August 26.

Constitution of the United States. 1787. "America's Historical Documents." College Park, MD: U.S. National Archives and Records Administration. http://www.archives.gov/historical-docs/document.html?doc=3&title.raw=Constitution%20of%20the%20United%20States (retrieved February 22, 2016).

Contorno, S. 2015. "Hillsborough's Environmental Commission Holds Firm on Politicking B an for New Director." *Tampa Bay Times*, June 24. http://www.tampabay.com/news/localgovernment/hillsboroughs-environmental-commission-holds-firm-on-politicking-ban/2234901 (retrieved October 5, 2015).

Cooper, T.L. 1982. *The Responsible Administrator: An Approach to Ethics for the Administrative Role*. Port Washington, NY: Kennikat Press.

———. 1984. "Citizenship and Professionalism in Public Administration." *Public Administration Review* 44 (March):143–149.

———. 1987. "Hierarchy, Virtue, and the Practice of Public Administration: A Perspective for Normative Ethics." *Public Administration Review* 47 (July/August):320–328.

——— (ed.). 2001. *Handbook of Administrative Ethics*. 2nd ed. New York: Marcel Dekker.

———. 2006a. *The Responsible Administrator*. 5th ed. San Francisco, CA: Jossey-Bass.

———. 2006b. Personal e-mail communication, February 27.

———. 2012. *The Responsible Administrator*. 6th ed. San Francisco, CA: Jossey-Bass.

Cooper, T.L., and D.C. Menzel (eds). 2013. *Achieving Ethical Competence for Public Service Leadership*. Armonk, NY: M.E. Sharpe.

Cooper, T.L., and N.D. Wright (eds). 1992. *Exemplary Public Administrators*. San Francisco, CA: Jossey-Bass.

Couloumbis, A. 2015. "Justice Eakin Suspended Over Emails." Philly.com. http://articles.philly.com/2015-12-24/news/69263832_1_michael-eakin-suspension-supreme-court-justice-j (retrieved March 9, 2016).

Council for Excellence in Government. 1992–1993. "Ethical Principles for Public Servants." *The Public Manager* 21:37–39.

Council of Governmental Ethics Laws (COGEL). 2004. *COGEL Blue Book: 2004 Ethics Update*. Jacksonville, FL: COGEL.

Cusick, R.I. 2010. "Director's Welcome Remarks." The 17th National Government Ethics Conference, May 10–14, Chicago, IL. www.usoge.gov/conference/pdf/17th_cusick_welcome.pdf (retrieved June 2, 2011).

Daily Mail Online. 2015. "Scandal-Hit Kids Company Spent £28,000 on £240-a-Session Harley Street Hypnotist Who Used 'Weird' Methods to Treat Young Drug Addicts." www.dailymail.co.uk/news/article-3298621/Scandal-hit-Kids-Company-spent-tens-thousands-pounds-sending-staff-clients-240-hour-Harley-Street-hypnotherapist.html (retrieved March 5, 2016).

———. 2016. "Shame of the Charity Cold Call Sharks: Mail Investigation Finds Britain's Biggest Charities Ruthlessly Hounding the Vulnerable and Elderly for Cash, Even if They Have Opted Out of Receiving Calls." http://www.dailymail.co.uk/news/article-3151533/Shamed-charity-cold-call-sharks-Britains-biggest-charities-ruthlessly-hound-vulnerable-cash-try-opt-receiving-calls.html (retrieved March 5, 2016).

Dao, J. 2005. "Governor of Ohio Is Charged with Breaking Ethics Law." *New York Times,* August 18 http://www.nytimes.com/2005/08/18/us/governor-of-ohio-is-charged-with-breaking-ethics-law.html (retrieved May 2, 2016).

Davey, M. 2008. "Illinois Governor Arrested in Inquiry into Filling Obama's Senate Seat." *New York Times,* December 9. www.nytimes.com/2008/12/09/world/americas/09iht-10illinois.18524701.html (retrieved February 22, 2016).

Davey, M., and E.G. Fitzsimmons. 2011. "Jury Finds Blagojevich Guilty of Corruption." *New York Times,* June 28:A1 http://www.nytimes.com/2011/06/28/us/28blagojevich.html (retrieved May 2, 2016).

Davey, M., and G. Ruethling. 2006. "Former Illinois Governor Is Convicted in Graft Case." *New York Times,* April 18.

Davis, M. 1999. Cited in R.W. Smith, "Local Government Ethics Boards: A Panel Discussion on the New York Experience." *Public Integrity* 1 (Fall):397–416.

Daytona Beach Morning Journal. 1954. Editorial. November 1.

Deadspin.com. 2015. "A Comprehensive Timeline of the Penn State Child Sex Abuse Scandal." http://deadspin.com/5859823/a-comprehensive-timeline-of-the-penn-state-child-sex-abuse-scandal (retrieved October 5, 2015).

deLeon, L. 1996. "Ethics and Entrepreneurship." *Policy Studies Journal* 24 (Autumn):496–514.

Denhardt, K.G. 1988. *The Ethics of Public Administration: Resolving Moral Dilemmas in Public Organizations.* New York: Greenwood.

———. 1989. "The Management of Ideals: A Political Perspective on Ethics." *Public Administration Review* 49 (March/April):187–192.

Denhardt, R.B. 1981. *In the Shadow of Organization.* Lawrence, KS: The Regents Press of Kansas.

de Tocqueville, A. 1840/2000. *Democracy in America,* trans. and ed. H. Mansfield and D. Winthrop. Chicago, IL: University of Chicago Press.

Dobel, J.P. 1999. *Public Integrity.* Baltimore, MD: Johns Hopkins Press.

———. 2009. "Value Driven Leading: A Management Approach." Case Teaching Resources from The Electronic Hallway at The Evans School of Public Affairs: University of Washington.

Dobuzinskis, A. 2011. "City Manager Pleads Not Guilty in Bell, California, Pay Scandal." Reuters, March 24. www.reuters.com/article/2011/03/24/us-pay-scandal-idUSTRE72N8HJ20110324 (retrieved February 22, 2016).

Dolan, M. 2015. "California Charities Must Disclose Major Donors, Court Rules." *Los Angeles Times,* May 1. http://www.latimes.com/local/lanow/la-me-ln-charity-court-20150501-story.html (retrieved November 6, 2015).

Dong, K.Y., H.S. Yang, and X. Wang. 2010. "Public Service Ethics and Anti-corruption Efforts in Mainland China." In *Public Administration in East Asia,* ed. E.M. Berman, M.J. Moon, and H. Choi. Boca Raton, FL: CRC Press, 95–116.

Drucker, P.F. 2004. Cited in S. R. Covey, *Seven Habits of Highly Effective People.* New York: Free Press, p.101.

Duggan, K., and K. Woodhouse. 2011. "A Code of Ethics That Packs A Punch." *Public Management* 93 (November): 6–10.

Dunlap, A. 1997. *Mean Business: How I Save Bad Companies and Make Good Companies Great.* New York: Fireside.

Eckhart, R. 2011. "Indicted Project Manager Received Gifts from Another Firm." *Herald-Tribune.com* (Sarasota, FL), May 10. www.heraldtribune.com/article/20110510/ARTICLE/110519964 (retrieved February 22, 2016).

Economist. 2011. "Charity at Home: Non-Profit Organisations in Japan." July 7. http://www.economist.com/node/18929259 (retrieved October 9, 2015).

Edmunds, F. 2011. Personal e-mail communication, March 3. Frank Edmunds is the city manager of Seminole, Florida.

Ellsberg, D. 2004. "Truths Worth Telling." *New York Times,* September 28. http://www.nytimes.com/2004/09/28/opinion/truths-worth-telling.html (retrieved May 2, 2016).

Eskridge, R.D., P.E. French, and M. McThomas. 2012. "The International City/County Management Association Code of Ethics." *Public Integrity* 14(2):127–150.

Executive Order 10939. 1961. "To Provide a Guide on Ethical Standards to Government Officials." May 5. http://www.thecre.com/fedlaw/legal15/eo10939.htm (retrieved November 18, 2011).

Executive Order 11222. 1965. "Prescribing Standards of Ethical Conduct for Government Officers and Employees." May 8. www.usoge.gov/laws_regs/exec_orders/eo11222.html (retrieved February 28, 2006).

Executive Order 12668. 1989. "President's Commission on Federal Ethics Law Reform." George H.W. Bush. *Federal Register*: 54 FR 3979, January 27. https://www.oge.gov/Web/oge.nsf/Resources/Executive+Order+12674+(Apr.+12,+1989):++Principles+of+Ethical+Conduct+for+Government+Officers+and+Employees (retrieved May 2, 2016).

Executive Order 12674. 1989. "Principles of Ethical Conduct for Government Officers and Employees," *Federal Register* 54 FR 15159, April 14, as modified by Executive Order 12731. April 12. https://www.oge.gov/Web/oge.nsf/Resources/Executive+Order+12674+(Apr.+12,+ 1989):++Principles+of+Ethical+Conduct+for+Government+Officers+and+Employees (retrieved May 2, 2016).

Executive Order 12834. 1993. "Ethics Commitments by Executive Branch Personnel." January 20. http://search.archives.gov/cs.html?url=http%3A//www.archives.gov/federal-register/executive-orders/pdf/12834.pdf&charset=iso-8859-1&qt=12834&col=1arch+social&n=1&la=en (retrieved November 18, 2011).

Executive Order 13490. 2009. "Section 1: Ethics Pledge." January 21. www.whitehouse.gov/the-press-office/ethics-commitments-executive-branch-personnel (retrieved June 5, 2011).

Fawcett, G., and M. Wardman. 2005. "Ethical Governance in Local Government in England: A Regulator's View." Paper presented at the Ethics and Integrity of Governance: The First Transatlantic Dialogue, Leuven, Belgium, 2–5 June.

FCCMA. 2015. "Ethics Policy." http://fccma.org/fccma-ethics-policy/ (retrieved October 7, 2015).

Ferrieux-Patterson, M.N. 2003. "Conflict of Interest—Vanuatu's Experience." Paper presented at the 4th Regional Anti-Corruption Conference of the ADB/OECD Anti-Corruption Initiative for Asia and the Pacific, Kuala Lumpur, Malaysia, December 3–5.

Fischenich, M. 2012. "Mankato City Council Cool to Values Proposal." *Mankato Free Press.* June 16. http://www.mankatofreepress.com/news/local_news/north-mankato-city-council-cool-to-values-proposal/article_ab28d541-936c-50d1-9ec3-99d0e1fa7b3c.html (retrieved October 7, 2015).

Florida Gulf Coast University. 2009. "Code of Ethics." In *2009–2010 MPA Student Handbook.* http://cps.fgcu.edu/PA/MPA/Files/handbook.pdf, pp. 13–15.

Florida Office of the Inspector General. 2005. *Contract Management of Private Correctional Facilities.* Internal Audit Report Number 2005–61, June 30.

Folks, S.R. 2000. "A Potential Whistleblower." *Public Integrity* 2 (Winter):61–74.

Follet, M.P. 1924. *Creative Experience.* New York: Longmans, Green.

Frederickson, H.G. 1992. "Elmer B. Staats: Government Ethics in Practice." In *Exemplary Public Administrators,* ed. T.L. Cooper and N.D. Wright. San Francisco, CA: Jossey-Bass, 214–240.

———(ed.). 1993. *Ethics and Public Administration.* Armonk, NY: M.E. Sharpe.

———. 1997. *The Spirit of Public Administration.* San Francisco, CA: Jossey-Bass.

Frederickson, H.G., and M.A. Newman. 2001. "The Patriotism of Exit and Voice: The Case of Gloria Flora." *Public Integrity* 3 (Fall):347–362.

Friedman, T. 2011. "Two Peas in a Pod." *New York Times,* November 8. http://www.nytimes.com/2011/11/09/opinion/friedman-india-and-america-two-peas-in-a-pod.html (retrieved May 2, 2016).

Fry, B.R. 1989. *Mastering Public Administration: From Max Weber to Dwight Waldo.* Chatham, NJ: Chatham House.

Gallup. 2014. "Honesty/Ethics in Professions." http://www.gallup.com/poll/1654/Honesty-Ethics-Professions.aspx?g_source=ETHICS&g_medium=topic&g_campaign=tiles (retrieved October 9, 2015).

García-Marzá, D. 2005. "Trust and Dialogue: Theoretical Approaches to Ethics Auditing." *Journal of Business Ethics* 57: 209–219.

Garvey, G. 1993. *Facing the Bureaucracy: Living and Dying in a Public Agency.* San Francisco, CA: Jossey-Bass.

Gawthrop, L.C. 1984. *Public Sector Management, Systems, and Ethics.* Bloomington, IN: Indiana University Press.

———. 1998. *Public Service and Democracy: Ethical Imperatives for the 21st Century.* Chappaqua, NY: Chatham House.

George C. Marshall Foundation. 2003. "George C. Marshall Foundation Award: A Gala Occasion Honoring Secretary of State Colin L. Powell." *Topics,* December (insert). www.marshallfoundation.org/pdfs/Topics-Gala-Insert.pdf (retrieved June 28, 2011).

Gerth, H.H., and C.W. Mills (eds and trans.). 1946. *From Max Weber: Essays in Sociology.* New York: Oxford University Press.

Ghere, R.K. 1996. "Aligning the Ethics of Public–Private Partnership: The Issue of Local Economic Development." *Journal of Public Administration Research and Theory* 6 (October):599–621.

Gibson, P. 2009. "Examining the Moral Reason of the Ethics Adviser and Counselor: The Case of the Federal Designated Agency Ethics Official." *Public Integrity* 11:105–120.

Gilman, S.C. 1995a. *The Management of Ethics and Conduct in the Public Service: The United States Federal Government.* Report, December. www.oecd.org/dataoecd/30/22/2731902.htm (retrieved January 2, 2006).

———. 1995b. "Presidential Ethics and the Ethics of the Presidency." *Ethics in American Public Service: The Annals of the American Academy of Political and Social Science* 537:58–75.

———. 2005. "Ethics Codes and Codes of Conduct as Tools for Promoting an Ethical and Professional Public Service: Comparative Successes and Lessons." Paper prepared for the Poverty Reduction and Economic Management (PREM) Network, the World Bank, Washington, DC. http://www.oecd.org/dataoecd/17/33/35521418.pdf (retrieved February 22, 2016).

———. 2006. Personal e-mail communication, July 6.

Gilman, S.C., and C.W. Lewis. 1996. "Public Service Ethics: A Global Dialogue." *Public Administration Review* 56 (November/December):517–524.

Ginley, C. 2012. "Policing the Politicians: State Ethics Commissions Lack Muscle." August 8. http://www.publicintegrity.org/2012/08/08/10588/policing-politicians-state-ethics-commissions-lack-muscle (retrieved March 3, 2016).

Glazer, M.P., and P.M. Glazer. 1989. *The Whistleblowers: Exposing Corruption in Government and Industry.* New York: Basic Books.

Global Financial Integrity. 2011. "Transnational Crime in the Developing World." Report, February. http://transcrime.gfip.org/ (retrieved February 13, 2011).

Global Integrity. n.d. "About Us." www.globalintegrity.org/about (retrieved July 15, 2011).

———. 2006. "Global Integrity Report." http://www.globalintegrity.org/information/downloads (retrieved February 22, 2016).

Goldsmith, S., and W.D. Eggers. 2004. *Governing by Network: The New Shape of the Public Sector.* Washington, DC: Brookings Institution Press.

Gong, T. 2000. "Whistleblowing: What Does It Mean in China?" *International Journal of Public Administration* 23 (11):1899–1923.

Gore, A. 1993. *Creating a Government That Works Better and Costs Less: The Report of the National Performance Review.* New York: Plume.

Gorman, S. 2011. "Voters in California's Corruption-Hit Bell Make Clean Sweep." Reuters, March 9. http://www.reuters.com/article/2011/03/09/us-corruption-bell-election-idUSTRE7286GZ20110309 (retrieved February 22, 2016).

Graham, K. 2005. "Parks Worker Accused of Taking Bribe." *St. Petersburg Times*, February 24.

Groeneweg, S. 2001. "Three Whistleblower Protection Models: A Comparative Analysis of Whistleblower Legislation in Australia, the United States and the United Kingdom. Public Service Commission of Canada." www.psc-cfp.gc.ca/research/merit/whistleblowing_e.htm (retrieved January 3, 2006).

Grosenick, L. 1995. "Federal Training Programs: Help or Hindrance?" *The Public Manager* 24 (4):43.

Guo, C., J. Xu, D.H. Smith, and Z. Zhang. 2012. "Civil Society Chinese Style: The Rise of the Nonprofit Sector in Post-Mao China." *Nonprofit Quarterly*. October 25. https://nonprofitquarterly.org/2012/10/25/civil-society-chinese-stylethe-rise-of-the-nonprofit-sector-in-post-mao-chinaby/ (retrieved October 9, 2015).

Hamilton, A. 1787. *The Federalist* #6. http://thomas.loc.gov/home/histdox/fed_06.html (retrieved February 22, 2016).

———. 1788. *The Federalist* #78. http://thomas.loc.gov/home/histdox/fed_78.html (retrieved February 22, 2016).

Hammack, D.C. 2002. "Nonprofit Organizations in American History." *American Behavioral Scientist* 45(11): 1638–1674.

Harlow, L.F. 1977. *Without Fear or Favor: Odyssey of a City Manager*. Provo, UT: Brigham Young University Press.

———(ed.). 1981. *Servants of All: Professional Management of City Government*. Provo, UT: Brigham Young University Press.

Harris, G. 2005. "Report Details F.D.A. Rejection of Next-Day Pill." *New York Times*, November 15. http://www.nytimes.com/2005/11/15/politics/report-details-fda-rejection-of-nextday-pill.html (retrieved May 2, 2016).

Hassan, S., B.E. Wright, and G. Yukl. 2014. "Does Ethical Leadership Matter in Government? Effects on Organizational Commitment, Absenteeism, and Willingness to Report Ethical Problems." *Public Administration Review* 74(3):333–343.

Haynes, W., and B. Gazley. 2011. "Professional Associations and Public Administration: Making a Difference?" In *The State of Public Administration: Issues, Challenges, and Opportunities*, ed. D. Menzel and H. White. Armonk, NY: M.E. Sharpe, 54–69.

Heifetz, R., A. Grashow, and M. Linsky. 2009. "Leadership in a (Permanent) Crisis." *Harvard Business Review* 87 (7/8): 62–69.

Hejka-Ekins, A. 1992. "Marie Ragghianti: Moral Courage in Exposing Corruption." In *Exemplary Public Administrators*, ed. T.L. Cooper and N.D. Wright. San Francisco, CA: Jossey-Bass, 304–323.

———. 2001. "Ethics in In-Service Training." In *Handbook of Administrative Ethics*, 2d ed., ed. T.L. Cooper. New York: Marcel Dekker, pp. 79–103.

Henry, N. 1995. *Public Administration and Public Affairs*. 6th ed. Englewood Cliffs, NJ: Prentice Hall.

————. 2011. "Federal Contracting: Government's Dependency on Private Contractors." In *The State of Public Administration: Issues, Challenges, and Opportunities,* ed. D. Menzel and H. White. Armonk, NY: M.E. Sharpe, pp. 221–237.

Herman, R.D. 2013a. "Ethical Decision Making." Cited in J.G. Pettey (2013). *Nonprofit Fundraising Strategy.* Hoboken, NJ: John Wiley.

————. 2013b. "Regulation in the Nonprofit Sector." Cited in J.G. Pettey (2013). *Nonprofit Fundraising Strategy.* Hoboken, New Jersey: John Wiley.

Hersh, S.M. 2004. "Torture at Abu Ghraib." *The New Yorker.* May 10. http://www. newyorker.com/magazine/2004/05/10/torture-at-abu-ghraib (retrieved October 9, 2015).

Hess, A. 2003. "Assessing the Ethical Judgment of a Potential Employee—II." *Public Administration Times,* September.

Hill, L.A. 2006. "Exercising Moral Courage: A Developmental Agenda." In *Moral Leadership: The Theory and Practice of Power, Judgment, and Policy,* ed. D.L. Rhode. San Francisco, CA: Jossey-Bass, 267.

Hillsborough County, Florida. 2011. "Disclaimer!" Official Citizen Participation Blog. http://hillsboroughfl.blogspot.com/ (retrieved June 7, 2011).

Hirt, M.J. 2003. "Assessing the Ethical Judgment of a Potential Employee." *Public Administration Times,* July.

Hoekstra, A., A. Belling, and E. Van Der Heide. 2005. "Beyond Compliance—A Practitioner's View." Paper presented at the Ethics and Integrity of Governance: The First Transatlantic Dialogue, Leuven, Belgium, 2–5 June.

Houston, D.J., and L.H. Harding. (2013–2014). "Public Trust in Government Administrators: Explaining Citizen Perceptions of Trustworthiness and Competence." *Public Integrity,* 16(1):53–76.

Hunt, M. 2005. "Ethics and British Local Government: The Relevance of Compliance Strategies." Paper presented at the Ethics and Integrity of Governance: The First Transatlantic Dialogue, Leuven, Belgium, 2–5 June.

Husock, H. 2014. "How Government Threatens Religious Charity: Lessons of New York's 'Met Council' Scandal." *Forbes,* July 31. http://www.forbes. com/sites/howardhusock/2014/07/31/how-government-threatens-religious-charity-lessons-of-new-yorks-met-council-scandal/ (retrieved October 5, 2015).

Hussey, K., and M. Santora. 2015. "Judge Sends Rowland, Ex-Connecticut Governor, Back to Prison." *New York Times,* March 18. http://www.nytimes. com/2015/03/19/nyregion/john-rowland-of-connecticut-sentenced-to-prison. html?ref=topics (retrieved October 8, 2015).

ICMA. 2015. *ICMA Code of Ethics with Guidelines.* http://icma.org/en/icma/ knowledge_network/documents/kn/Document/100265/ICMA_Code_of_Ethics_ with_Guidelines (retrieved March 2, 2016).

ICMA. 2016. *ICMA Code of Ethics: Rules of Procedure for Enforcement.* http:// icma.org/en/Search?s=ICMA%2BCODE%2BSANCTIONS (retrieved May 1, 2016).

Idealist. 2015. "Things a U.S.-Based Nonprofit Must (and Must Not) Do." http://www.idealist.org/info/Nonprofits/Mgmt4 (retrieved October 9, 2015).

IEEC. 2011a. *The Role of the EEC and the CPO in State Procurement.* http://www.illinois.gov/eec/Pages/TheRoleoftheEECandtheCPOin.aspx (retrieved March 3, 2016).

———. 2011b. *Annual Report. Fiscal Year 2010.* http://www.illinois.gov/eec/Documents/FY%202010%20%20AnnualRep.pdf (retrieved March 3, 2016).

Illinois Attorney General. 2010. "Ethics and Public Integrity." www.ag.state.il.us/government/ethics.html (retrieved July 1, 2011).

Independent Sector. 2015. "Principles for Good Governance and Ethical Practice: A Guide for Charities and Foundations." https://www.independentsector.org/principles (retrieved October 5, 2015).

Integrity Florida. 2015. http://www.integrityflorida.org/about-us/ (retrieved October 8, 2015).

International City/County Management Association (ICMA). 1998. "Code of Ethics." http://icma.org/en/icma/ethics/code_of_ethics (retrieved February 22, 2016).

———. 2005. "ICMA Rules of Procedure for Enforcement of the Code of Ethics." September. http://icma.org/en/icma/knowledge_network/documents/kn/Document/100266/ICMA_Rules_of_Procedure_for_Enforcement_of_the_Code_of_Ethics (retrieved April 20, 2011).

———. 2010. "ICMA Censures Former City Manager for Ethics Violation." December 20. http://icma.org/en/icma/newsroom/highlights/Article/100857/ICMA_Censures_Former_City_Manager_for_Ethics_Violation (retrieved April 20, 2011).

Iorio, P. 2011. *Straightforward: Ways to Live & Lead.* Tampa, FL: Pam Iorio.

Ivory, D., and K. Bradsher. 2015. "Regulators Investigating 2nd VW Emissions Program." *New York Times* October 9:B1–B5.

Jacobs, R. 2015. http://patimes.org/leading-doing-conducting-personal-ethics-audit/ (retrieved September 10, 2015).

Jeavons, T.H. 2012. "Ethics in Nonprofit Management: Creating a Culture of Integrity." p. 86 in Ott & Dicke 2012.

Jefferson, T. 1807/1824. *A Winter in Washington.* Memoir in two volumes by Margaret Bayard Smith. New York: E. Bliss and E. White.

Jelmayer, R. 2015. "Three Former Brazil Lawmakers Arrested in Petrobras Probe." *Wall Street Journal.* April 10. http://www.wsj.com/articles/three-former-brazil-lawmakers-arrested-in-petrobras-probe-1428674575?cb=logged0.92084113904275 (retrieved October 9, 2015).

Jenkins, C. 2005. "Penalty for Judge Is Seen Two Ways." *St. Petersburg Times,* November 19.

Jenkins, S. 2012. "Joe Paterno's first interview since the Penn State-Sandusky scandal." *The Washington Post.* https://www.washingtonpost.com/sports/colleges/joe-

paternos-first-interview-since-the-penn-state-sandusky-scandal/2012/01/13/
gIQA08e4yP_story.html (retrieved October 5, 2015).

Jennings, B., J.L. Nelson, and E. Parens. 1994. *Values on Campus: A Report.*
Braircliff, NY: Hastings Center.

Jiang, Z. 2001. "Keynote Speech at the Communist Party of China's 80th
Anniversary." China Internet Information Center, July 2. http://china.org.cn/
english/features/35725.htm (retrieved August 2, 2005).

Johnson, A. 2011a. Personal e-mail communication, April 28. Alan Johnson is the
executive director of Palm Beach County's Commission on Ethics (Florida).

———. 2011b. Personal e-mail communication, May 27.

Johnson, E. 2011. Personal e-mail communication, April 11. Eric Johnson is Director,
Strategic Planning and ERP Implementation, Hillsborough County, Florida.

Johnson, L.B. 1964. "Commencement Address, University of Michigan." http://
www.pbs.org/wgbh/americanexperience/features/primary-resources/lbj-
michigan/ (retrieved March 1, 2016).

Johnson, R. 2003. *Whistleblowing: When It Works—and Why.* Boulder, CO: Lynne
Rienner.

———. 2005. "Comparative Whistleblowing: Administrative, Cultural, and Ethical
Issues." Proceedings of 2005 International Conference on Public Administration,
October 21–22, Chengdu, P.R. China.

Jones, S. 2015. "Politicking Problems: Iowa Pastors Are Campaigning for
Presidential Candidates." Wall of Separation, April 8. https://www.au.org/
blogs/wall-of-separation/politicking-problems-iowa-pastors-are-campaigning-
for-presidential (retrieved October 5, 2015).

Jos, P.H. 1989. "In Praise of Difficult People: A Portrait of the Committed
Whistleblower." *Public Administration Review* 49:552–561.

Jurkiewicz, C.L., and G.M. Vogel. 2015. "The Ethics Audit: Measuring the
Effectiveness of Ethics Education across the Sectors." *Journal of Management
Systems.* 25(2):35–46.

Kant, I. 1785/1989. *Foundations of the Metaphysics of Morals.* 2d ed. Translated
from the German by Lewis White Beck. Upper Saddle River, NJ: Prentice Hall.

Kaptein, M. 2011. "Toward Effective Codes: Testing the Relationship with Unethical
Behavior." *Journal of Business Ethics* 99:233–251.

Kennedy, J.F. 1961. "Special Message to the Congress on Conflict-of-Interest
Legislation and on Problems of Ethics in Government." April 27. http://www.
presidency.ucsb.edu/ws/index.php?pid=8092#axzz1bkR1C1lc (retrieved May 2,
2016.

Kennedy, S.S. 2015. "Knowing One's Place: Ethics in a Multi-sectoral Context."
Journal of Management Systems 25(2):27–34.

Kernaghan, K. 2003. "Integrating Values into Public Service: The Values
Statement as Centerpiece." *Public Administration Review* 63 (November/
December):711–719.

King, M.L., Jr. 1963. "Letter from Birmingham Jail." April 16. http://abacus.bates. edu/admin/offices/dos/mlk/letter.html (retrieved March 5, 2011).

Kocieniewski, D. 2010. "Rangel Censured over Violations of Ethics Rules." *New York Times,* December 3:A1.

Kudo, H., and J. Maesschalck. 2005. "The Ethics Law and Ethics Code in Japanese Public Administration: Background, Contents, and Impact." Paper presented at the Ethics and Integrity of Governance: The First Transatlantic Dialogue, Leuven, Belgium, 2–5 June.

Kusnetz, N. 2015. "Only Three States Score Higher Than D+ in State Integrity Investigation; 11 Flunk." The Center for Public Integrity. http://www. publicintegrity.org/2015/11/09/18693/only-three-states-score-higher-d-state-integrity-investigation-11-flunk?utm_source=Integrity+Florida+Statement+on+updated+State+Integrity+Investigation&utm_campaign=Gov+Signs+Ethics+Reform+SB+846&utm_medium=email (retrieved November 9, 2015).

Lambert, B. 2005. "Audit Describes 8 Years of Looting by School Officials." *New York Times,* March 3.

Lasthuizen, K. 2008. "Leading to Integrity." Dissertation. Amsterdam: VU University.

League of Minnesota Cities. 2012. http://www.lmc.org/page/1/core-values.jsp (retrieved March 3, 2016).

Lee, C. 2006. "New Stamp to Honor WWII Envoy." *The Washington Post,* May 25, 2006. http://www.washingtonpost.com/wp-dyn/content/article/2006/05/24/AR2006052402467_pf.html (retrieved October 7, 2015).

Lee, T., and A.G. Bense. 2006. "Memorandum." The Florida Legislature. January 20.

Lee, Y.L., and V.M. Wilkins. 2011. "More Similarities or More Differences? Comparing Public and Nonprofit Managers' Job Motivations." *Public Administration Review* 71(1):45–56.

Leinbach, K. 2011. Personal e-mail communication, March 4.

Lewis, C.W. 1991. *The Ethics Challenge in Public Service: A Problem-Solving Guide.* San Francisco, CA: Jossey-Bass.

Lewis, C.W., and S.C. Gilman. 2012. *The Ethics Challenge in Public Service: A Problem-Solving Guide.* 3rd ed. San Francisco, CA: Jossey-Bass.

Lewis, M.J., A. Shacklock, C.M. Conners, and C. Sampford. 2013. "Integrity Reform in Developing Countries." *Public Integrity* 15(3):243–264.

Lewis, N.A. 2000. "Obituary: Elliot Richardson Dies at 79; Stood Up to Nixon and Resigned in 'Saturday Night Massacre.'" NYTimes.com—On This Day, January 1. www.nytimes.com/learning/general/onthisday/bday/0720.html (retrieved March 7, 2011).

Light, P.C. 1999. *The New Public Service.* Washington, DC: The Brookings Institution.

Liptak, A. 2010. "Justices Limit Use of 'Honest Services' Law Against Fraud." *New York Times,* June 24. http://www.nytimes.com/2010/06/25/us/25scotus.html (retrieved May 2, 2016).

Lipton, E., and D. Kocieniewski. 2010. "Panel in House Will Try Rangel in Ethics Cases." *New York Times,* July 23: A1.

Lipton, R. 2011. "G.O.P. Senator Resigning Post amid Scandal." *New York Times,* April 22:A1.

Los Angeles County Metropolitan Transportation Authority. 2011. "Codes of Conduct." www.metro.net/about/ethics/code-conduct/ (retrieved August 5, 2011).

Lovell, A. 2003. "The Enduring Phenomenon of Moral Muteness: Suppressed Whistleblowing." *Public Integrity* 1.5 (Summer):187–204.

Lovett, K. 2014. "Exclusive: Hotline Launched for State Government Staffers to Report Sexual Harassment and Other Complaints." *New York Daily News,* June 23. http://www.nydailynews.com/new-york/harass-hotline-set-state-government-workers-article-1.1839917 (retrieved March 2, 2016).

Lui, T.T. 1988. "Changing Civil Servants' Values." In *The Hong Kong Civil Service and Its Future,* ed. I. Scott and J.P. Burns. Hong Kong: Oxford University Press.

Lui, T.T., and I. Scott. 2001. "Administrative Ethics in a Chinese Society: The Case of Hong Kong." In *Handbook of Administrative Ethics,* ed. T.L. Cooper. New York: Marcel Dekker, 649–669.

Mackenzie, G.C. 2002. *Scandal Proof: Do Ethics Laws Make Government Ethical?* Washington, DC: Brookings Institution.

Madison, J. 1788. *The Federalist* #51. February 8. http://thomas.loc.gov/home/histdox/fed_51.html# (retrieved February 22, 2016).

Majorsky, K. 2015. "Enforcement Gap Reveals Difference between State Laws and Practices." http://www.stateintegrity.org/enforcement_gap_reveals_state_laws_practices (retrieved October 8, 2015).

Markkula Center for Applied Ethics. n.d. Santa Clara, CA: Santa Clara University. www.scu.edu/ethics/ (retrieved February 22, 2016).

Markus, M.L. 1994. "Finding a Happy Medium: Explaining the Negative Effects of Electronic Communication on Social Life at Work." *ACM Transactions on Information Systems* 12 (April):119–149.

Martirossian, J. 2004. "Russia and Her Ghosts of the Past." In *The Struggle Against Corruption: A Comparative Study,* ed. R.A. Johnson. New York: Palgrave Macmillian, 81–108.

Mayer, J.P. (ed.). 1969. *Democracy in America.* New York: Harper & Row.

McAllister, K. 2005. Personal e-mail communication, May 5.

McAuliffe, D. 2002. "Social Work Ethics Audits: A New Tool for Ethical Practice." Paper presented at the IIPE/AAPAE Conference, Brisbane, Australia.

McKeever, B.S., and S. L. Pettijohn. 2014. "The Nonprofit Sector in Brief 2014." Washington, DC: Urban Institute.

McKinley, J. 2015. "Harassment Suit Against Former Assemblyman Vito Lopez and Sheldon Silver Is Settled." *New York Times,* February 5, A20.

McWhirter, C. 2015. "Cancer Charities Called $187 Million Sham." *Wall Street Journal,* May 20. http://www.wsj.com/articles/four-cancer-charities-accused-of-fraud-1432063345 (retrieved October 8, 2015).

Mehta, N. 2009. "Nonprofits and Lobbying." *ABA Business Law Section.* 18(4):March/April   https://apps.americanbar.org/buslaw/blt/2009-03-04/mehta. shtml (retrieved October 5, 2015).

Menzel, D.C. 1992. "Ethics Attitudes and Behaviors in Local Governments: An Empirical Analysis." *State and Local Government Review* 24 (Fall):94–102.

———. 1993. "The Ethics Factor in Local Government: An Empirical Analysis." In *Ethics and Public Administration,* ed. H.G. Frederickson. Armonk, NY: M.E. Sharpe, pp. 191–204.

———. 1995. "The Ethical Environment of Local Government Managers." *American Review of Public Administration* 25 (September):247–262.

———. 1996a. "Ethics Complaint Making and Trustworthy Government." *Public Integrity Annual* 73–82.

———. 1996b. "Ethics Stress in Public Organizations." *Public Productivity and Management Review* 20:70–83.

———. 1997. "Teaching Ethics and Values in Public Administration: Are We Making a Difference?" *Public Administration Review* 57 (May/June):224–230.

———. 2001a. "Ethics and Public Management." In *Handbook of Public Management and Practice,* ed. K.T. Liou. New York: Marcel Dekker.

———. 2001b. "Ethics Management in Public Organizations." In *Handbook of Administrative Ethics,* 2d ed., ed. T.L. Cooper. New York: Marcel Dekker.

———. 2005a. "Research on Ethics and Integrity in Governance: A Review and Assessment." *Public Integrity* 7 (Spring):147–168.

———. 2005b. "Building Public Organizations of Integrity." Proceedings of 2005 International Conference on Public Administration, Chengdu, P.R. China, October 21–22.

———. 2009. "I Didn't Do Anything Unethical, Illegal, or Immoral." *Public Integrity* 11(4): 371–384.

———. 2010. *Ethics Moments in Government: Cases and Controversies.* Boca Raton, FL: CRC Press.

———. 2011. "Ethics and Integrity in Public Service: Issues and Challenges." In *The State of Public Administration: Issues, Challenges, and Opportunities,* ed. D. Menzel and H. White. Armonk, NY: M.E. Sharpe, pp. 108–124.

———. 2015a. "Leadership in Public Administration: Creative and/or Ethical?" *Public Integrity* 17(4):315–318.

———. 2015b. "Research on Ethics and Integrity in Public Administration: Moving Forward, Looking Back." *Public Integrity* 17(4):343–370.

Merle, R. 2004. "Long Fall for Pentagon Star: Druyun Doled Out Favors by the Millions." *Washington Post,* November 14: A01. http://www.washingtonpost. com/wp-dyn/articles/A48241-2004Nov13.html (retrieved October 7, 2015).

Miceli, M., and J.P. Near. 1985. "Characteristics of Organizational Climate and Perceived Wrongdoing Associated with Whistle-Blowing Decisions." *Personnel Psychology* 38:525–544.

Miller, C. 2011. "Hotline Analysis Dated August 2007–May 2011." Presented to the Council of the City of Jacksonville, Florida, June 14.

Miller, J. 2011. "Contractors Gather to Learn of New Cuyahoga County Ethical Standards." *Crain's Cleveland Business,* July 1.

Moilanen, T. 2007. "The Adoption of the Ethics Framework in EU Member States." Paper presented at the Conference on Public Integrity and Anticorruption in the Public Service, Bucharest, Romania. May 29–30.

Moilanen, T., and A. Salminen. 2006. *European Public Administration Network.* Brussels, Belgium: Human Resources Working Group, EUPAN.

Mosley, L. 1982. *Marshall: Hero for Our Times.* New York: Hearst Books.

Murse, T. 2015. What is dark money? About Politics. http://uspolitics.about.com/od/Money-In-Politics/a/What-Is-Dark-Money.htm (retrieved September 14, 2015).

Naplesnews.com. 2008. Quotations. August 2, September 4, September 30. http://www.naplesnews.com/news/local/investigation-clears-lee-county-manager-ep-401184567-344381582.html (retrieved March 2, 2016).

National Association of Schools of Public Affairs and Administration (NASPAA). 1989. *Standards for Professional Master's Degree Programs in Public Affairs and Administration.* Washington, DC: NASPAA

———. 2005. "NASPAA Member Code of Good Practice." October. http://www.coj.net/departments/ethics-office/docs/ethics-code-2011.aspx (retrieved March 5, 2016).

———. 2008. "Standards: 2008." January. https://naspaaaccreditation.files.wordpress.com/2014/04/old-accreditation-standards.pdf (retrieved March 5, 2016).

———. 2009. "NASPAA Standards 2009: Accreditation Standards for Master's Degree Programs." Commission on Peer Review and Accreditation, October 16. www.naspaa.org/accreditation/doc/NS2009FinalVote10.16.2009.pdf (retrieved June 7, 2011).

National Association of Social Workers. 2015. "Sanctions in Force." https://www.councilofnonprofits.org/tools-resources/code-of-ethics-nonprofits (retrieved July 6, 2015).

National Conference of State Legislatures. 2013. "Ethics Commissions: Who Can Initiate a Complaint?" November 1. http://www.ncsl.org/research/ethics/50-state-chart-ethics-commissions-who-can-initia.aspx (retrieved October 8, 2015).

———. 2015. "Gift Restrictions." http://www.ncsl.org/research/ethics/gift-restrictions.aspx (retrieved October 8, 2015).

National Council of Nonprofits. 2015a. https://www.councilofnonprofits.org/trends-policy-issues/government-grants-contracting (retrieved August 6, 2015).

———. 2015b. "Code of Ethics for Nonprofits." https://www.councilofnonprofits.org/tools-resources/code-of-ethics-nonprofits (retrieved July 6, 2015).

———. 2015c. "Conducting an Ethics Audit at Your Nonprofit." https://www.councilofnonprofits.org/sites/default/files/documents/Conducting%20an%20Ethics%20Audit%20at%20Your%20Nonprofit.pdf (retrieved October 7, 2015)

National League of Cities. 2010. "The Athenian Oath." http://nlc.org/build-skills-networks/resources/cities-101/the-athenian-oath (retrieved June 11, 2011).

National Personnel Authority (NPA). n.d.a. "Main Training Courses Conducted by the NPA." www.jinji.go.jp/english/fig/fig_15.htm (retrieved January 3, 2006).

———. n.d.b. "Training." www.jinji.go.jp/english/int_05.htm (retrieved February 22, 2016).

Nelson, M. 1999. "The Challenge of Implementing Codes of Conduct in Local Government Authorities." Paper presented at the Ninth International Anti-Corruption Conference, Durban, South Africa, October 10–15. http://9iacc.org/papers/day4/ws3/d4ws3_mnelson.html (retrieved February 22, 2016).

Newell, T. 2015a. "With So Many Ethics Laws, Why So Many Ethics Flaws?" The BLOG. March 25. http://www.huffingtonpost.com/terry-newell/with-so-many-ethics-laws_b_6937764.html (retrieved October 5, 2015).

———. 2015b. "Hiram Bingham: Courageous Dissent in Public Service." http://patimes.org/hiram-bingham-courageous-dissent-public-service/ (retrieved October 7, 2015).

New Land. 2015. "The Three Character Classic: Introductory." http://www.newland magazine.com.au/vision/article/1124 (retrieved March 4, 2016).

New York Times. 2009. "Editorial: Fed Up with Albany." October 19: A26.

———. 2010a. "Editorial: Untenable Judicial Ethics." November 28: 7.

———. 2010b. "Punishment in the House." November 19: A3. http://www.nytimes.com/2010/11/19/nyregion/19rangelside.html (retrieved February 22, 2016).

———. 2011. "Anna Hazare." http://topics.nytimes.com/top/reference/timestopics/people/h/anna_hazare/index.html?scp=10&sq=india%20corruption&st=cse (retrieved November 16, 2011).

———. 2015. "Timeline: The Penn State Scandal." http://www.nytimes.com/interactive/2011/11/11/sports/ncaafootball/sandusky.html?_r=2& (retrieved October 5, 2015).

Nixon, R. 2011. "G.O.P. Grants Reprieve to House Ethics Office." New York Times, January 21.

Obama, B. 2009. "President Barack Obama's Inaugural Address." January 20. http://www.whitehouse.gov/blog/inaugural-address/ (retrieved February 22, 2016).

O'Donnell, G. 2006. "Our 21st Century Civil Service—Creating a Culture of Excellence." Speech, June 6. www.egovmonitor.com/node/6303 (retrieved July 6, 2006).

OGE Institute for Ethics in Government. 2016. https://www.youtube.com/user/OGEInstitute (retrieved March 3, 2016).

O'Leary, R. 2006. The Ethics of Dissent: Managing Guerrilla Government. Washington, DC: CQ Press.

O'Neill, M. 2007. "The Future of Nonprofit Management Education." Nonprofit and Voluntary Sector Quarterly 36 (4) (suppl.): 169s–176s.

Organisation for Economic Co-operation and Development (OECD). 1997. "Managing Policy Ethics." PUMA Policy Brief. February. www.oecd.org/dataoecd/59/60/1899269.pdf (retrieved January 3, 2006).

————. 1998. "Principles for Managing Ethics in the Public Service." PUMA Policy Brief No. 4. May. https://www.kpk-rs.si/upload/datoteke/OECD_Public_service_2.pdf (retrieved March 5, 2016).

————. 2004. "OECD Reviews Progress in the Worldwide Fight Against Corruption." News release, January 12. http://www.oecd.org/document/30/0,23 40,en_2649_201185_33989854_1_1_1_1,00.html (retrieved January 3, 2006).

Osborne, D., and T. Gaebler. 1992. *Reinventing Government: How the Entrepreneurial Spirit Is Transforming the Public Sector*. Reading, MA: Addison-Wesley.

Ott, J.S., and L.A. Dicke. 2012. *Understanding Nonprofit Organizations*, 2nd ed. Boulder, CO: Westview Press.

Ott, J.S. 2015. United Nations Rule of Law. http://www.unrol.org/article.aspx?article_id=23 (retrieved August 20, 2015).

Ouchi, W.G. 1981. *Theory Z: How American Business Can Meet the Japanese Challenge*. Reading, MA: Addison-Wesley.

Paine, L.S. 1994. "Managing for Organizational Integrity." *Harvard Business Review* 72 (March/April):106–117.

Painter, R.W. 2009. *Getting the Government America Deserves: How Ethics Reform Can Make a Difference*. Oxford: Oxford University Press.

Palidauskaite, J. 2006. "Codes of Ethics in Transitional Democracies: A Comparative Perspective." *Public Integrity* 8:35–48.

Perry, J.L. 1993. "Whistleblowing, Organizational Performance, and Organizational Control." In *Ethics and Public Administration*, ed. H.G. Frederickson. Armonk, NY: M.E. Sharpe, pp. 79–99.

Peters, T.J., and R.H. Waterman. 1982. *In Search of Excellence*. New York: Harper & Row.

Pettey, J.G. (ed.). 2013. *Nonprofit Fundraising Strategy*. Hoboken, NJ: John Wiley & Sons.

Pevkur, A. 2007. "Compatibility of Public Administration Systems and Ethics Management." Tallinn, Estonia: State Chancellery of the Republic of Estonia, Department of Public Service, pp. 16–24.

Pfiffner, J.P. 2005. "Torture and Public Policy." *Public Integrity* 7(4):313–329.

Pierson, J. 2013. "How Big Government Co-Opted Charities." *Wall Street Journal*, July 17. http://www.wsj.com/articles/SB10001424127887324021104578553093991335514 (retrieved August 21, 2015).

Pinellas County, Florida. n.d. "Pinellas County Statement of Ethics." http://www.co.pinellas.fl.us/persnl/PCethics.pdf (retrieved February 22, 2016).

Plunkitt, G.W. 1903. "The Curse of Civil Service Reform." In *Plunkitt of Tammany Hall*, ed. W.L. Riordan. New York. http://www.yale.edu/glc/archive/993.htm (retrieved February 22, 2016).

Pope, J. 2000. "Source Book 2000—Confronting Corruption: The Elements of a National Integrity System." Transparency International. www.transparency.org/publications/publications/sourcebook2000 (retrieved January 3, 2006).

————. 2005. "Observations Concerning Comparative Administrative Ethics in Europe and the U.S." Paper presented at the Ethics and Integrity of Governance: The First Transatlantic Dialogue, Leuven, Belgium, June 2–5.

Pops, G. 2006. "The Ethical Leadership of George C. Marshall." *Public Integrity* 8:165–186.

Public Broadcasting Service. 2005. "Selecting State Judges." *NOW,* June 17. www. pbs.org/now/politics/choosingjudges.html (retrieved July 1, 2011).

Puccini. G.J., M. Mance, and J. Zacko-Smith. 2015. "Creative Leadership: Its Meaning and Value for Science, Technology and Innovation." http://www. academia.edu/1958027/CREATIVE_LEADERSHIP_ITS_MEANING_AND_ VALUE_FOR_SCIENCE_TECHNOLOGY_AND_INNOVATION (retrieved October 7, 2015).

Rabin, J. (ed.). 2003. *Encyclopedia of Public Administration and Public Policy.* 2 vols. New York: Marcel Dekker.

Raffel, J.A., S.M. Maser, and C. Calarusse. 2011. "Accreditation and Competencies in Education for Leadership in Public Service" In *The State of Public Administration: Issues, Challenges, and Opportunities,* ed. D. Menzel and H. White. Armonk, NY: M.E. Sharpe, pp. 70–88.

Rauh, J. 2015. "Predicting Political Influence on State Ethics Commissions: Of Course We Are Ethical—Nudge Nudge, Wink Wink." *Public Administration Review* 75(1):98–110.

Reamer, F.G. 2000. "The Social Work Ethics Audit: A Risk-Management Strategy." *Social Work* 45 (July):355–366.

————. 2007. "Conducting an Ethics Audit." *Social Work Today*, 7(1) http://www. socialworktoday.com/archive/EoEJanFeb07.shtml (retrieved October 7, 2015).

————. 2013. "Ethical Competence in Social Work." In *Achieving Ethical Competence for Public Service Leadership,* ed. T.L. Cooper and D.C. Menzel. Armonk, NY: M.E. Sharpe, pp. 163–188.

Reichenberg, N. 2015. Personal e-mail communication, August 12.

Reinke, S.J. 2006. "Abu Ghraib." *Public Integrity* 8(2):135–147.

Report of the National Performance Review. 1993. *Creating a Government That Works Better and Costs Less.* Washington, DC: U.S. Government Printing Office.

Republic of the Philippines. 1989. "Republic Act No. 6713." Congress of the Philippines, Metro Manila, Eighth Congress, February 20. www.lawphil.net/ statutes/repacts/ra1989/ra_6713_1989.html (retrieved June 25, 2006).

Richardson, E. 1996. *Reflections of a Radical Moderate.* New York: Pantheon Books.

Riordon, W.L. 1963. *Plunkitt of Tammany Hall.* New York: E.P. Dutton.

Roberts, R.N. 1988. *White House Ethics: The History of the Politics of Conflict of Interest Regulation.* New York: Greenwood.

Rohr, J.A. 1978. *Ethics for Bureaucrats: An Essay on Law and Values.* New York: Marcel Dekker.

————. 1986. *To Run a Constitution: The Legitimacy of the Administrative State.* Lawrence, KS: University Press of Kansas.

————. 1989. *Ethics for Bureaucrats: An Essay on Law and Values.* 2nd ed. New York: Marcel Dekker.

Ronquillo, A. 2007. "Ethics in Government: The Philippine Scenario." Paper presented at EUROPA, Tehran, Iran. November 18–22.

Rose-Ackerman, S. 1999. *Corruption and Government: Causes, Consequences, and Reform.* New York: Cambridge University Press.

Rosen, L. 2010. "Understanding Corruption." *The American Interest,* March–April. www.the-american-interest.com/article.cfm?piece=792 (retrieved February 13, 2011).

Rosenson, B.A. 2005. *The Shadowlands of Conduct: Ethics and State Politics.* Washington, DC: Georgetown University Press.

Ruth, D. 2015. "The Dangers of Dark Money." *Tampa Bay Times.* September 13. http://www.tampabay.com/opinion/columns/ruth-the-dangers-of-dark-money/2245181 (retrieved October 9, 2015).

Salt Lake County, Utah. 2011. "County Ethics Code." Salt Lake County, Utah, Code of Ordinances, Chapter 2.07, May 16. http://library.municode.com/HTML/16602/level2/TIT2ADPE_CH2.07COETCO.html#TOPTITLE (retrieved February 22, 2016).

Saul, S. 2011. "Charter Schools Tied to Turkey Grow in Texas." *New York Times,* June 6. http://www.nytimes.com/2011/06/07/education/07charter.html?mtrref=query.nytimes.com (retrieved October 9, 2015).

Scheer, R.. 1976. "The Playboy Interview: Jimmy Carter," *Playboy* 23(11) (November):63–86. http://www.arts.mcgill.ca/history/faculty/troyweb/courseweb/jimmycartertheplayboyinterview.htm (retrieved February 27, 2006).

Schneider, B. (ed.). 1990. *Organizational Climate and Culture.* San Francisco, CA: Jossey-Bass.

Schultz, D. 2010. "Ethics Regulation Across Professions: The Problem of Gifting." *Public Integrity* 12(2):161–172.

Schultz, D. 2011. "The Crisis of Public Administration Theory in a Postglobal World." In *The State of Public Administration: Issues, Challenges, and Opportunities,* ed. D. Menzel and H. White. Armonk, NY: M.E. Sharpe, pp. 453–464.

Schweers, J. 2005. "Concern Builds as Home Inspection Goes Private." *Florida Today,* July 25. http://www.floridatoday.com/article/20050725/NEWS01/50725 0330/Concern-builds-home-inspection-goes-private (retrieved October 9, 2015).

Scott, B. 2010. "Governor Paterson Fined $62k Over Free Yankees Tickets And Cover-Up." *New York Post,* December 21. http://nypost.com/2010/12/21/gov-paterson-fined-62k-over-free-yankees-tickets-and-cover-up/ (retrieved March 3, 2016).

Scott, W.G., and D.K. Hart. 1979. *Organizational America.* Boston, MA: Houghton Mifflin.

———. 1989. *Organizational Values in America.* New Brunswick, NJ: Transaction Publishers.

Senge, P. 1990. *The Fifth Discipline: The Art and Practice of the Learning Organization.* New York: Currency Doubleday.

Seper, W. 2013. "Inadequate Oversight of Millions in Federal Grants by Big Brothers Big Sisters." *The Washington Times,* June 24. http://www.washingtontimes. com/news/2013/jun/24/big-brothers-big-sisters-cant-account-23-million-f/print/ (retrieved October 7, 2015).

Shatteman, A. 2015. "Checklist for Illinois Charitable Organizations." Personal e-mail communication, October 29.

Sheyn, E.R. 2011. "Criminalizing the Denial of Honest Services After Skilling." ExpressO. Available at http://works.bepress.com/elizabeth_sheyn/2 (retrieved June 21, 2011).

Shreve, P. 2015. Personal e-mail communication, August 12.

Simmons, C.W., H. Roland, and J. Kelly-DeWitt. 1998. *Local Government Ethics Ordinances in California.* Sacramento, CA: California Research Bureau, California State Library.

Smith, M.K. 2001. "Peter Senge and the Learning Organization." *E-Journal of Organizational Learning and Leadership* 2 (1). www.leadingtoday.org/weleadi nlearning/msapr03.htm (retrieved December 6, 2005).

Smith, R.W. 2003. "Enforcement or Ethical Capacity: Considering the Role of State Ethics Commissions at the Millennium." *Public Administration Review* 63(3):283–295.

———. 2004. "A Comparison of the Ethics Infrastructure in China and the United States." *Public Integrity* 6 (Fall):299–318.

Smothers, R. 2005. "11 New Jersey Officials, Including 3 Mayors, Face Charges of Corruption." *New York Times,* February 25.

Stainer, L., A. Stainer, and A. Gully. 1999. "Ethics and Performance Management." *International Journal of Technology Management* 17 (7/8):776–785.

State of Florida. 2007. Office of the Governor Executive Order 07-01.

State of Florida. 2010. "Nineteenth Statewide Grand Jury, First Interim Report: A Study of Public Corruption in Florida and Recommended Solutions." Case No. SC 09-1910, December 17. http://myfloridalegal.com/webfiles.nsf/WF/JFAO-8CLT9A/$file/19thSWGJInterimReport.pdf (retrieved March 5, 2016).

State of Illinois. 1993. State Officials and Employees Ethics Act (Public Act 93–0617).

State Services Commission. 2001. *Walking the Talk: Making Values Real.* http:// www.ssc.govt.nz/upload/downloadable_files/Walking_the_Talk-_full_text.pdf (retrieved March 5, 2016).

Steinhauer, J. 2010. "Senate, for Just the 8th Time, Votes to Oust a Federal Judge." *New York Times,* December 9:A25.

Steinhauer, J. 2015. "Bob McDonnell, Ex-Governor of Virginia, Is Sentenced to 2 years for Corruption." *New York Times,* January 6. http://www.nytimes.

com/2015/01/07/us/bob-mcdonnell-ex-governor-virginia-sentencing-corruption.html (retrieved July 13, 2015).

Stillman, R.J. 1999. *Preface to Public Administration: A Search for Themes and Direction*. 2nd ed. Burke, VA: Chatelaine Press.

St. Petersburg, City. 2004. "Code of Ethics for City." http://www.stpete.org/city_departments/city_auditor/docs/ap010405.pdf (retrieved October 8, 2015).

St. Petersburg Times. 2005. "Editorial: Ethical Questions." March 20. http://www.sptimes.com/2005/03/20/Opinion/Ethical_questions.shtml.

Stone, M.M., and F. Ostrower. 2007. "Acting in the Public Interest? Another Look at Research on Nonprofit Governance." *Nonprofit and Voluntary Sector Quarterly* 36 (3): 416–438.

Stone, R. 2010. "A Wallet-Sized Code of Ethics." *Governing*, May 5. http://www.governing.com/columns/mgmt-insights/A-Wallet-Sized-Code-of.html (retrieved June 28, 2011).

Straus, J.R. 2008. "Honest Leadership and Open Government Act of 2007: The Role of the Clerk of the House and Secretary of the Senate." CRS Report for Congress, Order Code RL34377, July 22. www.fas.org/sgp/crs/secrecy/RL34377.pdf (retrieved March 30, 2011).

The Supreme Court of Florida. 2006. "Inquiry Concerning a Judge, No. 02-466, RE: Judge John Renke III. No. SC03-1846, May 25." www.floridasupremecourt.org/decisions/2006/sc03-1846.pdf (retrieved April 21, 2011).

The Supreme Court of Ohio. 1997. "Code of Judicial Conduct." May 1. www.supremecourt.ohio.gov/LegalResources/Rules/conduct/judcond.pdf (retrieved February 22, 2011).

Sussex, P. 2015. "Scandal-Hit Charities Need Strong Regulator." *The Guardian*, September 16. http://www.theguardian.com/society/2015/sep/16/scandal-hit-charities-strong-regulator-charity-commission (retrieved May 2, 2016)..

Tampa Bay Times. 2015. "Throw Some Light on Politics' Dark Money." September 14, p.8A.

Tapper, J. 2009. "President Obama Sets Rules on Ethics and Transparency." ABC News, January 21. http://blogs.abcnews.com/politicalpunch/2009/01/president-oba-3.html (retrieved March 28, 2011).

Taylor, F.W. 1911. *Principles of Scientific Management*. New York: Harper & Brothers.

Tenebaum, J. 2002. "Lobbying Disclosure Act of 1995: A Summary and Overview for Associations." June. www.asaecenter.org/Resources/whitepaperdetail.cfm?ItemNumber=12224 (retrieved January 2, 2006).

Terry, L. 1995. *Leadership of Public Bureaucracies*. Thousand Oaks, CA: Sage.

The Two-Way. 2012. "China's Communists Declare War . . . On Boring Meetings." http://www.npr.org/sections/thetwo-way/2012/12/05/166562850/chinas-communists-declare-war-on-boring-meetings (retrieved March 5, 2016).

Thompson, D.F. 1992. "Paradoxes of Government Ethics." *Public Administration Review* 52 (May/June): 254–259.

Thompson, D.F. 2014. "Responsibility for Failures of Governments: The Problem of Many Hands." *American Review of Public Administration* V. 44(3): 259–273.

Thornton, K. 2006. "Vagueness of Statute on Corruption Stirs Dispute." *San Diego Union-Tribune,* January 12. www.signonsandiego.com/uniontrib/20060112/news_1n12compare.html (retrieved April 17, 2011).

Time. 1971. "Illinois: Paul Powell's Nest Egg." January 18. www.time.com/time/magazine/article/0,9171,942440-1,00.html (retrieved April 15, 2011).

Transparency International India. 2005. *India Corruption Study to Improve Governance.* http://www.transparencyindia.org/resource/survey_study/India%20Corruption%20Study%202005.pdf (retrieved March 5, 2016).

Transparency International. 2012. "Codes of Conduct in Action: Continental Law States." http://blog.transparency.org/2012/08/24/codes-of-conduct-in-action-continental-law-states/ (retrieved March 16, 2016).

Treaster, J.B., and J. Desantis. 2005. "Storm and Crisis: The Police." *New York Times,* September 6.

Truelson, J.A. 1991. "New Strategies for Institutional Controls." In *Ethical Frontiers in Public Management,* ed. J.S. Bowman. San Francisco, CA: Jossey-Bass, pp. 225–242.

Twain, M. 1897. *Pudd'nhead Wilson's New Calendar.* New York: Charles L. Webster.

———. (n.d.a). "BrainyQuote.com." http://www.brainyquote.com/quotes/quotes/m/marktwain122044.html (retrieved November 19, 2015).

———. (n.d.b). Quotation. http://www.quotationspage.com/quote/225.html (retrieved March 1, 2016).

U.K. Committee on Standards in Public Life. 2001. "The First Seven Reports: A Review of Progress." September. https://books.google.com/books/about/The_First_Seven_Reports.html?id=dq5oMwEACAAJ (retrieved March 5, 2016).

U.K. Department for Communities and Local Government. 2012. "£250 Million Savings for Local Public Bodies Expected From Audit Commission Outsourcing." https://www.gov.uk/government/news/250-million-savings-for-local-public-bodies-expected-from-audit-commission-outsourcing--2 (retrieved March 5, 2016).

United Nations. 1999. *Public Service in Transition: Enhancing Its Role, Professionalism and Ethical Values and Standards.* New York: Department of Economic and Social Affairs, Division for Public Economics and Public Administration.

———. 2001. *Public Service Ethics in Africa*, Vol. 1. ST/ESA/PAD/SER.E/23. New York: Department of Economic and Social Affairs, Division for Public Economics and Public Administration. unpan000160.pdf (retrieved November 16, 2011).

———. 2006. "Starting Operations, New UN Ethics Office Fields Staff Requests for Advice." UN News Centre, January 17. www.un.org/apps/news/story.asp?NewsID=17185&Cr=UN&Cr1=staff (retrieved June 26, 2006).

United Nations Economic and Social Council. 1996. "Resolution 1996/8. Action Against Corruption (Annex—International Code of Conduct for Public Officials)." July 23. www.un.org/documents/ecosoc/res/1996/eres1996-8.htm (retrieved February 14, 2011).

United Nations Public Administration Network. n.d. http://www.unpan.org/ (retrieved November 18, 2011).

University of Wisconsin–Madison. 1992. "Statement of Professional Responsibility." Policies of the Wisconsin Certified Public Manager Program, October 27, p. 3. www.dcs.wisc.edu/pda/cpm/resources/CPMPolicies.pdf.

U.S. Census Bureau. 2009. "Local Governments and Public School Systems by Type and State: 2007." November 2. www.census.gov/govs/cog/GovOrgTab03ss.html (retrieved May 30, 2011).

U.S. Courts. 2011. "Code of Conduct for United States Judges." June 2. http://www.uscourts.gov/judges-judgeships/code-conduct-united-states-judges (retrieved May 2, 2016).

U.S. Department of Justice. 2005. "Religious Objections to the Postal Service Oath of Office." February 2. http://www.justice.gov/olc/2005/religious-objections.pdf (retrieved June 10, 2011).

U.S. House of Representatives. 2008. "Chapter 1. General Ethical Standards." In *House Ethics Manual, 2008 Edition.* Committee on Standards of Official Conduct, 110th Congress, 2d Session. Washington, DC: U.S. Government Printing Office. ethics.house.gov/Media/PDF/2008_House_Ethics_Manual.pdf (retrieved February 22, 2016).

U.S. Office of Government Ethics (U.S. OGE). 2015a. *Compilation of Federal Ethics Laws.* https://www2.oge.gov/Web/oge.nsf/0/0BC1FF0EB760D84A85257E96006A9256/$FILE/Compilation%20of%20Federal%20Ethics%20Laws%20(2015).pdf (retrieved March 4, 2016).

———. 2015b. *Mission and Responsibilities.* https://www2.oge.gov/web/oge.nsf/Mission%20and%20Responsibilities (retrieved March 4, 2016).

———. 2015c. *2014 Conflict of Interest Prosecution Survey.* https://www2.oge.gov/Web/OGE.nsf/All+Advisories/1C3D07B39FDE132B85257EC3003CC34A/$FILE/LA-15-10.pdf?open (retrieved March 4, 2016).

———. 2016. *Where to Report Misconduct.* https://www2.oge.gov/web/oge.nsf/Resources/Where+to+Report+Misconduct (retrieved March 4, 2016).

U.S. Office of Personnel Management (U.S. OPM). n.d. "Theodore Roosevelt." www.opm.gov/about_opm/tr/ (retrieved February 28, 2006).

U.S. Office of Special Counsel. 2010. "Introduction to OSC: Our Mission." January 21. https://osc.gov/Resources/ar-2010.pdf (retrieved March 5, 2016).

U.S. President's Commission on Federal Ethics Law Reform. 1989. *To Serve with Honor: Report and Recommendations to the President.* Washington, DC: U.S. Department of Justice.

U.S. Senate. 1884. "Oath of Office." http://www.senate.gov/artandhistory/history/common/briefing/Oath_Office.htm (retrieved June 11, 2011).

———. 1987. Joint Hearings Before the Senate Select Committee on Secret Military Assistance to Iran and the Nicaraguan Opposition and the House Select Committee to Investigate Covert Arms Transactions with Iran. 100th Cong., 1st Sess., 100–7 Part I, July 7, 8, 9, and 10.

U.S. Senate Select Committee on Ethics. 2002. "Letter of Admonition to Senator Robert G. Torricelli." July 30. http://ethics.senate.gov/downloads/pdffiles/ torricelli.pdf (retrieved February 22, 2016).

———. 2003. "Senate Ethics Manual." http://ethics.senate.gov/downloads/pdffiles/ manual.pdf (retrieved February 22, 2016).

———. 2015. "Annual Report for 2014." January 29. http://www.ethics.senate.gov/ public/index.cfm/annualreports?ID=47ecf54a-0773-4b5f-ac19-0898448397a5 (retrieved October 9, 2015).

Utah Nonprofit Association. 2015. "Standards of Ethics." https://www.councilof nonprofits.org/tools-resources/code-of-ethics-nonprofits (retrieved October 7, 2015).

Valmores, D.J. 2005. "Presentation on Fighting and Preventing Corruption." ASEAN+3 Senior Officials Consultative Meeting on Creative Management for Government, September 30–October 1, Bangkok, Thailand.

Van Blijswijk, J.A.M., R.C.J. van Breukelen, A.L Franklin, J.C.N. Raadschelders, and P. Slump. 2004. "Beyond Ethical Codes: The Management of Integrity in the Netherlands Tax and Customs Administration." *Public Administration Review* 64 (November/December):718–727.

Van Sant, W., J. Abel, and T. Blackwell. 2007. "Spratt Resigns, Saying it's Best." *Tampa Bay Times*, September 12. http://www.sptimes.com/2007/09/12/ Northpinellas/Spratt_resigns__sayin.shtml (retrieved October 5, 2015).

Van Wart, M. 2005. *Dynamics of Leadership in Public Service: Theory and Practice.* Armonk, NY: M.E. Sharpe.

———. 2008. *Leadership in Public Organizations.* Armonk, NY: M.E. Sharpe.

———. 2011. "Changing Dynamics of Administrative Leadership." In *The State of Public Administration: Issues, Challenges, and Opportunities,* ed. D. Menzel and H. White. Armonk, NY: M.E. Sharpe, 89–107.

Varian, B. 2005. "E-mails Get Tampa Workers in Trouble." *St. Petersburg Times,* April 19.

Walker, D.M. 2005. "Ethics and Integrity in Government: Putting the Needs of Our Nation First." *Public Integrity* 7 (Fall):345–352.

Wall Street Journal. 2015. "Show Us Your Donors." November 5, A14.

Washburn, R.H.A. 2011. Personal e-mail communication, August 10.

Wayne, L. 2005. "Boeing Chief Is Ousted After Admitting Affair." *New York Times,* March 8.

Wechsler, R. 2015. "A Good Example of Problems That Can Arise from Privatization." http://www.cityethics.org/print/1513 (retrieved October 9, 2015).

Weir, F. 2009. "Russia Corruption Costs $318 Billion—One-Third of GDP." *Christian Science Monitor,* Global News Blog, November 23. www.csmonitor.

com/World/Global-News/2009/1123/russia-corruption-costs-318-billion-one-third-of-gdp (retrieved 14 February, 2011).

Wells, I.B. 1892. Lecture. https://books.google.com/books?id=vgKYFgauOpQC&lpg=PP1&dq=to%20keep%20the%20waters%20troubled%20ida%20b.%20wells&pg=PA176#v=onepage&q&f=false (retrieved March 1, 2016).

West, J. 2005. Personal e-mail communication, August 23.

West, J.P., and E.M. Berman. 2004. "Ethics Training in U.S. Cities: Content, Pedagogy, and Impact." *Public Integrity* 6 (Summer):189–206.

Wex Articles. n.d. "Judicial Ethics." Cornell University Law School, Legal Information Institute. http://topics.law.cornell.edu/wex/judicial_ethics (retrieved July 1, 2011).

Whitaker, G.P., and J.C. Drennan. 2007. "Local Government and Nonprofit Organizations." Chapel Hill, NC: University of North Carolina. http://maaz.ihmc.us/rid=1M2FDPZM1-P5SH1Q-127P/ARTICLE-%20Local%20Government%20and%20Nonprofit%20Organizations.pdf (retrieved March 5, 2016).

White, L.D. 1926. *Introduction to the Study of Public Administration.* New York: Macmillan.

Whitton, H. 2007. "Developing the 'Ethical Competence' of Public Officials—A Capacity-Building Approach." *Public Policy and Administration* 1(21):49–60.

Wikipedia. 2011a. "Honest Services Fraud." June 16. http://en.wikipedia.org/wiki/Honest_services_fraud (retrieved February 22, 2016).

———. 2011b. "Ray Blanton." May 4. http://en.wikipedia.org/wiki/Ray_Blanton (retrieved November 18, 2011).

———. 2011c. "Thomas Porteous." June 5. http://en.wikipedia.org/wiki/Thomas_Porteous. (retrieved November 18, 2011).

———. 2015. "Cordell Hulls Telegram to Hiram Bingham, September 18, 1940." https://www.facinghistory.org/rescuers/cordell-hull's-telegram-hiram-bingham-september-18-1940 (retrieved October 7, 2015).

Wiley, C. 1995. "The ABC's of Business Ethics: Definitions, Philosophies, and Implementation." *Industrial Management* 37(1):22–27.

Williams, R.L. 1996. "Controlling Ethical Practices Through Laws and Rules: Evaluating the Florida Commission on Ethics." *Public Integrity Annual* 65–72.

Wilson, J.Q. 1993. *The Moral Sense.* New York: Free Press.

Wilson, W. 1887/1941. "The Study of Administration." *Political Science Quarterly* 56 (December):481–506.

Witt, E. 1992. "Is Government Full of Crooks or Are We Just Better at Finding Them?" In *Essentials of Government Ethics,* ed. P. Madsen and J.M. Shafritz. New York: Meridian/Penguin.

Wong, L., and S.J. Gerras. 2015. "Lying to Ourselves: Dishonesty in the Army Profession." U.S Army War College, Strategic Studies Institute, February. http://www.strategicstudiesinstitute.army.mil/pdffiles/PUB1250.pdf (retrieved October 5, 2015).

Wyatt-Nichol, H. & Franks, G. (2009–2010). "Ethics Training in Law Enforcement Agencies." *Public Integrity* 12 (1): 39–50.

Wye, C. 1994. "A Framework for Enlarging the Reform Agenda." *The Public Manager* 23:43–46.

Zajac, G., and L.K. Comfort. 1997. "The Spirit of Watchfulness: Public Ethics as Organizational Learning." *Journal of Public Administration Research and Theory* 7 (October):541–569.

Zauderer, D.G. 1994. "Winning with Integrity." *The Public Manager* 23:43–46.

Zhu, Q. 2000. "The Process of Professionalization and the Rebuilding of Administrative Ethics in Post-Mao China." *International Journal of Public Administration* 23 (11):1943–1965.

Index